WILLIAMSON COUNTY TENNESSEE

County Court Minutes

July 1812–October 1815

Carol Wells

HERITAGE BOOKS
2008

HERITAGE BOOKS
AN IMPRINT OF HERITAGE BOOKS, INC.

Books, CDs, and more—Worldwide

For our listing of thousands of titles see our website
at
www.HeritageBooks.com

Published 2008 by
HERITAGE BOOKS, INC.
Publishing Division
100 Railroad Ave. #104
Westminster, Maryland 21157

Copyright © 1994 Carol Wells

All rights reserved. No part of this book may be reproduced or transmitted in any form or by any means, electronic or mechanical, including photocopying, recording or by any information storage and retrieval system without written permission from the author, except for the inclusion of brief quotations in a review.

International Standard Book Numbers
Paperbound: 978-0-7884-0112-1
Clothbound: 978-0-7884-7488-0

Table of Contents

Foreword v

Court Minutes
  1812
    July 1
    October 13
  1813
    January 23
    April 34
    July 42
    October 53
  1814
    January 62
    April 69
    July 77
    October 87
  1815
    January 97
    April 105
    July 113
    October 124

Index 139

FOREWORD

Although Williamson County, Tennessee, was cut from Davidson County in 1799, the first surviving census is the 1820 enumeration. Other records must be used to throw light on families of those early years. Minute Book Two of the Court of Pleas and Quarter Sessions--the County Court--contains matters which passed before the justices of the peace from July 1812 to the end of 1815. In these pages can be found names of new settlers, landowners whose claims conflicted, or the wording of whose grants needed to be corrected, whose taxes were unpaid, or who were selling land in other counties or states. As new farms were created, old roads had to be changed and new roads laid off; names of men doing these tasks would show neighbors and possible relatives. Minutes also provide names and relationships in the proving of wills, providing for widows and children, guardians, dowers, apprentices, indigents, and illegitimate children.

In abstracting information from a microfilmed handwritten book, the spelling of names is often hard to determine. Clerks and justices wrote names as they heard them spoken. Usual spelling variations are complicated by the problem of reading hasty and sometimes careless penmanship. The reader should allow for uncrossed t's to be read as l; for r, s, and t to be confused; for n and u to look similar, for double r to appear as n. Names such as Handy and Hardy, Hale and Hall, Bennett and Burnett, which depend upon the careful formation of letters, may be indistinguishable. Lack of commas to separate names in jury lists also presents difficulties.

Carol Wells

ABBREVIATIONS

A&B	Assault & Battery
ac	acres
ackd	acknowledged
addl	additional
admr	administrator
agt	against
appt	appoint
atty	attorney
cr	creek
dam	damages
decd	deceased
dft	defendant
D/G	deed of gift
exd	excused
exn	execution
exr	executor
judgt	judgment
P/A	power of attorney
plf	plaintiff
rd	road
recd	received
retd	returned
sec	security
secy	security
will	last will and testament

JULY 1812

p.2 State of Tennessee. At a Court of Pleas and quarter Sessions held for the County of Williamson at the Court House in the Town of Franklin on Monday the 13th day of July 1812 Present the Worshipful George Hulme Sion Hunt and David Dickinson, Esquires.

Jurors summoned: Robt Hulme John Edmiston Jr Richard Reynolds Edward Elam Alexander Ralston Archibald Lytle David Edmondson exd John Edgar Jonathan Stepleton William G Boyd Edward Warren Cornelius Matthews Nicholas T Perkins exd Wm Hope William Shute Richd Hughes James S Clemm Andrew Johnson Chapman White Ewen Cameron John Williamson & Pleasant Russell. Constables Samuel Andrews exd; & Samuel Cox.

Grand jurors: Cornelius Matthews excused proved 5 days, Edward Warren Wm G Boyd Wm Hope Richd Hughes John Williamson Pleasant Russel Ewen Cameron Andrew Johnson James S Clemm Archibald Lytle foreman Robert Hulme Jonathan Stepleton discharged 6th day.

George Kinnard vs Julian Nail. John Garey surrendered Julian Nail in discharge of himself and his other security; Tristram Patton & John R Tankersly special bail.

Henry Barnes vs Chas S Legate Julian Neal & Wm Young. Execution awarded agt dfts.

Alexander and A Porter vs John Depriest & others. On motion. Present [justices above]. Plfs move judgt agt John Depriest late a constable and David Shannon & Wm Wilson his securities for a delinquency: exn dated 1809 Alex & A Porter agt Reuben Nance for $13.58 with interest collected by John Depriest but he failed to pay over same. Plfs recover agt dfts.

Alexr & A Porter vs John Depriest. Justices [above]. Plfs by atty Thomas H Benton p.3 agt John Depriest and his securities for delinquency; exn agt Reuben Nance for $37.83 with interest from 24 January 1808; John Depriest failed to pay over same. Plfs recover agt deft and David Shannon & Wm Wilson his securities.

Deed John L Fielder and Jane Fielder to David Cummins 213 acres & 8 poles ackd. Jane, wife of sd John L Fielder examined by David Dickinson and Sion Hunt Esqrs touching the execution of sd deed.

Robert Scales vs George Strambler. Stephen Barfield and Martin Stanley surrender George Strambler in discharge of themselves. Moses Chambers and John Douglass special bail for the appearance of George Strambler.

William Bateman vs George Strambler. [worded as above].

State vs Thomas Ragsdale. A&B. Caleb Manley surrenders Thos Ragsdale into custody of the sheriff.

State vs Thomas Ragsdale. Appearance bond.

Order Malachi Kerby oversee the road from Nashville towards Natchez from Capt Alexanders plantation up to dividing ridge.

p.4 Order James Gray oversee road from Sampson Sawyers from Sawyers to Britian

JULY 1812

Adams to Rutherford County line.

Order David Craig Senr oversee road from Franklin to John Buchanans on Arringtons Creek beginning at the five miles tree on Hayes creek and ending at the commissioners creek; hands from Col Craigs to Craftons to Eatons to Pages work thereon.

Order James Thompson oversee road from huse of Elisha Roads southwest to Natchez road and that John Hopkins Wm Demoss Henry Inman James Thompson Sampson Prowell Ambrose R Richards Vincent Cartwright Wm Quiling & Ambrose Sherald work thereon.

Order Nichs Perkins Senr oversee the road as lately laid off from West Harpeth to Davidson County; all hands on West Harpeth between N Perkins line & John Acols house thence to Federal road leaving Joseph Philips to the West, to County line including Samuel Williams, along county line including Thomas H Perkins knob plantation Martin Trantham & Jacob Tillman to the beginning work thereon.

Demsey Nash apptd overseer of road whereof he was formerly overseer.

William White allowed three Dollars for a wolf scalp by him killed in this county.

Pryor Reynolds allowed $8 for four wolf scalps killed by him in this county.

Deed Nicholas P Hardeman to George Parham 103 acres ackd.
Deed David Pinkston to Knacy Andrews 42 acres proven by Alexander Johnston and Benjamin Bugg.
p.5 Mortgage Thomas Sappington to John & Roger B Sappington ackd.
Deed Hendley Stone to William Floyd 227 acres ackd.
Deed Joseph Dean to Drury Warren for 116 acres ackd.
Deed Thomas Spratt to Andrew Spratt 62 acres proven by Sam Spratt & John Huston.
Supplemental inventory estate of Littleberry Epperson decd returned.
Account/sales estate of Littleberry Epperson decd returned.
Bill/sale David Jones & Elizabeth Jones to Thomas Jordan proven by Richard W Hyde.
Deed Daniel Brown to John Bayney 139 acres ackd.
Deed Robert Winsett to Silas Winsett 45 acres & 120 poles proven by Amos Winsett and William Winsett.
Deed Robert Winsett to Daniel Brown 45 acres 26 poles proven by William Winsett and Silas Winsett.
Deed Drury Warren to Joshua Cuchen 43 acres ackd.
Deed Robert Winsett to Wm Winsett 50 acres proven by Amos Winsett & Silas Winsett.
Deed Newton Cannon to Christopher Vannatto 70 acres ackd.
Deed Jas Campbell to Jno Sappington 160 acres proven by Robt C Currin & Thos Hulme.
Will of Patrick McCutchen decd proven by John Hardeman and Wm Marshall; Hannah McCutchan, Samuel McCutchan & James Marshall exx & exors qualified.
Order States business in future be taken up on Thursday of each term.
Court adjourns until Tomorrow morning 9 OClock.   G Hulme, Wm Nunn, C McDaniel.

Tuesday 14 July 1812. Present George Hulme William Nunn & Collin McDaniel Esqrs.
p.6 William Nunn Esqr paid to Clerk 75¢, a fine on Wm Crunk for profane swearing.
Letter/attorney Devinney Worlley to Thomas E Sumner ackd.
Hugh Pinkston apptd to oversee road whereof Samuel Wilson is overseer.

JULY 1812

Thomas Terry allowed $3 for a wolf scalp killed by him in this County over four months old.
Order Charles McCalister Hinchey Pettway Robert P Currin let to lowest bidder the repairs of the Court house.
Enoch Galloway allowed $24 for maintenance of Bird Taylor an object of charity for last year.
Release Archibald Wilsons heirs from double tax on 225 acres for present year.
Release William H Bellow from double tax on 1 white poll for year 1812.
Release Robert Wilson from double tax on 3 slaves & 1 stud horse at $3 and the white poll is to be struck off as he did not give it in.
Release George Calhoun from tax on 1 Black Poll.
Appoint James Gordon Charles McAlister & John Sample to sell the old county Jail.
Jesse Sparkman resigns his office of a constable for this County.
Order Philip Maury have certificate to County Trustee for balance due him for building the County Jail.
Release John Fitzgerald from double tax on 1 White Poll 2 Slaves & 50 acres.
Release Alexr McClaran from double tax on 2 White Polls 2 Slaves & 160 acres.
Order Sion Hunt and George Hulme Esqrs let to lowest bidder Betsey Carlile and Robert Carlile children of Robert Carlile deceased who are to be maintained at
p.7   charge of this County.
Order Hinchey Pettway John Witherspoon and Nicholas Scales Esqrs examine the marks and descriptions of Will Hill Sally Hill & Joseph Hill children of James Hill a free man of color.
Order jurors summoned on the original pannel since last appropriation be allowed fifty cents each per day for their attendance.
Allow Elisha North $3 for wolf scalp he killed in this County over 4 months old.
Allow John Hardeman $3 for wolf scalp he killed in this County over 4 months old.
Release Joseph Cowan from double tax on 3 Slaves 1 White Poll & 239 acres & 1 Town Lot, but he is to pay single tax on same.
Release Andrew Cathey from double tax on 1400 acres, but pay single tax on same.
Release Ann Harrison from double tax on 1 Slave, but pay single tax.
Release Daniel Guman[German?] from double tax for present year.
Release John Haley from double tax on 1 White poll & 2 Slaves.
Allow Elisha Williams $3 for wolf scalp he killed in this County over 4 months old.
Thomas Hoggs heirs released from double tax on 3976 acres for present year.
Release George Fellman from tax on 5 slaves for present year.
Release Enoch Bateman from double tax on 1 Slave for present year.
Release Isaac Bateman from payment of 1 White poll for present year.
Release David McCord from double tax on 227 acres & 1 Slave.
Release Moses Turner from double tax on 123 acres & 1 White poll for present year.
Release Charles Buford from double tax 134½ acres for present year, pay single tax.
p.8   Jacob Gray discharged from double tax for present year.
Release Isaac Forgerson from tax on 1 White Poll for present year.
Release James Merritt from double tax on 3 Slaves for present year.
Release John Neelly from double tax on 1 White Poll & 1 Slave for present year.
Release Thomas Harding from double tax on 102 acres for present year.
Release John Neelly Senr from double tax on 418½ acres 1 white poll & 5 Slaves for present year.
Release Benjamin Roberts from double tax 1 White Poll & 2 Slaves for present year.
Release George Mansker Junr from double tax 100 acres & 1 White poll present year.

JULY 1812

Release Lewis Mansker from double tax on 1 White poll for present year.
Release Isaac Neelly from double tax on 1 White poll for present year.
Release Thomas Gooch from double tax for present year.
Release estate of Joel Parrish from double tax for present year.
Release John S Street from double tax for present year.

William Denson Thomas Walker Freeman Walker Drury Pulliam & James Cavender report they turned the road from Franklin to 5 Mile tree on Hayes Creek leading by Michael Kinnards for the benefit of the inhabitants & the publick in general.

Allow David McEwen Richard Steele Ewen Cameron George Hulme & James Hicks $7.86 each for attendance as commrs to let & superintend the building of the County Jail.

Allow David Squier $18.18¾ for washing sweeping & keeping Court house in repair
p.9   from April 1811 to July 1812 & other repairs done to Court house.

David Squire licensed to keep an ordinary at his dwelling house in this County; bond $2500 with Nichs Perkins & Ewen Cameron his securities.

Order John Moore oversee road from Franklin to Chambers ferry from 10 mile tree to Maury County; residents on Walkers branch Leepers fork to Duck river ridge to Big Carter leaving out Wm Simpson work thereon under his directions.

Order John R Boyd oversee road from ridge between Arringtons & Wilsons creek to Nelsons creek; hands from new meeting house near Nicholas Scales to Nelsons Creek including John Bosticks hands to Rutherford County work thereon.

Letter/atty Thomas Graham to Edward Graham proven by Robert P Currin & John Sample.

Enoch Galloway bond with Luke Patterson his security for maintenance of Bird Taylor an object of charity returned into Court by Saml Akin & Jesse White Esqrs.

Deed Cary Bibb to Richard Herbert 100 acres proven by Jno Mayfield & Nathl Herbert.
Will of Jane Wheaton decd proven by James Shannon & Wm Black.
Deed Moses Oldham to Conaway Oldham 280 9/20 acres proven by Elisha R Oldham & Moses Oldham.
Deed Moses Oldham to Moses Oldham Junr 25 acres proven by Con Oldham & Elisha R Oldham.
Inventory of estate of Patrick McCutchen decd returned.
Deed Abram Maury to Samuel McCleary Lot 35 in Franklin ackd; assignment thereon from sd McCleary to David Coonrod proven by William Legate.
Deed Samuel Seers atty/fact for David Coonrod to William P Harrison Lot 35 in Franklin proven by Nathaniel Harrison & Ewen Cameron.
p.10   Deed Burrell McLamore to Ann Harrison 89 1/10 acres ackd.
Deed William Duberry to Allen Cotton 63 acres proven by Henry Rutherford & Saml Edmiston.
Inventory of estate of John Seay decd returned.
Deed John Hunter to John Duberry Senr 160 acres proven by Hezekiah Jordan & Charles A Duberry.
Deed William Hulme Sheriff to Wm M Bell 555 acres ackd.

JULY 1812

Deed Wm M Bell to Abraham Brantley 555 acres ackd.
Bill/sale Abraham Walker to Alson Edney ackd.
Deed Thomas McCrory to josiah Knight part of lots 102 & 103 in Franklin ackd.
Deed Pleasant Russell to Thomas mcCrory part of lots 109 119 110 ackd.

Deed Thomas Old & Betsey his wife to David C Jones 439 acres in Dinwiddie County Virginia ackd by sd Thomas Old. Order David Dickinson james Black & Tristram Patton Esqrs take private examn of sd Betsey relative to her voluntary exn of sd deed.

Allow Wm Houston $3 for wolf scalp killed by him in this County 4 months old.

Ewen Cameron Robert P Currin James Stewart James S Clemm & Pleasant Russell report on turning the road from Franklin to the bridge at Parrishes old mill round Andrew Johnstons lot.

Release Elisha North from double tax on 8 Slaves & 1 White poll for present year.

Allow Philip Maury $118.27½ for extra work done to County Jail.

p.11   Elect Jordan Phipps Constable in Capt James Anglins Company; bond $625 with William Bond Senr and Robert McMillan his securities, and qualified.
Elect James J Thomas Constable in Capt Temples Company; bond $625 with Joseph Hassell and James Hardgrave his securities, and qualified.
Elect Vincent Green Constable in Capt Garretts Company; bond $625 with George Hulme & Jacob Garrett his securities, and qualified.
Elect William Bond Jr Constable in Capt Davis Company; bond $625 with Kemp Holltime and Wm Bond Senr his securities, and qualified.
Elect Tapley B Andrews Constable in Capt Geo Mebanes Company; bond $625 with Alexander Mebane George Mebane Edward Ragsdale securities, and qualified.
Elect Caleb Manley Constable in Capt Giddens Company; bond $625 with Henry Cook & Elisha North his securities, and qualified.

Robert McMillin Wm Dowdy Wm Tucker John Curry & Abraham Castleman report they had marked a road from Dickson County line to Davidson County line near Shannons.

Order Abraham Castleman Wm Dowdy Robert McMillan Joshua Barham Ivy Barham Daniel Underhill & Deliverance Gray any 5 lay off a road from Davidson County line near Shannons ponds to Dickson line passing by houses of Robert McMillan and William Dowdy so as to cross Turnbull at Ryners waggon ford below sd Ryners dwelling house and report to next Court.

Order Caleb Willis oversee road from Wm Nolens shop to Liberty meeting house road running to east fork of Mill Creek to include Luke Pryor Jr Caleb Willis & Samuel Haggard John Vaults David Nolen to work thereon under his directions.

Wm Nolen Thomas Simmons Benja Kidd John P Irion & Nelson Fields report they viewed part of the road from Nashville to Harpeth Lick which passes through Wm Anthony's
p.12   land which is the nearest and best way & ought to run through the same.

Order David Chrisman Moses Steele David Gillaspie Aaron Christman Samuel Brown

JULY 1812

Zacheus Wilson Haden Tillman & Isaac Gillaspie any 5 mark out a road through Woods Gap in Duck River ridge to meet a road from Columbia in Maury County between David Gillaspies & James Scotts northwardly to Nashville near John Walkers or James Allisons Esqr as they think best; report to ensuing County Court.

Ltrs/admn granted Richard Puckett on estate of John Shepherd decd; bond with George Hulme and Saml Shelburne securities, and qualified. Inventory estate of John Shepherd decd returned; order Richard Puckett sell chattel property mentioned.

Authenticated papers relative to the emancipation of James Hill a man of color presented and ordered to be recorded. James Hill gave bond with John Reed Thomas Old Isaac Bizzell & Demsay Deans his securities to indemnify Sally Hill Moses Hill Will Hill & Joe Hill from becoming chargeable on the parish of this County.

Jurors to next Circuit Court: John Witherspoon David Dunn Burrill McLemore Alexr Mebane Wm Bond Senr Abram Walker Burwell Temple Thomas Wilson Samuel Shelburne Wm Logan Lewis Stephens Joel Stephens Wm Martin Eleazer Hardeman Horatio Pettis James Andrew Stephen Childress Nichs T Perkins James McCutchan Jacob Gray James Simms Wm Simpson George Brooks Sherwood Green Nichs Scales Saml Perkins. Constables Peter Pinkston and John Nunn.

Jurors to next County Court: Jesse Sparkman Wm Sparkman Charles Robinson David Robinson Barnett Donalson Benjamin May Meredith Holm Moses Chambers Drury Pulliam James Turner Thomas Ridley Benja Roberts Benja Gholson Wm Nall Wm Dowdy Thomas Walker Saml F Glass John Swinney Henry Walker John Parks Jr James Sneed Richd Hightower Joel Riggs Jesse Tarkington Senr Thomas Cash John Neelly. Constables Caleb Manley and William Bond.

p.13 Jimmey Hill a free man of color appeared in open Court & set forth that he was emancipated by Benjamin Crawley of Amelia County Virginia by deed dated 25 January 1787, that 1 March 1798 purchased of Wm Mosely of Chesterfield County Virginia his wife Sarah and her two children Sally & Moses in authenticated bill/sale produced in Court, that he and sd Sarah lived as husband and wife till she died leaving her four other children the issue of her marriage with petitioner, praying permission to emancipate four of sd children, viz Sally about 17, Moses about 16 with scar on left thumb and scar on instep of right foot, Will age about 15, and Joe age about 13 years. Sd petition upon bond having been entered into was granted and certificates of Record ordered for benefit of sd slaves so emancipated.

Anthony Walker by Nichs Perkins his atty produced an exn issued by James Allison Esqr agt John Gillaspie & Wm Hooker for $16.31¼ & costs which exn Constable Nelson Chapman executed, levied on 100 acres property of sd John Gillaspie on Flat creek where he now lives; order of sale to issue to shff.
[Another, worded as above, for $6.50.]

Saml Dodson by Alfred Balch his atty produced an execution issued by Hinchey Pettway Esqr agt Wm Glover for $51.39 & costs, put in hands of Constable Caleb Manley who levied on 89 acres on McCrorys Creek adj Duck River; ordered sold.

Motion of Henry Rutherford by John Hardeman his atty, judgt granted agt Griffith W

JULY 1812

Rutherford for $54.79½, the amt of judgt & costs W Bell assee recovered agt sd Henry as security for sd Griffith W Rutherford besides costs of this motion.

Court adjourns untill Tomorrow morning 9 O Clock.
                                Robert McMillin Thomas Wilson HDLY Stone

Wednesday 15th July 1812. Present Charles Boyles John J Henry Robt McMillin Esqrs. Appt Sion Hunt & Geo Hulme Esqrs to settle with the admx of the estate of James McCutchen decd.

Charles McAlister vs Hayes & Drew. Name of Nuvit Drew struck therefrom.

p.14   Joseph Mairs vs Jacob Harder. Motion of plf by atty N Perkins. Gersham Hunt Hendley Stone Robt McMillin. Motion of Joseph Mairs by atty shews he was security for Jacob Harder the deft; William T Lewis recovered j udgt agt sd Harder & sd Mairs 15 Jany 1812 for $108 & costs. Plf recovers agt dft sd sum & costs of motion.

Order Sheriff pay Philip Maury the sum allowed him for building the bridge across Harpeth opposite the town of Franklin.

Charles McAlister & wife admrs of John Wright decd vs John Hays & Newit Drew. Attachmt $700. Court G Hunt Henly Stone Robt McMillin. Jury Nicholas T Perkins Edward Elam Chapman White Wm Bateman Jacob Harder Dixon Vaughan Michael Robertson William McKenzie William Peebles Joseph Braden Joseph Hassell George Kinnard. Defts recover agt plfs their costs in their defence expended in this behalf.

Settlement of estate of Hardy Pate as respects his daughter Nancy Pate now Nancy Simmons made by C Boyles & John Witherspoon under order of last Court and settled with Lancaster Glover guardian to sd Nancy is now returned into Court.

Order John W Manier oversee road from John Walkers to top of Tennessee ridge; hands formerly working under Saml Gentry with addition of sd Maniers hands David Edmiston Robert Wilson & Thomas Wilson Junr work thereon under his directions.

Following persons who lately worked under Moses Ridley viz James Sanders Mark Black Wm Logan Benjn Smith Wm Dixon & Abram Hill work under James Joice overseer of road from Nashville to Fishing Ford on Duck River.

Order Henry Cook Daniel Perkins & Robert McLemore to divide estate of Metcalf Degraffenreid decd and allot to Metcalf Degraffenreid Jr a son & heir to decd his proportionable part of sd estate.

p.15   Will of Samuel Wilson decd proven by Zacheus Wilson & Moses Wilson. Martha Wilson & Zacheus Wilson extx and extr qualified as such.

Deed Abraham Truett to James B Thompson 140 acres ackd.

Jesse Tarkington vs William Willett. Motion of Jesse Tarkington by atty Nicholas Perkins. Sd Jesse recovered judgt agt Wm Willett on 9 April last for $11.62 & costs

JULY 1812

before John Witherspoon J P. Constable Kemp Holland levied on 500 acres on West Harpeth belonging to sd Wm Willet adj Jordan Reese; order of sale to issue.

John Berkley vs John G Pickings. Damage $300. Defendant brings into Court Samuel B McKnight & William G Boyd who stand special bail for him.

Bill/sale John J Henry to Zachariah Betts for negro woman and child ackd.

Order Thomas W Stockett Jacob Garrett & Sion Hunt Esqrs any 2 take deposition of William McGaugh relative to improvements boundaries or specialties called for in a grant to Charles Brown 640 acres on beach creek of Little Harpeth, 1 Sept next.

David Lewis allowed $14 for 7 wolf scalps killed by him in this county.
Nicholas T Perkins is excused as juror; proved his attendance 3 days.

Wm McCalpan & George Mayfield vs Silas Tompkins. Covenant Dam $500. Justices Hinchey Pettway Robert McMillin John J Henry. Jury Edward Elam Chapman White Wm Bateman Jacob Harder Dixon Vaughan Michael Robertson Wm McKenzie Wm Peebles Joseph Braden Joseph Hassell Sterling Davis Robt P Currin. Dft recovers agt plf his costs by him about his defence in this behalf expended. Plfs are granted appeal to the
p.16   Circuit Court, giving John Mayfield their security.

Bill/sale Robert P Currin to Andrew Johnson ackd.
Deed Abram Maury & Chapman White admrs of Joel Parrish decd to Andrew Johnson 14 acres 60 poles ackd.
Bond of Wm Houston with Isaac Tignor his security for maintenance of Wm Houston Jr returned into Court by James Black & David Dickinson Esquires.
Indenture/apprenticeship from Nancy Wooldridge to Harrison Boyd proven by Moses Davis & Joel T Rivers.

King & Carson vs William Parker. Plf came not; non suited & pay to dft his costs. Court adjourns until tomorrow morning 9 O Clock.
                         Hinchey Pettway Robert McMillin John J Henry.

Thursday 16 July 1812. Present Hinchey Pettway Robert McMillin John J Henry Esqrs.

Wm Bradshaw assee vs John Bond. Debt $123.86 Dam $100. Justices [above]. Jury Edwd Elam Wm Denson James Gee David Caldwell John Gee Wm Hill John Bridges Wm Parks John McKinney Fras M Dean Stephen Smith John Johnston. Plaintiff recovers agt defendant.

p.17   Nathaniel Simmons vs Stephen Smith. Debt $430.25 Dam $100. Justices [above] Jury Edwd Elam Wm Denson James Gee Wm Hill John Bridges Wm Parks John McKinney Francis M Dean John Johnston James McGavock. Plf recovers agt deft.

Rodian Poe vs John Gary. Debt $300 Dam $100. Justices [above]. Jury Edwd Elam Wm Denson James Gee David Caldwell Wm Hill John Bridges Wm Parks John McKinney Francis M Dean John Johnston James McGavock John Gee find dft hath not paid debt.

Pettway & Maury vs Charles Kavenaugh. Debt $235 Dam $100. Justices Chs McAlister

JULY 1812

Robt McMillin John J Henry. Jury Edwd Elam Wm Denson Jas Gee David Caldwell John Gee Wm Hill John Bridges Wm Parks John McKinney Francis M Dean John Johnston James McGavock. Plfs recover agt dft.

John Camp vs John White. Debt $100 Dam $50. Justices [above]. Jury [above]. Plf recovers agt dft.
p.18

David McGavock assee vs Thomas H Perkins. Debt $750 Dam $100. Justices [above]. Jury [above] say Dft hath paid part, balance of $296.33½ remains.

Saml Wilson assee vs Wm Glover & Burrell McLemore. Debt $170 Dam $100. Justices [above]. Jury [above]. Plfs recover agt deft.

Edmond Powell vs Charles Kavenaugh. Debt $130 Dam $60. Justices [above]. Jury [above]. Plf recovers against the deft.

p.19 Bethel Allen vs Guilford Dudley. Debt $200 Dam $100. Justices [above]. Jury [above]. Plf recovers agt deft.

Robert Scales vs George Strambler. Debt $158.25 Dam $60. Justices [above]. Jury [above]. Plf recovers agt deft.

State vs Jacob Garrett. Jacob Garrett personally appeared at instance of Isaac Wright who heretofore required security of sd Jacob Garrett to keep peace toward sd Isaac Wright. Recognizance $1000 with securities Vincent Greer & Ephriam Brown $500 each.

p.20 Order Richd Puckett Oliver Williams & Samuel Williams Esqrs settle with John Crafton & Daniel Wilkes admrs/estate of James Crafton decd.

State vs Allen Morriss. On Indictment. Dft fined at last court for A&B on Caleb Manley. Sheriff levied on property of defendant.
State vs John Bridges. Indictment for an affray. Justices [above]. Jury [above except Chapman White & Peter Holladay for John Bridges and John McKinney] find deft guilty; fine $10 & costs.
State vs Elisha Williams. Affray. Isaac Crow deft's security produced him into custody of Sheriff.
State vs John Epps. Affray. Isaac Crow, deft's security, [as above].
State vs John H Crockett. Presentment overseer of road. Justices Thomas W Stockett Robt McMillin John J Henry. Deft amerced $3 and costs.
State vs Thomas Ragsdale. Affray. Justices [above]. Deft amerced $10 & costs.
Deed James Robertson to Stephen Stockett 113¾ acres 10¾ perches proven by Loyd Adamson and Joseph H Stockett.

Archd Patten produced certificate from Joel Lewis & Jas Herndon formerly commrs to liquidate debts between this & Davidson County wherein it appears Jas Herndon was entitled to $2.12¼. County trustee to pay this sum if not heretofore paid.

p.21 Order Jacob Garrett pay fine $10 & be in custody of sheriff till he pays; this fine for misbehaviour and treating the court contemptably.

JULY 1812

Deed James Robertson to Jacob Garrett 160¼ acres 3/4 perch proven by Loyd Adamson and Joseph H Stockett.

State vs Thomas H Perkins & Thomas McCrory. Affray. Justices R McMillin Gersham Hunt John J Henry. Deft Thos H Perkins saith he is guilty; amerced $1 and costs.

State vs Isaac Crow. Affray. Justices [above]. Jury Isaac Wright James Hardgrove Nichs Wilburn Shiner[?] Merritt Sterling Davis Ethelston Andrews Dixon Vaughan James House Robert Waite Nathaniel Smithson Lancaster Glover John Nichols who find deft guilty; amerced $10 and pay costs.

State vs John McKinney. Affray. Justices G Hunt Robt McMillin John J Henry. Jury Wm Shute Edwd Elam Wm Denson Jas Gee John Gee Wm Hill Wm Parks John Johnson James McGavock Chapman White Danl Perkins Saml Estes Sr find deft guilty. Fine $10 & costs.

William Nawl bound to answer complaint of Thomas Younger for surety/peace bound in sum $500. Thos H Perkins Robt McMillin & Daniel Perkins his securities $166⅔ each.

William Bateman vs George Strambler. Debt $375. Dam $100. Justices Hinchey Pettway Ro McMillin John J Henry. Jury Isaac Wright James Hardgrave Nichs Wilburn Dixon Vaughan James House Lancaster Glover John Nichols Joseph Crenshaw Robert P Currin
p.22   Martin Stanley Daniel McMahon Ethelston Andrews. Plf recovers agt deft.

Ephriam Andrews exs vs Lancaster Glover. Debt $143.56½ Dam $100 Justices [above]. Jury [above, except Wm Parks & Robt Waite for Lancr Glover & Ethelston Andrews]. Plfs recover against defendant.
Ephriam Andrews exors vs William Glover. Debt $143.56½ Dam $100 [as above].

William Neelly vs James Neelly. On motion Wm Neelly by atty Thos H Benton produced a bond: James Neelly & William Neelly bound unto Benjamin Carter of Kershaw Dist SC $3224.20 1 November 1809 with obligation to pay sd Carter $662.10 with interest 6% before 1 August 1811. Witness: Robt Neelly Rt Neelly Jur. Wm Neelly claimed to
p.23   be security of James Neelly though not so stated in the bond. Jury: Isaac Wright James Hartgrave Nicholas Wilburn Dixon Vaughan James House John Nichols Joseph Crenshaw Robert P Currin Martin Stanley Daniel McMahon Wm Parks Robert Wait say Wm Neelly signed sd bond as security of sd James Neelly. May term 1812 Benjamin Carter obtained judgt agt Wm Neelly. Wm Neelly recovers agt James Neelly $693.73 and his costs about this motion in that behalf expended.

Dolly Law made oath before William Anthony & Gersham Hunt Esqrs that she is with child, a bastard which may become chargeable to this county, that George Standfield begat sd child. George Standfield gave bond $100 with securities Ephriam Standfield and Shackspier Standfield for maintenance of sd child.

Gabriel Buford vs Thomas McCrory. Debt $130 Dam $50. Justices Hinchey Pettway Robt
p.24   McMillin John J Henry. Jury [above]. Plf recovers agt dft.

James Gordon & Co by Nicholas Perkins their atty produced an execution issued by Hinchey Pettway J P agt Francis M Dean for $47 & costs. Constable Samuel Cox levied on Lot #93 in Franklin on 2 Jul 1812. Order of sale issue to Sheriff to sell same.

JULY 1812

On motion of Isaac Roberts Joseph Brown Wm Frierson & John Lindsey commrs of Columbia by John White their atty exn is awarded them agt Richard Orton Samuel Cox & Thomas Bell on their replevin bond given for stay of exn in favour of sd commrs agt Richd Orton for $164.75 with interest & costs of sd suit and this motion.

On motion of William Frierson Joseph Brown Isaac Roberts & John Lindsey commrs of Columbia by John White their atty exn is awarded them against Charles B Neilson Newton Cannon James Wilson & Patrick McCutchen...$329.50 [as above]
Court adjourns untill Tomorrow morning 9 0 Clock.
                                        Hinchey Pettway C Boyles Robert McMillin

Friday 17 July 1812. Present Hinchey Pettway Charles Boyles & Robt McMillin Esqrs.

Appt Thomas W Stockett overseer of road whereof he was formerly overseer.

p.25   State vs George J Poindexter & Nicholas Tomlin. Affray. Justices Hinchey Pettway Robt McMillin Thos W Stockett. Poindexter fined $10 and pay costs.

Campbell & Stewart vs Richard Orton. Debt $149.16¾ Dam $100. Justices [above]. Jury Chapman White Edwd Elam Wm Shute James Moore Saml Estes Sr John Sample Jacob Harder Jno Johnston James McGavock Saml Estes Jr John Gee Jas Hicks. Plf recovers agt dft.

Campbell & Stewart vs Stephen Smith. Debt $244.37½ Dam $100. Justices [above]. Jury [above]. Plfs recover agt deft.

Charles McAlister vs John Depriest John Hill & Thomas Simmons. On Motion. Present C Boyles H Pettway T W Stockett. Elizabeth Wright who has married plf Charles McAlister on 11 Oct 1810 before Nicholas Scales J P obtained judgt agt Sampson Sawyers for $20.90 & costs. Constable John Depriest held sd exn 20 and more days. Sd Charles McAlister recovers agt John Depriest and John Hill & Thos Simmons his
p.26   securities sd $20.90 and costs of motion.

Grand Jury returned Bills/Indictment agt Daniel Carter John Carter John Jones Edward Tignor Jones Tignor Thomas Brooks Jeremiah Terry David Terry Graves Thomson John McMeans for a riot, true bill.

Acct/sales estate of Dudley Porter decd returned by Sarah Porter admx.

Allen & Christopher Degraffenreid vs Gilbert G Washington. Present C Boyles R McMillin Jas Boyd. Jury Edwd Elam Wm Shute Jas Moore Jno Sample Jacob Harder James McGavock Jesse Tarkington John Nichols Josiah Wooldridge Benjn Bugg Wm Bateman Geo Kinnard. Plf recovers of dft damages $312.50 also costs of suit.

John J Henry vs Henry Cook Garner McConnico & Peggy Sharp extrs & extx of Anthony Sharp decd. Present James Boyd William Wilson R McMillin. Exrs & extx produced will of Anthony Sharp decd. John J Henry claimed interest in the estate in right of his wife Sally Henry formerly Sally Sharpe daughter of sd Anthony and alledged that sd will was invalid; Anthony Sharp was of unsound memory; will is not attested as law requires; will not written as sd Anthony directed when in better senses; will con-

JULY 1812

tains multitude of erasures and interlineations; will contains different devises of same property, is contradictory, and unintelligable; will not dated. Jury E White p.27   Joseph H Scales Burrell McLemore Saml Winstead Joel Stephens Martin Stanley Jas House Henry Walker Jas Skelly John Nichols Nicholas Wilbourn James S Clem who cannot agree on their verdict. Order Sheriff conduct Jurors and safely keep them together in some convenient place.
Court adjourned untill Tomorrow morning 8 0 Clock.
             Nicholas Scales James Boyd Robt McMillin

Saturday morning 18th July 1812. Present William Wilson Robert McMillin James Boyd. John J Henry vs Henry Cook & others. Jurors afsd Isaac Wright [name spelled White in previous list, other jurors above]. Paper purporting to be last will & testament of Anthony Sharpe deceased is not last will & testament of sd Anthony. John J Henry recovers agt the defendants his costs.

Order John Love oversee road from James Boyds to intersection with road from Franklin to James Neellys whereof he was formerly overseer.

Samuel Chambers vs Charles Boyles. Debt. Writ/error granted Chas Boyles to Circuit Court; who gave bond with Thomas H Benton & Harrison Boyd his securities.

Nicholas T Perkins vs Robert Estes. Motion of Nicholas T Perkins by Nichs Perkins his atty shewing that sd Robert Estes was bound with sd Nichs T & Thomas H Perkins as joint securities for Eli Stacy in a guardian bond for his guardianship of Chas B Simpson, also shewing judgt recovered agt him sd Nichs T Perkins in this Court by George Hulme & others for use of sd Chas B Simpson. Nicholas T Perkins recovers agt p.28   Robert Estes his proportionable part of sd judgt & costs of motion.

Order Wm G Boyd Robert Sharp Jas McKnight & John McClellan be included in bounds of hands to work on road between ridge of Mill Creek & Arringtons Creek to top of the ridge between Arringtons & Wilsons Creek whereof Wm Polk is overseer.

Charles McAlister & wife admrs of John Wright decd vs John Hays's admx. Attachment $900. Justices H Pettway R McMillin J Boyd. Nonsuit set aside; plf granted leave to amend declaration on paying costs of suit from last term to this time. Continued.

Order Richard Puckett Oliver Williams & Saml Shelburne Esqrs any two to settle with Joseph Love exr of William M Love decd and report to next Court.

Whereas John Sample & Co by John Hardeman atty produced an exn issd by David Mason Esqr at instance of Sample & Co Francis M Dunn for $12.75 & costs; Shff Wm Hulme levied on Lot 93 in Franklin; order of sale issues.

Ilai Metcalf vs Cary Bibb. Debt $230. Justices Geo Hulme Robt [Mc]Millin Hendley Stone. Dft came not; plf recovers agt dft his debt damages and costs.

George Kinnard vs Julian Neal. Dft to take deposition of Wm Anderson of Bedford Co.

Report of division of land & negroes of estate of Jesse Benton decd returned.

JULY 1812

George Kinnard vs Jacob Whitehead. Justices Geo Hulme Robt McMillin Hendley Stone.
p.29   Dft confesses judgt $10 & costs. Plf recovers debt & costs.

John Holloway by Nicholas Perkins his atty produced execution issd by Richard Puckett Esqr agt Francis M Dean for $14 & costs; Constable Caleb Manley levied on Lot 93 whereon F M Dean now lives; order of sale to issue to Sheriff.

Anthony Gilliam vs William Shute. Dam $200. Justices [above]. Jury Edwd Elam Ewen Cameron Andw Johnson Richd Hughes Wm Hope James Pinkerton Michael Layton Chapman White John Gee Jacob Harder Pleasant Russell Wm Jones. Plf recovers agt defendant.

Letters/admn granted Henry Cook and Peggy Sharp on estate of Anthony Sharp decd; bond $8000 with Chapman White & Samuel Shelburne their securities.

John Bukley[Berkley?] vs Jno G Pickens. Justices R McMillin H Stone Chas McAlister. Dft not appearing, plf recovers damages sustained by nonperformance in declaration mentioned; amount of damages to be enquired of by a jury at next Court.

Ephriam Andrews exrs vs Newton Cannon. Debt $422. Justices [above]. Dft not appearing, plf recovers debt, damages and costs.

p.30   Campbell & Boyles vs Archibald Lytle. Debt. Justices Geo Hulme Ro McMillin Chs McAlister. Dft confesseth balance of debt is due $352.09. Plf recovers.

Attendance as jurors proved by Chapman White 6 days Edwd Elam 6 & Wm Shute 6 days.

David McGavock assee vs Thomas H Perkins. Debt. Deft is granted writ/error to Circuit Court; gave bond with Daniel Perkins & Nicholas Perkins Senr his securities.

Thomas Shannon vs Thomas Alexander. Debt. Justices C McAlister R McMillin G Hulme. Deft came not. Plf recovers debt, damages, and costs.

Deed William King to Hugh Campbell part of 3 Lots in Rogersville proven by Robert P Currin.

Jno Cockrell assee vs Thos Sappington. Debt $190 Dam $100. Justices [above]. Contd.

Thomas West resigned his office of a Constable.
Court adjourns untill Court in Course.
                                    Hinchey Pettway   CHS McAlister   G Hulme

p.31   Monday 12th October 1812. Present the Worshipful George Hulme Samuel Akin and John J Henry Esquires.

Jurors summoned: Jesse Sparkman Wm Sparkman Charles Robinson David Robinson Barnett Donelson Benjamin May Meredith Helm Moses Chambers Drury Pulliam Thomas Ridley Benjn

OCTOBER 1812

Roberts exd Benjamin Gholson Wm Nall Wm Dowdy exd Thomas Walker Samuel F Glass John Swinney Henry Walker John Parks Junr James Sneed Richd Hightower Joel Riggs exd Jesse Tarkington Senr Thomas Cash exd John Neelly. Constables Caleb Manley Wm Bond.

Grand Jurors James Sneed foreman Henry Walker Jesse Sparkman John Parks Junr Barnet Donelson Thomas Ridley Moses Chambers John Swinney Benjamin Gholson Charles Robinson Wm Sparkman Drury Pulliam Jesse Tarkington Senr.

Order Thomas Walker oversee road whereof Arthur Fulgham was formerly overseer. Nathaniel Casey produced licence to practice law and is admitted.

State vs Edward Gossage. Recognizance to keep peace. Samuel Andrews one of defts securities surrendered him to custody of sheriff. Moses Chambers and George Strambler defts security for his appearance from day to day until discharged.

Jacob Myers vs Israel Mayfields heirs. Debt $107 Dam $50. Justices Saml Akin Collin McDaniel John J Henry. Jury Wm Dowdy Thos Walker Joel Hobbs Robt Guthrie Saml Merritt Thos Merritt Lancaster Glover Geo Strambler Andw Craig Jas Berry Saml Moore David Craig say plf sustained damages by reason of detention of debt to $13.49, that £24.13 Kentucky money is equal to $82.16. Therefore plf recovers agt dft debt £24.23 Ky money equal in cash to $82.16 and interest on the debt from 1 Mar 1805.

p.32   Drury Nobles, confined in county jail, to appear before Grand Jury.

George Burnett Senr vs Walter Burnett. Attachment. Justices Geo Hulme Saml Shelburne Richd Puckett. Jury Stephen Smith Alexr Smith Andrew Goff Swanson Johnson Wm Peebles Burrell McLemore Andw Dorton David Caldwell Demsey Nash Benjn White Ephriam Simpson John Johnston who find for plf his damages and costs.

Jlai Metcalf vs Cary Bibb. On execution. Richard Horbert summoned as garnishee.
Bond Stephen Hale to Richard Brown title to 1 acre 56 poles ackd.
Deed Josiah Wooldridge to Andw Berryman 272 acres proven by Francis Flournoy and Drury Scruggs.
Deed Abraham Kennedy to William Boring 6 acres 8 poles proven by Richard Brown and Robert Bigger.
Deed G Reed to Bethel Allen 200 acres proven by Thomas Allen.
Deed Charles Calhoon to Richard Brown 11½ acres 34 poles proven by Jesse Bugg.
Deed William Haile to Richard Brown 30 acres proven by Robert Price and Wm Borris [Boind?]
Mortgage Henry G Kearney to Andrew Goff proven by Joel T Rivers as to Kearney and ackd by Andrew Goff.
Deed Andrew Harriss to Geo Barnett 20 acres proven by Glen Owen & Woodson Hubbard.
Deed Richard Brown to Wm Jackson 40½ acres 24 poles ackd.
Deed William McGee to Ephriam Andrews 100 acres proven by Edward Ragsdale and Geo Andrews.
p.33   Bond William Christmas to General Lee Nolen proven by Wm Nolen.
Deed Berry Nolen to Genl L Nolen 95 acres ackd.
Bill/sale James Vaughan to Henry Bailey proven by John Bailey.
Deed Wm Haile to Robert Price 100 acres proven by Robert Bigger & Stephen Haile.
Deed Robert Winsett to Milly Winsett & Jason Winsett 65 acres 36 poles proven by

OCTOBER 1812

Daniel Brown and Silas Winsett.
Will of James Sullards decd proven by R W Shannon & David Kaiglar.
Deed Wm Glover to John R Tankersly 100 acres proven by Alexr & Julian Neal.
Deed James Gullett to David Dunn 27½ acres proven by James Wilkins.
Will of Robert Winsett decd proven by Daniel Brown & Silas Winsett & Milley Winsett Wm Winsett and Amos Winsett exx & exrs qualified.
Deed Thomas Hardeman to Thomas J Hardeman & Bailey Hardeman 546 acres ackd.
Deed John Gillaspie to David Christman 27 acres 18 poles proven by George Tillman & Aaron Christman.
Deed Joseph Mullin to Joseph T Elliston 1 seventh part of 552 acres proven by Chapman White and James Gordon.
Deed Wm Mullin to Joseph T Elliston 1 seventh part of 552 acres proven [as above].
Deed Bethel Allen to Theoderick Bland Dudley 200 acres ackd.
Deed Alexander Cathey to James Gullett 200 acres proven by James Wilkins.
Deed Wm Glover & Burrell McLemore to Ann Harrison 89 acres ackd.
Will of Andrew Harris decd proven by James House Senr & Glen Owen; Ede Harris Eph-
p.34   riam Sampson & George Burnett the executors named qualified.
Inventory/estate of Anthony Sharp decd returned into Court. Admrs ordered to sell perishable property except Negroes.

Order Benjamin Parks oversee road from east of Joseph Love to James Neelly.

Order Thomas Gooch oversee road from Liberty Meeting House to Davidson Co; residents on west side Nelsons Creek and Thomas Gooch Moses Holmes Luke Pryor James Kimbrough on east side work thereon.

License Samuel Winstead to keep an ordinary at his dwelling house; bond $2500 with David Squier and Andrew Goff his securities.

Order Thomas Duty oversee road from Franklin to knob south of Major Porters; James Williams George Neelly Thomas Neelly Watson John Hay George Slesker Nathan Bullock Amos Bullock John McKinney Charles Boyles Andrew Cowsart George Burnett James Terrill James House Mr Gillaspie Thomas Duty Baalam Ezell Jesse Tarkington John Tarkington Richard Swanson Robert Dysart Mr Dobson Ephriam Sampson work thereon.

Order Andrew Reid oversee commissioners trace from Robert Johnsons to Liberty Meeting House road; residents from Robert Johnstons to Mr Nortons to Mr Montgomery to John Gray on Spencers Creek to Joel Stephens to road from Mr Goffs to McConnicos Meeting House leaving John Goff on Liberty road work thereon.

Settlement with John Crafton and Daniel Wilkes admrs/estate of James Crafton decd returned.

Appoint Daniel Wilkes guardian of Richard Crafton and Daniel Crafton minor orphans of James Crafton decd; bond $5000 with Robert Crafton and David Craig securities.

Appoint John Crafton guardian of George Crafton and Dennis Crafton minor orphans of
p.35   James Crafton decd; bond $500, Saml Shelbourne & Richd Puckett securities.

Ltrs/admn granted to David Riggs on estate of Wright Riggs decd; Bond $2000 with

OCTOBER 1812

Joel Riggs and George Tillman his securities.
James Wooten arrested for contempt/court fined $10 and remain in custody of sheriff until he pay said fine and costs.
Settlement with James Wilkins exr of William Wilkins decd returned.
Division/partition land of Metcalf Degraffenreid returned.
License William Bond to keep an ordinary at his dwelling house in this County; bond $2500 with Alexander Smith his security.
On petition of Andrew Cole and Sarah Cole his wife late Sarah Crafton setting forth that they are entitled to dower of estate of James Crafton decd of personal property only; order sheriff summon a jury to lay off to them according to law.
Order James Allison Thomas Wilson David Edmiston James Robertson Josiah Wilson Richd Reynolds and General Lee Nolen surveyor lay off and partition 700 acres above Harpeth Licks granted to James Wilson decd and allot to Jacob Howdeshall, one of legatees, his proportionable part and report thereof.
Court adjourns until tomorrow morning 9 OClock

G Hulme Robert McMillin John J Henry

Tuesday 13th October 1812. Present [justices above].
Thomas Mastersons exors vs Abraham Walker. Debt $300 Dam $100. Justices Geo Hulme John J Henry Saml Akin. Jury James House Senr John B Gibson Wm Parham Terry Bradley John Williamson Robt Waite Nicholas T Perkins Michael Kinnard Lancaster Glover
p.36   Walter Hill John Gholson Wm Dowdy. Plfs recover agt deft $309.75 & costs.

Order James Wooten released from fine imposed yesterday after he pays prison fees.
James Allison paid into Court 37½¢ being fine on James Shumate for swearing 3 oaths & $6.50 a fine on Constable Wm Alexander for swearing 26 oaths.
Isaac Crow imprisoned four hours & until he pays fees for contempt/court.
Supplemental inventory/ estate of Littleberry Epperson decd returned.
Deed James McCarrill to John Blackman 190 acres proven by Wm Smith & John Swinney.
Will of John Manier decd proven by Thomas Wilson & John Walker.
Deed Robt Davis to James Gocey 95 5/6(?) acres proven by Jas Gordon & Edwd Bevell.
Ephriam Sampson released from value of steer; same proven away by Thomas Polk.
Deed Abraham Walker to Saml Blackburn Lot 97 in Franklin ackd.
Deed George Strambler to Sion Hunt 119 acres proven by Saml Moore & Thos Hulme.
Deed Isaac Crow to Jason Hopkins 1/2 Lot 32 in Franklin proven by Archibald Potter and John Sample.
Deed James Brisbey Rosey Brisbey Lewis Martin & Ann Martin to James Frazier 2560 acres ackd. Ordered Robert McMillin & Collin McDaniel Esqrs take private examination of sd Rosey & Ann who report the same is their act.
p.37   Inventory/estate of Wright Riggs decd returned.
Deed David Gillaspie to Clement Wall 61¼ acres proven by Saml Brown & John Walker.
Deed Henry Critchlow to Joseph T Elliston 1/7 part of 552 acres proven by John Witherspoon and Robert McLemore.

Robt McMillin Daniel Underhill Abraham Castleman & Wm Dowdy apptd last Court to lay off road near Shannons pond to Dickson County line passing house of Robert McMillin & Wm Dowdy, also to cross Turnbull at Ryners ford below Ryners house report.
Order Deliverance Gray oversee the new road.

OCTOBER 1812

Order William House oversee road from McGavocks branch; residents at Nicholas Mill Lytles Thomas Bell John Morses hands those on Henry G Kearneys old place Walter Hill William Hill & Benjamin Gresley work thereon.
Hadijah Collins released from double tax on 3 slaves but pay single tax.

Order Jacob Halfacre oversee road from McConnicos meeting house to near Hayes Creek; hands including Wm Marshall and Wm Thomas and as far as Pulliams branch at upper end of David McElwees to John Rickards Michael Kinnard Charles Harrald and Wm Denson to the beginning work thereon.
Release Thomas Gooch from appraised value of stray mare proven away by John Price.
Order so much of road under superintendance of John Williamson from George Kinnards p.38 still house to McCalls Gap be discontinued as a public road.
Release James Carson from appraised value of cow posted by him & since proven away by Clement Cannon.
Order Andrew Goff and David McEwen be included in bounds of hands to work on road whereof James McEwen is overseer and sd James McEwen given leave to get a crowbar & sledge for purpose of breaking and raising rocks in sd road.
Solomon Barnett released from appraised value of mare which has been proven away.
James Carson released from appraised value of cow proven away by Clement Cannon.

Order David Squier Gurden Squire Samuel Cox Benjn White Thomas Sappington & Robert P Currin any 5 lay off a road from Harpeth bridge to road from John Buchanans.
Wm McEwen released from tax on 100 acres & 1 black poll for present year.
Edward Gossage released from appraised value of bull since proven away by Joseph Denton.
Elect Nelson Fields constable in Capt Charles Johnsons Company; bond with Thomas Simmons & Gersham Hunt his securities.
Elect Isaac N Henry constable in Capt Crocketts Company; bond with John J Henry and Sion Hunt his securities.
Elect David Briggs constable in Capt Hookers Company; bond with David Riggs and George Tillman his securities.
License Stephen Barfield to keep an ordinary at his house in Franklin; bond $2500 with John Blackman and Thomas Walker his securities.
License John [name written over: Brytsas? Krytsai?] to keep an ordinary who gave bond $2500 with Richard Orton and Henry Rutherford his securities.
p.39 Allow John Young $5 for two wolf scalps killed by him in this county, one over and one under four months old.
Allow Jonathan W Martin $3, wolf scalp killed in this county over four months old.

Order Reuben Parks James Williams Finch Scruggs John Parks any 5 lay off public road from James Neelys to Cannons Mill so as to go round his meadow.
Ltrs/admn granted James Craig & Samuel Buchanan on estate of David Craig Junr decd; bond $1000 with Andrew Craig and Daniel Wilkes securities. Inventory returned.
Order hands east of Caney Spring creek road and west of fishing ford road work on road whereof James Joyce is overseer in addition to other hands ordered to him.

Jurors to ensuing County Court: Zacheus German Ephriam Brown Samuel Gentry Tignal Martin Luke Pryor Junr Charles Johnston Britain Adams Wm Marshall Wm Denson Michael Long Sampson Prowell John Hopkins Andrew Craig James Neelly Thomas B Walthal John Bond George Andrews Guilford Dudley Berry Nolin David Nolin John Winstead Knacy

OCTOBER 1812

Andrews Joseph Robertson John Buchanan Burton Jordan Robert P Currin. Constables Richard W Hyde and Isaac N Henry.

Following persons apptd to take lists of Taxable property for 1813: Thomas W Stockett Esq in Capt Garretts Compy; Thos Garrett Esq in Capt W McKeys Co; Hinchey Pettway Esq in Capt Joel T Rivers Co; John Crawford Esq in Capt Thomas McCrorys Co; James Davis Esq in Capt Geo Barnes Co; John J Henry Esq in Capt Joseph Crocketts Co; Samuel Shelburne Esq in Capt Dilliards Co; Robert McMillin Esq in Capt Anglins Co; David Dunn Esq in Capt David Dunns Co; Jesse White Esq in Capt James Simms Co; Tristram Patton Esq in Capt Isaac Pattons Co; James Black Esq in Capt Jas Giddens Co; Edward Ragsdale Esq in Capt Geo Mebanes Co; Wm Logan Esq in Capt Wm Hookers Co; James Allison Esq in Capt John Daltons Co; Wm R Nunn Esq in Capt James Ridleys Co; Samuel Perkins Esq in Capt James Gantts[Gaults?] Co; Nicholas Scales Esq in Capt Wm Hickmans Co; Wm Anthony Esq in Capt Charles Johnsons Co; Richard Puckett Esq in Capt James Shannons Compy.

Commrs of Franklin granted leave to erect a market house on southwest corner of the p.40 public square 18 ft from Thomas Crutchers lot & 20 ft from main street to be 40 ft long & 18 ft wide.
Court adjourns untill Tomorrow morning 9 0 Clock.
            Hinchey Petway John J Henry Robert McMillin

Wednesday 14th October 1812. Present George Hulme Robt McMillin John J Henry Esqrs. Chs McAlister & wife admrs John Hayes admx. Attcht. Justices Geo Hulme Jas Davis Robt McMillin. Thomas H Benton is admitted prosecution bail the room of John Barkley who is released. Jury Wm Dowdy Kinchin P Bass Thomas T Maury Benjn White Beverly Reese John Gee Silvanus Sturdevant Wm Peebles Thos Haynes Wm Shute Wm Banks Geo Neelly. Plfs recover agt deft their debt and costs.

John Sample & Co vs Geo Strambler. Debt. John Sample one of the partners of sd John Sample & Co says Thomas Masterson one of the partners of the firm Jno Sample & Co died, and sd Jno Sample having suggested that C White & Thomas Washington had qualified as executors to will of Thomas Masterson, therefore ordered by Court that they be admitted parties to sd suit jointly with John Sample; by consent of counsel on both sides, sd order rescinded, and sd suit proceeds in name of John Sample surviving partner of the firm aforesaid.

John Sample surviving partner vs Geo Strambler. Justices Geo Hulme Saml Shelburne John Witherspoon. Jury Archd Lytle John Johnston Gregory Wilson Daniel McMahon Saml F Glass Thos Walker Andw Craig Robt Sayers Andw Dorton Wm Alexander Wm Wharton p.41 David Houston. Jno Sample recovers agt dft his debt, damages, costs.

John Nichols vs John Reed. Justices Saml Shelbourne Geo Hulme Jno Witherspoon. Jury James Craig John Johnston Gregory Wilson Danl McMahon Saml F Glass Thos Walker Andw Craig Robt Sayers Andw Dorton Wm Alexander Wm Whinton[Wharton?] David Houston. Dft recovers agt plff his costs in this behalf expended.

Exors of E Andrews vs George Mebane. Debt. Geo Mebane admits he owes $123.36¼ and interest $5.59. Plaintiff recovers agt dft.

OCTOBER 1812

John H Eaton vs Robert Crafton. Covenant. Justices O Williams H Pettway John J Henry. Jury Archibald Lytle Benjn White Wm Banks John Nichols Sylvanus Sturdevant John Gee Wm Dowdy Kinchen P Bass Wm Peebles Thomas Haynes Beverly Reese Thos T Maury. Plf recovers agt dft his damages and costs.

Order John R Boyd oversee road from ridge between Arringtons and Wilsons Creeks to Nelson Creek; residents from Nicholas Scales to John Bostick and Reps O Childress to Burton Jordan John D Hill Johnson Wood John Sammons James Lawrance Charles Adams to Thomas Jordan and Hartwell Miles work thereon under his directions.

Court fine Wm Shute and George Neelly Senr each 50¢ for not attending as jurors.
p.42 Henry Lyon licensed to keep an ordinary at his dwelling house in this town; bond $2500 with Thomas McCrory and Benjn White his securities.

John W Crunk vs Daniel Perkins. Appeal. Suit referred to determination of Chapman White and Thomas Ridley whose award is to be judgt of this Court.

Felix Staggs vs Arthur Stewart. Debt $110 Dam $50. Justices Saml Shelburne Geo Hulme John Witherspoon. Jury James Craig John Johnston Gregory Wilson Danl McMahan Saml F Glass Thos Walker Andw Craig Robt Sayers Andw Dorton Wm Alexander Wm Wharton David Houston. Plf recovers agt deft his debt, damages, and costs.

Joseph Carson vs Samuel Wilson. Debt $500 Dam $200. Justices O Williams H Pettway Jno J Henry. Jury Archd Lytle Benjn White Wm Banks John Nichols Sylvanus Sturdevant John Gee Wm Dowdy Kinchen P Bass Wm Peebles Thos Haynes Beverly Reese Thos T Maury. Plf recovers agt dft his debt, damages, and costs of suit.

John Berkley vs John G Pickens. Case. Dam $300. Justices Oliver Williams H Pettway J J Henry. Jury [above]. Plf recovers agt dft his damages and costs.

p.43 Gasper Mansker vs Thomas McCrory. Debt $1100 Dam $500. Justices O Williams H Pettway J J Henry. Jury [above] say dft hath not paid the whole debt. Plf recovers agt dft $300, damages, and costs.

Tillman Dixon vs Henry Lyon. Debt $243.75 Dam $100. Justices [above]. Jury [above]. Plf recovers agt dft his debt, damages, and costs.

Deadrick & Sitter vs William Smith. Debt $121.31 Dam $60. Justices [above]. Jury [above]. Plfs recover agt deft their debt, damages, and costs.

Elihu S Hale & Co vs Thomas Simmons. Debt $138.74 Dam $50. Justices [above]. Jury
p.44 [above]. Plf recovers agt dft his debt, damages, and costs.

Currin & Mason vs Wm Wolf. Debt $110 Dam $50. Justices [above]. Jury [above]. Plfs recover agt dft their debt, damages, and costs.

Saml Shelburne vs John Bond. Debt $294.78 Dam $100. Justices [above]. Jury [above] say dft hath not paid whole debt. Plf recovers agt dft $267.18, damages, and costs.

John Sample & Co vs Wm McKey. Debt. Cont in name of Jno Sample surviving partner.

OCTOBER 1812

p.45   John Sample surviving partner of John Sample & Co vs Wm McKey. Justices O Williams Hinchey Pettway John J Henry. Jury Archd Lytle Benjn White Wm Banks John Nichols Sylvanus Sturdivant John Gee Wm Dowdy Kinchen P Bass Wm Peebles Thos Haynes Beverly Reese Thos T Maury. Plf recovers agt dft his debt, damages, and costs. Court adjourns untill tomorrow morning 9 Oclock.

G Hulme S Shelburne C McDaniel

Thursday 15th October 1812. Present Geo Hulme Saml Shelburne Collin McDaniel Esqrs. Appt Ephriam Sampson overseer of road whereof Charles Kavenaugh was overseer.

State vs Andrew Craig. Presentment overseer of a road. Justices John Witherspoon John J Henry Collin McDaniel. Dft fined $5 and costs.

State vs Daniel Carter. Riot. Justices O Williams S Shelburne C McDaniel. Jury Wm Dowdy Thos Walker Saml F Glass Wm Hill Wm Banks Metcalf Degraffenreid John Allen Wm O Perkins Michael Layton Wm Mansker David Houston Thos T Maury find dft not guilty.

p.46   State vs Archibald Anterbury. Sci Fa. Deft came not. Order state have exn agt him for $50 in scire facias mentioned together with costs.

State vs James House Senr. Presentment overseer of road. Justices G Hulme S Shelburne C McDaniel. Dft says he is guilty, fined $5 and costs.

Order Oliver Williams Richd Puckett & Saml Shelburne Esqrs settle with Joseph Love exr of William M Love decd; report thereof to next Court.
Settlement with Lewis Stevens & Michael Kinnard admrs/estate of Michael Kinnard decd returned.
Bill/sale John Bukley[Berkley?] & Thos Bradley to Gersham Hunt ackd.
Deed/gift Robt McLemore[McLemon?] to Bethenia Ann Green McLemore[McLemon?] ackd.

Janie Sharp over age 14 chose Henry Cook her guardian; bond $5000 with Caleb Manley David Dunn Stephen Childress & Robert McLemore his securitys.
Nancy Sharp over age 14 chose Henry Cook her guardian [as above].
Appt Henry Cook gdn of Salie Sharp minor orphan of Anthony Sharp decd bond [above].
Appt Henry Cook gdn of Searcy Davis Sharp [as above].
Appt Henry Cook gdn of Sumner Martin Sharp [as above].
p.47   Appt Henry Cook gdn of Peggy Nelson Sharp [as above].
Wm Dowdy excused as a juror this Term, proves attendance 4 days.

Zacheus Wilson Haden Tillman Isaac Gillaspie Moses Steele Samuel Brown and Aaron Christman apptd last Court to mark out a road report they marked from between Thomas and David Gillaspie at Maury Count line through Woods Gap on Duck River ridge to Nashville road at John Walkers plantation. Appt David Gillaspie overseer of sd road to the ridge; residents including Wm Alexander work thereon. Order Samuel Brown oversee road from ridge to intersection with Nashville road, hands including Richard Sampson work thereon under his directions.
Court adjourns until Tomorrow Morning 9 OClock.

O Williams J P   Hinchey Pettway J P   T W Stockett

OCTOBER 1812

Friday 16 October 1812. Present Oliver Williams Hinchey Pettway John J Henry Esqrs. State vs Nicholas Tomlin. A&B. Alexander McCown dfts bail surrendered him; dft committed to custody of Sheriff.
State vs Edward Gossage. Recognizance to keep peace. Dft to keep peace toward
p.48   Drury Nobles; recognizance renewed, $250; Moses Chambers and George Strambler his securities.

State vs Henry G Kearney. Recognizance to keep peace. Dft to keep peace toward Lucy D Kearney, $1000; Securities Jas Gordon Robt McLemore Andw Goff Danl Perkins Thos H Perkins Moses Chambers Atholston Andrews Danl McMahon George Neelly Geo Strambler.

Attendance as jurors proved by Samuel F Glass 3 days Thos Walker 5 days.
Deed George Neelly to John Swinney Lot 152 in Franklin ackd.

Order William May oversee road from Franklin to McGavocks branch; residents including Burwell McLemore Old Mr Ashman work thereon.

Deed Jos German to John Sappington Lots 2 17 25 26 proven by Wm Hulme & Thos Hulme.

p.49   State vs Nicholas Tomlin. A&B. Justices O Williams D Dunn Jno J Henry. Jury Burrell McLemore Chas A Duberry William Banks Thos T Maury Samuel F Glass Thomas Walker Jason Hopkins Andrew Goff Jno Bridges Jno Bond William W Cunningham William Hunter find dft not guilty. Dft recovers his costs agt plf.

State vs Thomas Brooks. Riot. Justices O Williams D Dunn David Dickinson. Dft confesses guilt; fined 50¢ and pay costs of prosecution.
State vs John McMeans. Riot. Justices [above]. Dft in proper person saith he is guilty; fined 50¢ and pay costs of prosecution.
State vs Graves Thurman. Riot. Justices [above]. Fined 50¢ & pays costs.
State vs John Carter. Riot. Justices [above]. Fined 50¢ & pays costs.
State vs John Jones. Riot. Justices O Williams C McDaniel Wm Wilson. Dft in proper person saith he is guilty; fined 50¢ and pays costs of prosecution.
p.50   State vs Edward Tignor. Riot. Justices [above] Fined 50¢, pays costs.
State vs Jeremiah Terry. Riot. Justices [above]. Fined 50¢, pays costs.
State vs Daniel Carter. Riot. Justices [above]. Fined $10, pays costs.
State vs John McCutchen. A&B. Justices [above]. Fined $10, pays costs.

John Cockrell Junr vs Thomas Sappington. Debt. Justices Daniel Dunn Collin McDaniel John Crawford. Jury Samuel F Glass Thos Walker John Bond John Bridges David Houston Andw Cuff Wm Peebles Daniel Carter Senr John McKinney Lancaster Glover Alexr Smith Alexr Lester. Plf recovers agt dft his debt, damages, costs.

Abraham Maury Jr vs Joel T Rivers. Appeal. Justices Collin McDaniel John J Henry Hinchey Pettway. Jury [above]. Dft recovers agt plf. Appeal granted, N Perkins and John White securities.

p.51   William Mitchell vs Wm Peebles. Debt. Justices Hinchey Pettway Geo Hulme Collin McDaniel. Jury [above except Martin Stanly for Wm Peebles] find for dft.

Drury Nobles appearance bond to prosecute Edward Gossage for A&B in January next.

OCTOBER 1812

Order Sheriff summon to next Court Mary Wooldridge Loving Wooldridge Thomas Wooldridge & Elizabeth Wooldridge children of John Wooldridge decd.

Groves Sharp Isham Cole & Owen Hughs called but came not; sci fa to issue. Wm Spencer Alexr Smith & John West came not; sciri facias to issue agt them. Owen Hughes Elizabeth Hughes & Robt Gray came not; sci fa to issue agt them. Court adjourns untill Tomorrow morning 10 OClock.

                                                              G Hulme   H Pettway   John J Henry

Saturday 17 October 1812. Present George Hulme John J Henry Collin McDaniel Esqrs.
p.52   State vs James Tigner. Riot. Justices [above]. Fined 50¢ & costs.
Joseph Carson vs Samuel Wilson. Debt. Dft granted appeal to Circuit Court; bond with John Hardeman & Archd Lytle his securities.
Ltr/admn to Mary Rolland on estate of Jacob Rolland decd; bond $2500 with George Neelly and Daniel Carter Senr securities. Inventory returned.
Deed Turner Saunders to David Dunn 260 acres ackd.
Deed James Gullett to David Dunn 27½ acres proven by Turner Saunders.
Deed Alexander Cathey to James Gullett 200 acres proven by Turner Saunders.
Isaac Crow vs Francis Gunter. Certiorari. H Pettway S Shelburne C McDaniel. Warrant issued is quashed and deft recovers agt plf.

Andrew Dorton vs Wm Wharton. Certiorara. Justices G Hulme S Shelburne C McDaniel. Suit quashed; dft recovers agt plf his costs. Plf obtained appeal to Circuit Court giving bond with Henry Crenshaw and John Wilkins his securities.

Ltr/atty Green Hill to Jorden Hill ackd.

Order Meredith Helm oversee road to Chambers ferry from Nicholas P Hardemans line to ten mile tree; hands from sd lane to Murfrees east boundary including Wm Simpson
p.53   to Walkers branch to ridge between Leepers and Murfrees forks including Joseph Cowan work thereon under his directions.

Ltrs/admn granted to Thomas T Maury on estate of Jane Wheaton decd with will annexed; bond $10,000, David Dunn Hinchey Pettway Henry Lyon & John Reed securities.

John Nichols vs John Reed. Appeal. Justices G Hulme C McDaniel D Dunn. Judgment entered in this cause set aside; new trial to be had. Deposition of Ezekiel Graham to be taken by plf.

Tapley B Andrews vs Curtis Hooks. Justices [blank]. Note of Tapley B Andrews and Curtis Hooks to pay Knacy Andrews and Benjamin Bugg exrs estate of Ephriam Andrews decd $123.36¼. Test John R Tankersley. Tapley B Andrews suggests to Court that he executed sd bond as security of sd Curtis Hooks; judgt this day passed agt him. Jury Geo H James James Shannon Jas Gordon Geo Mebane Jno Gholson Jno Wilkins Jas Pinkerton Burwell McLemore Edward Warren Lan Glover Ruffin Brown Joel Hobbs who say T B Andrews did execute sd bond as security; he recovers agt Curtis Hooks.

Henry Cook vs Charles B Neilson. Attachment. Chas B Neilson came not; plf recovers; jury at next Court to determine his damages.

JANUARY 1813

John Sample surviving partner vs Robert Carter. Debt. Dft came not; plf recovers his debt, damages of detention, and costs of suit.

Ltrs/admn granted Jno Wilkins on estate of James Wilkins Jr; bond $500 with James Wilkins his security.

p.54 Henry Cook vs Charles B Neilson. Attachment. Wm Hulme garnishee, as sheriff sold stud horse called Royalist; after satisfying execution there remained $141.61 on which he levied this attachment at instance of sd Henry Cook.

Motion of Joseph B Porters admr of Reese Porter decd, judgt granted him agt John L Fielder late constable & John Edmondson Joel Riggs & Saml Edmiston his securities, the amt of judgt & interest recovered by plf agt John F Maury and which was collected by sd Fielder who hath failed to pay over same to plf.

Court adjourns till the Court in Course.

G Hulme Dd Dunn C McDaniel

Court of Pleas and Quarter Sessions for County of Williamson at the Court House in the Town of Franklin on Monday the 11th day of January 1813. Present the Worshipful George Hulme Charles McAlister & David Shannon Esquires.

Jurors summoned: Berry Nolen Chas Brown Ephriam Brown Guilford Dudley exd Jno Buchanan Wm Denson Jas Neely Thos B Walthall John Bond David Nolen Andrew Craig Burton Jorden exd Knacy Andrews George Andrews Zacheus German Joseph Robertson Luke Pryor John Winstead Wm Marshall Britian Adams. Constables Richd W Hyde Isaac N Henry.

Grand Jurors Wm Denson foreman Berry Nolen Benton[Burton?] Jordan Ephriam Brown Zacheus German William Marshall Joseph Robertson Knacy Andrews George Andrews Britian Adams Andrew Craig Luke Pryor John Winstead.

Deed/gift Nathan Chaffin to Polly Johnson proven by John Johnston.
Deed Wm Peebles to Wm Spencer 92 acres ackd.
Deed James Davis to John Primm 11 acres 40 poles proven by Joel Riggs and Jeremiah Primm.
Deed James Davis to Jeremiah Primm 132 acres proven by Joel Riggs & John Primm.
p.55 Deed Elizabeth Spencer to James Brooks 150 acres proven by Shack Speer Standfield and John Gray Senr.
Deed John Baldridge to Edmond Chitwood 110 acres proven by Anslem Nolen.
Deed James Craig to Thomas Almond 80 acres proven by Wm Banks & John Coffey.
Deed James Robertson to Elijah Hunter 129 acres proven by Garner McConnico and Robert P Currin.
Deed Samuel Haggard to Mary McClore 140 acres proven by General L Nolen.
Deed John Jones to Thomas E Jones 100 acres proven by John Jones Jr & Wm Jones.
Deed John Jones to John Jones Junr 142 acres proven by Thos E Jones & Wm Jones.
Deed John Davis to Thomas E Jones 12 acres proven by James Gordon & Jason Hopkins.
Deed John Jones to Wm Jones 225 acres proven by Thomas E Jones & John Jones Jr.
Deed John Davis to Wm Jones 10 acres proven by James Gordon & Jason Hopkins.
Deed Hartwell Miles to Wm Taylor $127\frac{1}{2}$ acres proven by Richd W Hyde & Geo M Taylor.

JANUARY 1813

Deed Robert Rogers to Minos Cannon 150 acres ackd.
Deed John Hill to Thomas Hardrick 100 acres ackd.
Deed Joseph Cowan to Richard Graham 66 acres 16 poles proven by John Blackman and John Gray.
Deed John Porter to Able Garrett 25 acres ackd.

Return of Lists of Taxable property for 1813 made by Hinchey Pettway Esq in Capt Joel T Rivers Compy, Wm R Nunn Esqr in Capt Jas Ridleys Compy, Richd Puckett Esqr in Capt James Shannons Compy.
Inventory/estate of Robert Winsett decd returned.
Acct/sales estate of Samuel Wilson decd returned.
p.56   Order Nicholas Perkins Senr Daniel Perkins Robert McLemore and Edward Warren any three settle with Hendley Stone guardian of Peter Pryor and Green Pryor orphans of John Pryor decd & report thereof to next County Court.
Division of land of James Wilson decd to his heirs received.
Ltrs/admn granted to Nancy Bugg David Pinkston & Ephriam Bugg on estate of Benjamin Bugg decd; bond $10,000; Jesse Bugg & Knacy Andrews their securities.
Ltrs/admn granted to Moses Ridley & Dianna Elam on estate of Stephen Elam decd; bond $1000; James Allison & Richd Ogilvie their securities. Inventory returned.
Ltrs/admn granted to Joseph Crenshaw on estate of John Crenshaw decd; bond $500; Joel T Rivers & Oliver Crenshaw securities. Inventory returned.

Appt Henry Rutherford guardian of Washington Pinkney Crawford, orphan of John Crawford decd; bond $3000; John Witherspoon Richd Hightower & Richd Orton securities.
Appt Henry Rutherford guardian of James Johnston Crawford orphan [as above].
Appt Henry Rutherford guardian of Henry Rutherford Crawford orphan [as above].

Order Coorod Richardson oversee road from Nelsons Creek to Big Harpeth; hands from Cannons Horse Mill to Rutherford County line work thereon.
Order Francis McDaniel oversee road from Joel Hobbs to McDaniels ford; hands of Jas Gee Thomas Blair Richard Hughes Robert Guthrie Francis McDaniel Wm McDaniel John McDaniel Turner Saunders David Dunn Moore Bragg and on Leepers lease work thereon.
p.57   Order Richard Hughes oversee road from John Witherspoons to Wm Bonds; residents from John Witherspoons to Samuel Williams to Hugh Dobbins to Richard Steeles including Hendley Stone and Wm Bonds hands work thereon.
Order James Smith oversee road from Ephriam Browns to near Hogues old place; residents in bounds from McCutchens Creek to Lytles Knob up Harpeth to Thomas H Perkins horse mill leaving out his hands to Newsoms Mill to Donelsons Creek leaving out Ephriam Browns plantation work thereon.
Order William Williams oversee road from John Clicks or his former place of residence to Bufords Ford on West Harpeth; hands from Herrins to Giddens road including Elisha Hassell & Michael Gunter to Cornelius Wilson to Mark Andrews to James Herrins including James Boyd & Edward Ragsdale up Harpeth to McBanes work thereon.

Appoint Alexander Mebane Esqr to take List/Taxable property & persons in Captain George Mebanes Company of Malitia for present year in room of Edward Ragsdale.

Order Simon Roach have $3 for wolf scalp killed by him in bounds of this County over four months old.
David Dickinson records his stock mark.

JANUARY 1813

David McEwen vs Joseph Mairs. On motion of sd David McEwen by John Hardeman his atty; Harris Ogilvie recovered judgt agt Joseph Mairs on 24 Feby 1812 before Charles McAlister Esqr for $79.30 & costs; paid by David McEwen as security; David p.58 McEwen recovers agt Joseph Mairs sd sums & costs of his motion.
Order Samuel Younger have $3 for wolf scalp killed by him in this County over four months old.
Richard Orton vs John Johnston. Motion.
Court adjourns untill Tomorrow Morning 9 OClock.

G Hulme R Puckett James Davis J P

Tuesday 12th January 1813. Present George Hulme Richard Puckett James Davis Esqrs. Edward Buford vs Edward Ragsdale. Debt $250 Dam $100. Justices [above]. Jury John Buchanan James Neelly Henry G Kearney John Cox Andrew Johnson Loammi Stephens Andrew Goff Wm Martin Thomas Haynes David Caldwell Archd Lytle John Johnston. Plf recovers agt dft his debt damages and costs.

William Adams vs John Tillman. Certiorara. Justices [above]. Jury Richard Ogilvie Michl Kinnard Saml Williams Richd Steele Jeremiah Hardin Nimrod Fielder Wm Glover George Kinnard Wm Willett Moses Chambers Henry Dobson Thomas Scott. Plf recovers agt dft his debt and costs of suit.

p.59   George Seaton vs James McCracken. Richd Ogilvie defts bail surrendered him; James Andrews and Robert Davis bail for deft.
Order Gersham Hunt & James Davis Esqrs let to lowest bidder Wm Deakins an object of Charity.
Abraham Little exonerated from Poll tax for present year.
Collin McDaniel apptd to take List/Taxable property & persons in Capt Thos McCrorys Company in room of John Crawford deceased.
Order Philip Maury have balance of money allowed him heretofore for building bridge across Harpeth River opposite Franklin as soon as collections are sufficient.
Allow Elisha Fly $24 for support of Wm Deakins an object of Charity.
Order Richard Puckett Oliver Williams & Wm Denson settle with different guardians of orphans of John Page decd & report to next Court.
Order Hinchey Pettway George Hulme & Charles McAlister settle with Lancaster Glover guardian of orphan Hardy Pates.
Appt Saml Wells Esqr to take list of Taxable property in Capt Wilsons Company.

Jurors to next Circuit Court: George Hulme John Witherspoon Jacob Garrett Richard Puckett Thomas Wilson John Echols Wm Denson Wm R Nunn James Davis Henley Stone Owen T Watkins Daniel Carter Samuel Akins Wm Jones James Boyd Michael Kinnard Henry Rutherford Matthew Johnston Wm Perry Wm Wilson Isham R Trotter Spencer Buford Sion Hunt Chapman White Robert McMillin Daniel Perkins. Constables Nelson Fields Caleb Manley and Saml Andrews.

p.60   Order Thomas Gooch oversee road from Liberty meeting House to Davidson County; hands of Luke Pryor Thomas Taylor Green Scott John T Street Wm Kidd Nathanl Barnes James Williams Daniel Hamer John Hamer Senr Wm Hamer John Hamer Jr Harris Hamer Jesse Council John Defries Joel Riggs Nimrod Fielder Henry Robertson Solomon Humphreys Benja Humphreys work thereon.

JANUARY 1813

Isham R Trotter qualified as a Justice of the Peace for this County.
Order Henry Hunter oversee road to Samuel Bentons; residents in bounds to Leepers Fork to John Bonds to Samuel Bentons to John Hunters old place to Murfrees fork to work thereon under his directions.

Order William House oversee road from McGavocks branch; hands at Nichols's mill Lytles Thos Bell John Manses lease, Henry G Kearneys old place Walter Hill Wm Hill Benjamin Gurley David Houston Isham House & John Bridges work thereon.

Order Joseph Robinson oversee road from James Allisons toward Fishing Ford on Duck River; hands from Thomas Wilsons fence to Thomas Wilson Esqr including him to James Allisons to Philip Munars including Drury Bennett to John Ogilvies to David Spains work thereon under his directions.

Order David Campbell oversee Natchez road from where John Johnston formerly lived to Edward Gossages to Maury County; residents from John Johnstons old place to John Hopkins to Leepers Creek work thereon under his directions.

Order John Williamson Jones Glover John Roberts Richard Tanner David Lancaster Geo Kinnard & Frederick Taylor any five lay off a road from Glovers Gap Duck river ridge to intersect Harpeth Lick road between James Gibsons & Hurricane Creek.

Order David Squier Gurdon Squier Samuel Cox Benjamin White Thos Sappington Robt P
p.61   Currin any 5 lay off a road from Harpeth Bridge to intersect road from Jno Buchanans.
Order all hands on Spring creek of Duck to Bedford County line work on road whereof James Joyce is overseer.
Release Isaac Bateman from value of mare & colt posted by him which since proven away by Isaiah Hogin.
Lists/Taxable property & persons for 1813 returned by Thomas W Stockett Esqr in Capt Jacob Garretts Compy Jesse White Esq in Capt Wm Simpsons Compy Robert McMillin Esqr in Capt Jas Anglins Compy Samuel Shelburne Esqr in Capt Dilliards Compy Tristram Patton Esqr in Capt Pattons Compy James Black Esqr in Capt Jas Giddens Compy Wm Logan Esqr in Capt Wm Hookers Compy Wm Anthony Esqr in Capt Chas Johnsons Compy.

Grant license to James Pewitt to keep an ordinary at his dwelling house in this County; bond $2500 with Wm Bond Senr & Wm Bond Jr securities.
Grant license to Gurden Squier to keep an ordinary at his dwelling house in Franklin; bond $2500 with Samuel Cox & Andrew Johnston securities.
Ltrs/admn granted Charlotte Willett on estate of Richd Willett decd; bond $600 with James Pugh & Eleazer Andrews her securities.

County tax for 1813: white poll $11\frac{1}{2}$ cts, slave 23 cts, town lot 24 cts, stud horse the price of the season of one mare; on each merchant $5.
Court lay Bridge Tax over Big Harpeth opposite Franklin: white poll $11\frac{1}{2}$ cts, 100 acres $11\frac{1}{4}$ cts, each slave 21 cts, each town lot 23 cts.
Poor Tax for 1813: white poll 3 cts; slave 6 cts; town lot 6 cents.

Order Pleasant Russell have $64.98 for repairs done to Courthouse.
Allow John H Eaton county solicitor for 1812 $42 for exofficio services.

JANUARY 1813

Allow Wm Hulme Shff $41.40 for exofficio services.
p.62   Elect Wm H Downing constable; bond $625 with James Gault & John Coffee his securities.
Elect Samuel Cox constable in Capt Joel T Rivers Company; bond $625 with James Gordon & Robert P Currin securities.
Elect Richard W Hyde constable; bond $625 with Nicholas Scales and John Bostick securities.
Elect David Black constable; bond $625 with Isaac Ferguson and James Giddens securities.
Elect Wm Wells constable in Capt Wells Company; bond $625 with Thomas Wells and Danl Clift securities.
Elect John Marchant constable in Capt Ridleys Company; bond $625 with James Joyce & Littleberry Epperson securities.
Elect James Hill constable; bond $625; John Hill & Nicholas Scales securities.

Grant ltrs/admn to Edith Harris on estate of Josephine Harris decd; bond $1000 with George Bennett and James Black her securities.

Bond of Archibald Lytle and John Nichols to George Hulme chmn of Court of Pleas for Williamson County $150 condition that Lovell Tom John Rolly & Betsey Wooldridge children of late John Wooldridge shall not become chargeable to the County for their support during year 1813.

Ltr/atty Ebenezer Darbey to Angus McPhail proven by John Sample and John Hardeman.
Deed Abraham Walker to James Patton 107 acres ackd.
Deed Shff Wm Hulme to Thomas McElwee 100 acres ackd.
p.63   Acct/sales estate of David Craig Junr decd returned.
Deed Thomas McElwee to Thos Gillaspie 116½ acres ackd.
Deed Abraham Walker to Andrew Johnson 5 Lots in Franklin ackd.
Inventory/estate Richard Willett decd returned.
Inventory estate of Andrew Harris decd returned.
Deed Young A Gray to Gideon Blackburn 150 acres proven by Abram Maury Senr and Robert P Currin.
Deed William Bond Senr to Hugh Dobbins 50 acres ackd.
Deed Berton Jordan to Thomas Anderson 174 acres ackd.
Deed John McDaniel to Benard Richardson 37½ acres proven by John K Campbell and Francis Worley.
Deed Newton Cannon to Alexander McClaran 160 acres ackd.
Bill/sale David Robinson to Michael Robinson proved by Charles Robinson and John Robinson.
Inventory/estate of John Crawford decd returned.
Deed Shff Wm Hulme to John Sample Wm Peebles & Thos Hulme 100 acres ackd.
Settlement with Hannah McCutchen admx/estate of James McCutchen decd returned by Sion Hunt & George Hulme Esqrs.

Order Samuel Williams Presley Hardin John Parks Senr James Merritt Thomas Merritt & David Houston any 5 alter road to run between Joel Dilliard & Samuel Merritt.
p.64   Order Joseph Robinson John Ogilvie James Ridley Moses Ridley John W Manier Thomas Wilson & James Reed any 5 lay off a road near John Walkers to the County line towards Murfreesborough.

JANUARY 1813

Appoint Terner Saunders Abraham Maury Jr David Dunn Oliver Williams Thomas Old Garner McConnico & John Watson to divide lands of which Hardy Murfree decd died possessed equally between David Dickinson & Fanny his wife Matthias B Murfree William H Murfree Isaac Hilliard and Mary his wife James Maney and Sally his wife Levina Murfree and Martha Ann Murfree joint heirs of sd Hardy Murfree. Petition of David Dickinson & Matthias B Murfree two of sd heirs pray division of following described lying in several counties in this state [page of land description follows including: tract granted by NC to James Martin on 14 March 1786; in Rutherford several tracts granted by NC 7 March 1786: 389 acres to Henry Winberne; 318 acres Wm Pender[Ponder?]; 640 ac to John Wills; 274 ac to Ezekiel White; 320 ac to Thomas Powel; 228 to John Butler; 342 ac to Bryant Smith; 274 ac to Joseph Mitchell; 640 ac to Anthony Gaines; 768 ac to Clement Hall; 320 ac to Dempsey Jinkins. In Wilson County 321 ac by NC to Wm Slade on 18 May 1789; 640 ac by NC to David Bezzel on 14 March 1786; 94 ac to Robertson on Stones Creek; 200 ac granted Mosson Williams & conveyed to H Murfree; 62¾ ac adj Bezzel. In Smith County 1508 ac granted by NC to John Benten 20 May 1793; 773 ac granted by NC to Archibald Henderson 14 March 1786. In Robertson County 640 acres granted by NC to Nancy Shepperd and conveyed by her and O Smith to H Murfree; 400 ac part of tract from NC to Abraham Burgess 7 March 1786; 71 ac part of grant by NC to John B Hammond 18 May 1789; 384 ac part of tract p.65 granted by NC to Thomas Calender on 14 March 1786; 640 ac granted by NC to Nancy Shepperd on 8 Decr 1787. In Dixon County 490 ac part of grant by NC to Hardy Murfree on 24 May 1793. In Montgomery County 640 acres granted by NC to B Archer on 7 March 1786; 640 acres granted by NC to Letitia -- 7 March 1786; 228 ac granted by NC to James Coleso-- on 7 March 1786; 174 acres part of grant by NC to John Hargrove 20 Decr 1791; 440 acres part of grant by NC to Benjn Mailey 14 March 1786; 67 ac part of grant by NC to John Madiaris on 6 Decr 1797; 640 ac granted by NC to John Madiaris 6 Decr 1797. In Davidson County 256 ac part of grant by NC to John Pierce 7 March 17--; 390 ac by NC to Benjn Johnson 20 May 1793; Lot in Nashville.

Order John Tillman Francis Tillman Jesse Kennedy Richard Reynolds Benjn Smith James Carson & John Johnston any 5 lay off a road from road that crosses the ridge at Woods Gap to begin near George Tillmans old mill to near John Hills horse mill to intersect the road leading to Warren Courthouse.
Court adjourns until tomorrow morning nine O Clock.
            John Witherspoon T W Stockett James Davis

Wednesday 13th January 1813. Present Jno Witherspoon Thomas W Stockett James Davis. Order Abraham Maury Senr oversee road whereof he was formerly overseer.

John Nichols vs John Reed[?]. Appeal. Justices Jas Davis James Boyd Jacob Garrett. Jury John Buchanan James Neelly John Allen John L Fielder Henry G Kearney John Cox Wm Hemphill Moses Chambers Jesse Bugg Samuel Cummins Wm Banks David P Anderson. Dft recovers agt plf his costs of suit.
p.66 Lists/taxable property & persons for 1813 returned by James Allison Esqr in Capt Daltons Compy; David Dunn Esqr in Capt Dunns Compy.
Orphan John Wilson bound unto Moses B Francis until age 21 to be taught the art mystery or occupation of a Farmer and further that he be taught to read and write to rule of simple interest; at end of apprenticeship to be furnished with horse saddle and bridle at value of $55 & decent suit of homespun clothes.

JANUARY 1813

James Priestly vs Richard Compton. Justices O Williams Nichs Scales David Dunn. Jury John Hardin Ruffin Brown Thomas Berry John Nichols Michael Kinnard Joammi Stephens Wm Bateman Wm C Deverox Andrew Dorton Joel Stephens Wm Alexander John Cox. Deft recovers agt plf his costs. Plf granted appeal to Circuit Court; gave bond with Lemuel P Montgomery and Wm Smith is securities.

Order Jesse Bugg oversee road from Kinnards Still House to Nashville road; hands in bounds from Joseph Bridgers to Alexr Johnson to Knacy Andrews to Wm Borins to Stephen Hails to Charles Calhoons work thereon under his directions.

Acct/sales of estate of Jacob Rolland decd returned.

George Kinnard vs Julian Nail. Slander. Deft in open Court says the error charged by plf agt him he utterly disavows and prays suit may be dismissed. Plf agrees to pay his own witnesses. Plf recovers agt dft his damages and costs.

p.67   Deed James Bullock to Nathan Bullock 37½ acres ackd.
Acct/sales estate of Anthony Sharp decd returned.
Bill/sale James Taylor to John H Nichols proven by Jesse Harden.
Deed James Davis to Daniel Hamer[Haince?] 200 acres ackd.
Mortgage Parham S Kirk to Andrew Dorton proven by David Dunn & Wm Bond.
Deed Sampson Prowell & Sarah Prowell to Andrew Dorton 75 acres proven by Richard Graham and Charles Kavenaugh.

Order Thomas E Sumner oversee road from Sampson Sawyers to ridge between Arringtons and Wilsons creek with hands from John Hills lane to North of Thos E Sumners farm. Court adjourns until tomorrow morning 10 0 Clock.
                                        Richd Puckett   C H McAlister   James Davis   Dd Dunn

Thursday 14th January 1813. Present George Hulme Richard Puckett Charles McAlister. State vs Jacob Halfacre. Overseer of road. Justice Geo Hulme. Jury James Neelly John Buchanan John McSwine Wm McMullin Hugh Pinkston John Cox Nicholas T Perkins John Allen Isham Cole Wm Hemphill Grove Sharp Arthur Fulgham find dft not guilty.

State vs Wm Mansker. A&B. Justices Geo Hulme Collin McDaniel David Dunn. Dft confesses guilt; fined $10 and costs.
Deed Samuel Blackburn to Henry R Balance ackd.
Deed Samuel Jackson to Wm parks 250 acres proven by James Neelly & John Thomas.

p.68   State vs Arthur Fulgham. Presentment Overseer of road. Justices G Hulme David Dunn Jacob Garrett. Jury [above except Moses Chambers and Matthew Johnson for Nichs T Perkins & Arthur Fulgham]. Juror John White is withdrawn and cause continued untill next Court.

State vs Collin McDaniel. Preentment overseer of road. Justices James Davis Richd Puckett Jacob Garrett. Jury John White John Gray Burwell Temple Edward Gossage Thomas Ridley Joel Stephens George Parker Thos Scott Arthur Fulgham Thos Haynes John Nichols James Cavinder. Juror John White withdrawn; cause contd to next Court.

JANUARY 1813

State vs Nathan Scuggs[Scruggs?]. Presentment overseer of road. Justices Geo Hulme Jacob Garrett Hendley Stone. Dft confesses guilt; fined 50 cents & costs.

Order James Cavinder oversee road from Franklin to five mile tree on Hayes creek as far as McConnicos meeting house; hands from Big Harpeth to Drury Pulliams branch to David McElwees plantation to Wm Marshall including hands that heretofore worked under Henry Ingram as overseer work under his directions.

Deed Thomas Smith to Henry Lyon Lot 131 in Franklin proven by John Reid and John M Armstrong.

State vs John White. Presentment overseer of road. Justices Hendley Stone Nichs
p.69   Scales George Hulme. Jury John Buchanan Jas Neelly John McSwine Hugh Pinkston John Cox John Allen Grove Sharp David P Anderson Peter Estes Wm McMullin Isham Cole Richd Swanson find dft guilty; fined $1 and pay costs.

State vs May. Preentment overseer/road. Justices G Hulme H Stone Jas Boyd. Dft in proper person submits to Court; not fined.

List/taxable property & persons in Capt Hickmans Compy returned by Nicholas Scales. List taken by Thomas Garrett Esqr retd.
Grant license to Collin McDaniel to keep an ordinary at his dwelling house in this County; bond $2500 with Nicholas Perkins & Wm P Harrison security.
Deed Benjn White to Henry R Ballance Lot 114 in Franklin ackd.

Orptian boy John T Anderson age 15 on 3 September 1812 bound to John Mallory to age 21 to be taught art mystery or occupation of a house joiner; at expiration of time to be given a horse saddle & bridle, a sett of bench tools & a good freedom suit, & to learn him to read write & cypher to understand rules of interest.

Ltrs/admn granted to Young A Gray on estate of Sally L R Gray decd; bond $2000 with John H Eaton & Peter R Booker his securities.
Order hands that live on Flat Rock branch and hands at Smiths lower mill on Little Harpeth work on road whereof John White is overseer.

Order Jacob Halfacre Freeman Walker Jas Harden Ebenezer Alexander & Robt Davis partition Negroes of estate of James Crafton decd between widow and his four children to wit George Crafton Dennis Crafton Richd Crafton & Daniel Crafton dividing same into 5 equal parts and report to next County Court.

John Epps, recognizance $150 for affray with John Bridges and Archer Beasley his securities $75 each, called and came not. Scire facias to issue against them.
p.70   Elisha Williams Isaac Crow & John Bridges [as above].
William Gurley Jeremiah Gurley & isaac Crow [as above].

Order Nicholas Perkins Junr oversee road from SE corner Franklin to McGavocks branch; hands on John Donelsons plantation Moses Moore and others on McGavocks and sd Nicholas Perkins hands work thereon under his directions.
Court adjourns until tomorrow morning nine O Clock.
               G Hulme   R Puckett   C H McAlister

JANUARY 1813

Friday 15th January 1813. Present George Hulme Richd Puckett Charles McAlister. State vs Isaac Crow. A&B. Justices G Hulme Oliver Williams R Puckett. Jury James Neelly John Buchanan Joseph Love Wm Mansker Hugh Pinkston Felix Staggs John Harden Wm Hemphill Jeremiah Harden David P Anderson James Cavender Wm McMullin. Deft found guilty; fined $10 and pay costs. Dft granted appeal to Circuit Court giving bond; Jeremiah Gurley and Tristram Patton his securities.

John Doe Lessee of John Sample & others vs Richard Herbert. Ejectment. John Herbert admitted a defendant.

State vs Ruffin Brown. A&B. Moses Chambers prosecutor. Justices George Hulme James
p.71   Boyd Gersham Hunt. Jury John Cox Jacob Gray Robert Gray Stephen Smith Jason Hopkins Abraham Secrest Thomas Ridley Edward Warren Joseph Love James Cavender John Buchanan Wm C Deverix say deft not guilty. Moses Chambers pays all costs.

Deed/gift James Gray to Sally L R Gray proven by Peter R Booker.
Bill/sale Archer Jordan to Gabriel Barton. Berton Jordan made oath the signature of Archer Jordan is hand writing of Archer Jordan & Richard Orton made oath that hand writing of James McCutchen is hand writing of James McCutchen.
Deed William Willett to Hamiah[Hannah?] Ashman Willett Lewis Ashman Willett Absalom Tatum Willett Joseph W Willett Sally Clift Willett & James Tyrrell Willett proven by John Berkley & John Johnston.
Inventory/estate of Sally L R Gray decd returned; Order Young A Gray admr sell perishable part of sd estate.

Order Abraham Maury Senr Stephen Childress Nicholas T Perkins Sion Hunt & Thomas Old divide personal estate of Anthony Sharp decd among heirs of sd decedent, heirs of sd Sharp being present in Court and consented to sd order.

Mortgage from Samuel McBride to Thomas E Sumner is ordered to be registered, it appearing that Samuel Pepper a subscribing witness thereto is not an inhabitant of this state.
William Adams vs John Tillman. On motion of sd John Tillman appeal is granted him to Circuit Court; bond with Wm Alexander & Wm Mansker securities.
Reuben Nance vs Wm Alexander. On motion of sd Wm Alexander, appeal is granted him to Circuit Court; bond with John Tillman & Wm Mansker securities.
Benjamin White vs Lemuel White. On motion of sd Benjn White by Nicholas Perkins his atty, and sd Benjn White paying $49.60 as security for sd Lemuel White to James
p.72   Wier, sd Benjn White recovers agt Lemuel White $49.60 & costs of suit.

Appearance bond to Circuit Court, Isaac Crow, Walter Hill & Wm Hill his securities.
Appearance bond to Circuit Court, Samuel Cox, to prosecute Isaac Crow.

Court adjourns untill tomorrow morning 9 0 Clock.
                              C H McAlister   Richd Puckett   John J Henry

Saturday 16th January 1813. Present Chs McAlister Richd Puckett & John J Henry Esq. Petition of Lucy D Kearney praying a commission be apptd to set apart one third of estate of Henry G Kearney to her separate use. Order Abraham Maury Senr Robert P Currin & Archd Lytle enquire into real & personal estate of sd Henry G Kearney,

JANUARY 1813

also debts due from him at time of granting the divorce and after setting aside sufficient for paymt of debts; report to next Court. Henry G Kearney granted appeal to Circuit Court; bond with Atholston Andrews & Nichs Dilliard his securities.

Lytle and Richardson vs Ewen Cameron bail of David Trimble. Plfs by atty; Ewen Cameron called. Plf granted execution agt dft for debt damages and costs.

p.73   Deed Andrew Johnston to Henry R Bateman ackd.
Lists/taxable property & persons for 1813 in Capt McKays Compy retd by Sion Hunt Esq & by John J Henry in Capt Joseph Crocketts Compy.
John Harden vs James Neelly. Justices G Hulme R Puckett J Boyd. Demurrer of deft sustained.

James Williams vs Charles Boyles. Debt. Justices C H McAlister R Puckett Jas Boyd. Jury Wm Denson Berry Nolen Zacheus German Wm Marshall Joseph Robertson Knacy Andrews George Andrews Britian Adams Andw Craig John Winstead John Buchanan David P Anderson say dft hath not paid the debt. Plf recovers his debt, damages, and costs.

Robert Brown vs Young A Gray. Debt. Justices G Hulme R Puckett J Boyd. Dft withdraws his plea of payment; plf recovers his debt damages and costs.
Campbell & Stewart vs Andrew McKorkle & Andw Spratt. Debt. Justices [above]. Dfts withdrew plea of paymt; plf recovers debt damages and costs.
John W Simpson vs Henry Lyon. Debt. Justices G Hulme R Puckett Saml Shelburn. Dft p.74   withdraws plea of paymt; plf recovers debt damages & costs.
David McGavock vs Thomas Berry & Thomas Cowden. Dft came not; plf granted execution agt dft for debt, damages, costs of original suit, costs of this suit.
Ltrs/admn granted James House Senr on estate of Green House; bond $200 with Wm House & Robt McLemore securities. Inventory/estate returned.

Henry Cook vs Charles B Neilson. Attachment. Justices John Witherspoon David Dunn John J Henry. Jury Wm Denson Berry Nolen Zacheus German Wm Marshall Joseph Robinson Knacy Andrews George Andrews Britian Adams Andrew Craig John Winstead John Buchanan David P Anderson. Plf recovers agt dft his damages and costs of suit.

Joshua White allowed $6 for two wolf scalps killed by him within this County over four months old.
Deed Wm McKenzie 100 acres ackd.

6 January 1813. In open Court L P Montgomery Esqr moved to have judgt entered in name of Charles B Neilson agt Nicholas P Hardeman Clerk of this Court and his securities for $141.60 deposited in his hands by sheriff being the balance of money made on execution issued from this Court at suit of Commrs of Columbia agt Charles B Neilson Newton Cannon James Wilson & Patrick McCutchan. Sd motion overruled; no judgt in this case entered; plf by atty objected.

p.75   Wm Hulme Sheriff and collector/taxes for 1812 makes report: taxes unpaid on following lands and he found no goods or chattels whereon he could distrain for sd taxes: John Armstrong 128 acres Carey Bell 100 acres William C C Claiborne 1 town Lot Archibald Craig 640 acres James Caruthers 50 acres John Davis 1227½ acres Jonathan Davis Junr 300 acres John Gillaspie 1000 acres Wm Hayes 1250 acres ditto

JANUARY 1813

1060 acres John Hopkins 100 acres 1 pole Thomas H Jones 1028 acres Samuel Jackson 460 acres M Lewis heirs town Lot Benjamin McCuiston 125 acres George McLean 1000 acres Frasis Ramsey 2200 acres Sampson Sawyers 64 acres Robert Smith 39 acres Absalom Tatom estate 640 acres Joseph Watkins 66 acres John Gray Blount 2560 acres; whereupon ordered by Court that foregoing shall be sold November next.
List of insolvent taxable property for 1812 sworn to by Wm Hulme Shff.

Following proved attendance as Jurors: Britian Adams 2 days Jas Neelly 6 days John Buchanan 6 days Wm Denson 2 days Berry Nolen 1 day.
Edward Buford vs Edward Ragsdale. Motion for new trial. Justices Jno Witherspoon Jno J Henry David Dunn. New trial granted.
Inventory/estate of John Atkinson decd returned.
Settlement with Joseph Love exr of Wm L Love decd returned.

Joseph Pollard vs Ebenezer Coleman. Attacht. Dft not appearing, plf recovers agt damages as in declaration mentioned; damages to be enquired of at next Court.
Ltrs/admn granted to Baalam Hay on estate of John Atkinson decd; bond with Garner McConnico his security in sum $500.
John Hardin vs James Neelly. Plf came not. Deft recovers his costs.
p.76 Charles Halsey vs Archer Beasley. Appellant came not. Judgt affirmed & deft amerced costs.
Jos Wilson use John Sample vs William Shute. Debt. Plf came not. Dft recovers of plf his costs of suit.

Order $141.60 from sale of horse Royalist deposited in hands of Clerk/Court in case Commrs of Columbia agt Charles B Neilson Newton Cannon and others be paid to Henry Cook by Clerk in part of satisfaction of Judgt, and sd Cook recovers agt sd Charles B Neilson, and that fiari facias issue to make balance of sd judgt & costs of sd Cooks. 1813 Jany 19th recd above sum of Clerk. H Cook.

Pleasant Russell vs Jacob Jacoby. Attachment. Attacht stayed for nine months.
William Glover vs Samuel Jackson. Plf by atty. Dft not appearing, plf recovers agt deft damages; amount to be enquired of by a jury at next Court.
Court adjourns until the Court in Course.   Dd Dunn C H McAlister John J Henry

At a Court of Pleas and quarter Sessions held for County of Williamson at Courthouse in Franklin on Monday 12th April 1813. Present the Worshipful George Hulme Edward Ragsdale and Isham R Trotter Esquires.

Jurors summoned: Joel Stephens Drury Pulliam Saml McCutchen James Ridley Thos Merritt Jas Pewitt David Nolen Jas Giddens Thos Ridley Wm Bond Andw Herrin Wm Williams Chapman White exd Wm Banks Henry Lyon Jas Thompson Henry Inman Joel Riggs Jas Sneed John Keystar exd Edward Gossage. Constables John Marchant & David Black.

Grand Jurors Saml McCutchan foreman James Giddens David Nolen Joel Stephens Drury Pulliam Jas Sneed Wm Banks Jas Ridley Wm Bond Thos Ridley Thos Merritt Joel Riggs

APRIL 1813

Andrew Hamer David Black constable.

p.77   Settlement with Hendley Stone guardian of Peter Pryor & Green Pryor orphans of John Pryor deceased returned.
Bill/sale Joseph Farrar to Henry Bailey ackd.
Bond John Crawford to Zacheus Jarman for title to land proven by John Morrow.
Bond John Crawford to John Morrow for title to land proven by Zacheus German.
Deed Lancaster Lovatt to Nathan Stancill 337 acres proven by Wm Anthony & Don F Bostick.
Deed Thomas[Theron?] W McGaugh to John Swancey 127 acres ackd.
Deed Abraham Brantley to Langhorn F Watson 145 acres proven by Finch Scruggs and John Thomas.
Letter/atty Neavel Gee & Wm Dunnright to Richard Turner proven by John H Eaton.
Deed James Boyd to Mary Thomas Phineas Thomas Finch Scruggs executors of Jesse Thomas decd 210 acres proven by John P Shelburne & Jesse Walton.
Deed Lerois Garrett to Turner Saunders for Town Lot in Franklin ackd.
Deed Daniel Ross[Rap?] to Samuel McCutchan 32¼ acres proven by John Porter and James McCutchen.
Ltr/atty George Andrews & Wm Dunnright to Nevil Gee & Wm Dunnright Junr.
Deed Abram Brantley to Jacob Garrett 555 acres proven by Geo Hulme & Ephriam Brown.

Will of Jordan Reese decd proven by James Hicks Leonard Dunergut & Fendall Crump. John Watson one of exrs therein named qualified.
Will of William Ogilvie decd proven by John White who made oath that John Masine [Mason?] now dead subscribed as a witness in his presence. James Allison and Richd Ogilvie the executors therein named qualified.
Account/sales estate of Willliam Stine[Hine?] decd returned.
p.78   Inventory estate of Benjamin Bugg decd returned.
Settlement with Wm Parham gdn of James & Henry Hill orphans of Wm C Hill decd retd.

Order Gersham Hunt & James Davis Esqrs settle with William Brown admr/estate of Joseph Roberts decd and report to next Court.
Inventory/estate of Wm Ogilvie decd returned.
John Watson apptd guardian of Patrick Reece a minor orphans of Jordan Reece decd; bond $40,000 with Abraham North & Thomas Old his securities.
Abner Lambert is bound apprentice to John Ogilvie until he arrived to age 21 to be taught the art mystery or occupation of a Farmer, taught to read and write and arithmetic to include the rule of three, to give him a horse saddle and bridle to be valued at seventy five Dollars & a good suit of homespun clothes at the expiration of his time of apprenticeship.
Lists/taxable property for 1813 returned by Samuel Perkins Esq. & Alexr Mebane Esq.
Order Samuel Shelburne & Richard Puckett Esqrs settle with Michael Kinnard & Lewis Stephens admrs on estate of Michael Kinnard decd.

Order Charles Mason oversee road; residents beginning where Col Murfrees line crosses Murfrees fork to John Popes branch crossing ridge at Popes Gap to opposite Isaac Fergusons including him to James Neelly to Col Murfrees work thereon.

Order James Terrill oversee the public road from N P Hardemans lane on Murfrees fork to the Natchez road at Joel Hobbs; residents from fork to Jesse Tarkingtons to

APRIL 1813

Willetts mill to John Griffiths Sr work thereon under his directions.
Division of Negroes of James Crafton decd ordered to be recorded.

Order Shemi Merritt oversee road from Jas Neellys to Wm Wilsons mill to west bound-
p.79   ary of John Hardeman; hands down Neellys Creek including James Kinnard to
Shemi Merritt to James Williams work thereon.
Order David Pinkston oversee from Natchez road to Methodist meeting house; James
Lord[Lard?] Isaac Jones Joel Jones Benjn Pritchett Frederick Ivey Jas Jackson Eli-
jah Spencer Thos Forehand John Jones hands John West Burwell Temple work thereon.

Order David Chrisman oversee road from McCalls Gap in room of Martin Nawl who has
removed; hands on head of Rutherfords Creek from Wm Allens work thereon.

Samuel Woods vs Oliver Woods. Plf by atty suggests plf paid $464.87½ as security
for deft to George Tillman. Jury Wm Williams Henry Inman Edward Gossage Wm
McCandless John Buchanan John Mairs John S Campbell John Cox Knacy Andrews
Archibald Lytle Zacheus German Robert Hill find plf was security for deft; plf
recovers agt dft $464.87½ and costs.
Court adjourns untill tomorrow morning 9 0 Clock.
                                        Richd Puckett   John Hill   Edward Ragsdale

Tuesday 13th April 1813. Present Richard Puckett John Hill Edward Ragsdale Esqrs.
Will of Peter Perkins decd proven by Thos H Scales & John Bostick. Nichs Perkins
and Nichs Scales exrs therein named qualified.
Deed Michael Kinnard to Jesse Jackson 50 acres proven by W Webb & John Pickard.
p.80   Bond Patrick McCutchen to Benjamin Roberts for title to land proven by
Nicholas Scales & Jacob Halfacre.
Deed Wright Williams to Thomas Malloy 640 acres proven by John Sample & Jas Sample.
Lease Thomas S West to John West ackd.
Deed Anderson Berryman to John Nichols Senr 272 acres ackd.
George Hulme & William Anthony Esqrs apptd to settle with different guardians of
John Jordan decd.
Bill/sale Burrell McLemore to Wm Sample proven by Robert P Currin & Edward Bevill.
Inventory/estate of Josephus Harris decd returned.
Acct/sales estate of Green House decd returned.
Bill/sale Austin G Sandridge to Henry Hunter proven by Reuben Cofee.
Bill/sale Charles Harrell & Mary Harrell to Abraham Harrell ackd.
Deed Samuel Brown to John Morton 66⅛ acres ackd.
Deed John Wells to Samuel Wells 140 acres proven by John W Linster and Wm Wells.
Deed Wm Spencer & Elizabeth Spencer 6¼ acres proven by Wm Peebles & Peter Potts.
Deed John McDaniel to Bernard Richardson 29 acres ackd.
Settlement with Samuel Crockett gdn of Stokely Page & Harvey Page orphans of John
Page decd returned.
Settlement with Samuel Wilson Gdn of David Page Jacob Page & John Page orphans of
John Page deceased returned.
Settlement with Owen T Watkins gdn of Frederick Page & Patsey Page orphans of John
Page decd returned.
Deed Beverly Reese & Susannah his wife to Abram Maury 35½ acres ackd by Beverly
Reese; order Charles McAlister and Hinchey Pettway Esqrs take the privy examn of sd

35

APRIL 1813

p.81   Susannah touching her voluntary execution of said deed.
License Wm Spencer to keep an ordinary at his dwelling house in this County; bond $2500 with John Cox and Robert P Currin his securities.
Acct/sales of estate of Richd Willett decd returned.
Settlement with Nicholas Scales gdn of Susannah G Jordan orphan of John Jordan decd returned.
Settlement with Oliver Williams gdn of Nancy Jordan orphan of John Jordan decd returned.
Elect Daniel Perkins County Trustee for two ensuing years; bond $2000; Thomas H Perkins Robert McLemore Nicholas Scales & Nicholas Perkins Senr his securities.
Elect Robert Sample Junr constable in Capt Joseph Crocketts company; bond $625 with John Sample & John T Bennett his securities.
Elect Nelson Chapman constable in Capt John Daltons Company; bond $625 with John Walker and Thomas Wilson his securities.
Elect John Carothers constable in Capt Thomas McCrorys Company; bond $625 with Thomas S West and Collin McDaniel his securities.
Letrs/admn granted Ewen Cameron on estate of Frankey Cameron; bond $2000 with Nicholas P Hardeman and Jason Hopkins his securities.
Order hands of Sally Reese Thomas Old Malinda Reese & Beverly Reese work on road whereof Beverly Reese is overseer.
Jurors to next County Court: John Morrow Alexander Smith Billington Taylor John Watson Abraham North Bernard Richardson Wm Thomas Wm Marshall Thos Wilson Jr Ephraim Andrews Moses Turner Edward Buford George Mebane Thos B Walthal Jas Neely James Berry Geo Oliver Jas S Clemon Ben Gholson Robert Rogers Wm Jones Thomas Cash John Hailey Thos Old Daniel Perkins Alson Edney. Constables Robt Sample John Carothers.

Nicholas P Hardeman allowed $1.50 for repairs to Court house.
p.82   Settlement with Lancaster Glover guardian of Pason[Person?] Pate orphan of Hardey Pate decd returned.
Order Young Gray & Gideon Blackburn alter road by them to make it run on the line between them and that Abram Maury George Hulme John H Eaton Wm McKey Philip Maury Robert P Currin & John Sappington lay off the same.
David Squier allowed $3 for care of the court house from July session 1812 untill this Court.
Order Jonathan Wood oversee road from Wilsons rd to Arringtons creek rd leaving out Wm Deason[?] Michael Kinnard Chas Harrell & John Racord then up Hays Creek to Frederick Davis including his hands to near Alexr Simpsons Denne[?] Hills work thereon.

Order Coonrod Richardson oversee road from Wilsons Cr; hands from Nelsons Cr to Alexander Ralston down Harpeth to Williamsons mill to crossing of Nelsons Creek work thereon.
Order James Hicks oversee road from Franklin to near Joel Hobbs; Moses Friersons hands James Grays James Hobbs Swanson Johnson Moses Parks John Parks David Gee Peter Edwards Solomon Hobbs & John Hobbs or residents in their places work thereon.

Order David Gillaspie oversee road from Maury County line to Duck River ridge; hands on Flat creek except David Christman work thereon.
Order Jesse Sparkman oversee road from John Andrews to old Natchez rd west of John Johnstons formerly David Dobbins; hands from John Andrews to David Robinsons to John Johnsons to County line to Hunters trace to John Armstrongs to John Andrews

APRIL 1813

work thereon under his directions.
Richard Farmer John Williamson Frederick Taylor David Lancaster Jones Glover apptd last court to lay off a road from Glovers Gap to Harpeth Lick road between James Gibsons and Hurricane Creek report they laid off same.
Order John Williamson oversee road from Glovers Gap to Harpeth Lick road between
p.83   Gibsons & Hammonds creek; hands from Widow Harrisons including Frederick Taylor to David Lancaster to Harpeth Lick rd including Patrick & John Gibson work thereon under his directions.
Order John Walker George H Allen David Spain Josiah Wilson Jr John Ogilvie Joseph Robinson Jonah Wilson Senr any five lay off a road from Thomas Wilsons north.
Wm Sargant released from appraised value of a mare posted by him as she run away from him soon after she was posted.
Order James Davis & Collin McDaniel Esqrs let to lowest bidder Polly Hinds who is to be supported at the charge of this County.
Order Joseph Braden Thomas Williamson John J Henry Henry Walker Garner McConnico Michael Kinnard & Wm Marshall any five lay off a road from Harpeth bridge to Jefferson rd at some convenient place & report to next Court.
Grant leave to Joel T Rivers to make a door in the back of the Jailors room provided he does it on his own expence.
Order Burtis[Bentis?] Allford oversee road from east of Wm L Watsons to crossroads; hands of Bartholomew Stovall John Duffill Thomas Nolen Mark Thomas Israel McCarrell Chitwood Burns Hak[Hale?] Mason Isaac Mason Jr Joseph Mason Wm Sharp Abraham Mason Anslem Nolen Wm Astan Joseph Howell John G & Wm Simpkins work thereon.
Order Samuel McBride oversee rd from Sawyers to Rutherford County line; to include sd McBride to Sawyers to Abram Crisman to Jas Taylor work thereon.
Order George Burnes John L Fielder Nimrod Fielder John Primm John Hamer John Edmondson (B) David Cummins & Gersham Hunt any five lay off a road from John L Fielders plantation near the bridge near Liberty Meeting House to run the nearest & best way to North end of David Cummins lane near the County line.
p.84   Order John H Eaton Owen T Watkins Garner McConnico Amos Rounsevall Wm Stephens Charles Stephens & Lewis Stephens any five alter the road at Atkinsons Blacksmith shop to go round a bad mud hole and hill about 100 yards from the other road if they deem the same most expedient.
Simon Roach is released from appraised value of a filly taken up by him as same has been proven away from him.
Order George Kinnard oversee road from Hurricane Creek to George Kinnards still house; hands in bounds from Knacy Andrews including Squire Garretts hands leaving out David Lancaster and F Taylor including Richard Tankersley to Duck River ridge.

Order John Watson oversee road from Andrew Cowsars to north of Joshua Colemans; residents from John Watsons including Richd Swenson to mouth of Devers Branch above Robert Reads leaving out Joshua Coleman & Hightower Dodson work thereon.
Order John Bond John Williamson Wm Williams Richard Hay George Kinnard & Jones Glover any five lay off a road from Thomas Mayfields to Glovers Gap to intersect road from Little Hurricane to Glovers Gap and report thereof.
Order Wm Edmondson Joseph H Scales Richd W Hyde John D Hill Johnson Word Samuel Perkins & Nicholas Scales any five lay out a road from Murfreesborough road to Franklin and report thereof to next County Court.
Order Thomas Morton oversee Natchez road from John Andrews to intersection with old road half mile west of where David Dobbins formerly lived; hands that worked under

APRIL 1813

Benjamin May late overseer work thereon under his direction.
Court allow jurors on original pannell 50¢ each per day for attendance.
Court allow Wm Huston $100 for support of Wm Huston Jr an object of Charity.
p.85   Order John Tillman Francis Tillman Jesse Kennady Richd Reynolds Benjamin Smith James Carson John Johnston & Joseph Read any five lay off a road from near Columbia road at Woods Gap near George Tillmans mill best way to near John Hills horse mill to intersect road to Warren Court House.
Order James Davis & Collin McDonnell Esqrs let to lowest bidder John C Wilson an object of Charity to be supported at charge of this County.
Nicholas P Hardeman apptd to take care of Court House for twelve months and keep keys of same & it may not be compulsory on him to open the doors thereof except for different Courts & for Hours of Divine Worship for for the Masonic Lodge.
Order James Patton oversee road from Henry Childress to Natchez Road whereof Abram M Degraffenreid was formerly overseer.

Charles B Nelson vs Saml H Williams Shff of Maury County. Motion for costs of suit making an improper return on an execution Chs B Neilson vs Wm Gilberts heirs. Justices O Willliams David Shannon Wm Wilson. James Holland waived all errors; considered by Court that plf recover agt dft $26.25 & 5 mills.

James Black vs James Pugh. Debt. Justices [above]. Dft in proper person waives all errors & confesses judgt. Plf recovers debt & his costs. Plf agreed to stay execution till October Court next.
Court adjourns till Tomorrow morning 9 0 Clock.   Wm Anthony R Puckett Geo Tilman

Wed. 14 April 1813. Present the Worshipful Wm Anthony Richard Puckett Geo Tillman.
Ltrs/admn granted to Ann Ballow & Alexander Smith on estate of Thomas Ballow decd; bond $1000 with David Johnston & Wm Bond securities.
p.86   Division of Negroes of Anthony Sharp decd returned.

Wm Willett vs Andrew Dorton. Certiorara. Justices [above]. Dft recovers expenses.

Owen T Watkins vs Moses Chambers. Justices Wm Anthony George Tillman James Allison. Jury James Thompson Wm Williams Henry Inman Jesse Tarkington Joseph Pollard William McCandlass Wm Pogue George Andrews Eli Hope Felix Staggs Newton Cannon Robert Powers. Plf recovers agt dft his damages $50 and costs.

Claiborne Williams vs George Parker. Covenant. Justices Geo Hulme Richd Puckett Robt McMillin. Jury Wm Hill John Cox Tenner Pinkston John Ricard Charles Stevens George Strambler Walter Hill James Terrill Walter Ridley Walter Ridley James Terrill Thomas Ridley James Giddens John Nichols Hugh Pinkston. Plf recovers agt dft his damages and costs of suit.

Hamilton & Walker vs Abraham Secrest. Certiorara. Dft to take deposition of John B Haynes of Madison County Mississippi Territory.
On motion of Daniel Williams & appearing he is man of good moral character, has attained age 21, was resident of this County before he commenced study of law, therefore considered by the judges [blank]
Court adjourns until tomorrow morning 9 0 Clock.   H Pettway Jes White E Ragsdale.

APRIL 1813

p.87 Thursday 15th April 1813. Present Hinchey Pettway Jesse White Edward Ragsdale Esquires.
Bucknell Harwell and others vs Henry Lester. Debt. Motion to amend. Plf granted permission to amend the original writ.
John Doe Lessee of John Sample & others vs Richard Herbert. Ejectment. Justices [above]. On affadavit of Richd Herbert & also on record of Jany Session, mistake by entering John Herbert admitted deft instead of John Alford was there made. Court admits that John Alford may be defendant in this case and that John Herbert is not known in it, and plfs to pay costs of this order.
State vs David Craig Senr. Indict as overseer. Justices[above]. Jury James Thompson Benj Roberts Thos Berry Wm Williams Jas Pinkerton Wm White Edwd Gossage Geo Andrews Gregory Wilson Henry Inman Archd Lytle Geo Kinnard find deft not guilty.
State vs Wm McKey. Indictment stopping road. Justices [above]. Jury above except Alexr Smith for Wm White. Deft not guilty.
State vs Wm Hooker. Justices Geo Tillman Jesse White Robt McMullin. Dft in proper person cannot deny he is guilty. Fined one cent and costs.
State vs Collin McDaniel. Overseer. Justices Geo Tillman Jesse White Wm R Nunn. Jury John S Campbell Zacheus German Henry Rutherford Joseph Pollard John Cox Benjn White Wm J Bomar Elisha Williams James Gray Hugh Pinkston John Nichols John Andrews
p.88   find dft guilty; fined one cent and costs.

Deed George Strambler to Francis Burrows 110 acres ackd.
Inventory/estate of John Crawford decd retd.
Order shff summon Jury to lay off to Elizabeth Crawford widow of John Crawford decd her dower of perishable property of estate.
Supplementary inventory/estate of Sally L R Gray decd retd.
Account/sales estate of John Atkinson decd returned.
List/taxable property for 1813 retd by Collin McDaniel Esqr.
Deed Thomas Ridley to John Adam Laypoor ackd.
Inventory/estate of Thomas Ballow decd retd.
Order William Robbins oversee road from Hollly Tree Gap to forks of Nashville Rd; residents north of sd Gap as far as McDaniels east to include James Armstrong west to Wm Robbins Nathan McFashion & Abraham Hunter work thereon.
Order James Y Green oversee Natchez Rd from West Harpeth to John Andrews; residents including David Dunn Turner Saunders Elijah Hunter & John Wilkins thence south to include John McCrackin to John Andrews work thereon.
Order Wm Campbell oversee road from Northeast of Big Harpeth bridge to old road to Nashville, as the one mile tree being discontinued by order of Court, bounds of hands that formerly worked thereon work under his direction.
Order Hugh Pinkston oversee road from John Currys to Widow Woods lane following the marks made by jury of review; hands within bounds from plantation where John Curry did live thence to George Manskers to Frederick Davis to Widow Woods lane to Jason
p.89   Wilsons work thereon under his directions.

State vs David Terry. Riot. John Johnston prosecutor. Justices James Black George Tillman Edward Ragsdale. Jury James Thompson Wm Williams Edwd Gossage Henry Inman Geo Andrews Gregory Wilson Benjn Roberts Thos Berryt Alexr Smith Jos Carson Wm McCandlass Wm Pogue say dft is not guilty; plf pays costs.

State vs Robert Rogers. Justices Jas Black Robt McMillin Geo Tillman. Dft saith he

APRIL 1813

is guilty; fined $5 and costs of prosecution.

State vs James Gentry. Justices [above]. Dft saith he is not guilty; fined $5 and costs.

State vs John Cox. Justices R McMillin Wm R Nunn Wm Anthony Geo Tillman. Dft saith he is not guilty. Jury Wm Williams Henry Inman Jas Thompson Edwd Gossage Elisha Williams Owen T Watkins Thos Berry Henry Rutherford Geo Stramblar Wm McCandless Robt Gray Wm Aslin. Jury could not agree; mistrial; continued to next Court.

Order Nicholas Scales & Wm Anthony Esqrs settle with Richard Puckett guardian of heirs of Benjamin Coddington decd of whom he is guardian.
Court adjourns until Tomorrow Morning 9 O Clock.   Wm Anthony   R Puckett   Geo Tilman

Friday 16th April 1813. Present Wm Anthony Richard Puckett George Tillman Esquires.
Inventory/estate of Jordan Reese decd returned.
p.90   Account/sales the estate of Peter Reeves decd returned.
Bond John Eaton by his agent John H Eaton to Robert Crafton for title to land ackd.
Inventory/estate of Peter Perkins returned.
Order Young A Gray admr estate of Sally L R Gray decd sell property of sd estate that a division of sd estate may be had amongst the heirs.

Order Benjamin Roberts oversee road to John Buchanans on Arringtons creek from the Commissioners Creek to John Buchanans; residents from Robert Sayers to James Roland to Robert McClellands to Mr Edmistons to Patrick McCutchans work thereon.

John Den lessee of John Sample & others vs John Allford. Ejectment. Plf and dft both claiming title derived from John Wooten; agreed by parties that sd Wooten had legal title.

Order David Dickinson Hinchey Pettway Alexander Clark Edward Swanson & Wm Parham any three divide personal estate of Jordan Reese decd.

Order James Allison Thomas Wilson & Jacob Garrett settle with Knacy Andrews surviving executor of Ephriam Andrews decd.

Samuel K Blythe & Co vs Henry Lyon. Debt. Justices Wm Anthony Richd Puckett Geo Tillman. Dft withdraws his plea of payment. Plf recovers agt dft his debt $100.15, damages of detention $10.20, and costs of suit.

Wm Glover vs Samuel Jackson. Covenant. Justices Wm Anthony Richd Puckett Andw Jordan. Jury Wm Williams Jas Thompson Newton Cannon Daniel Williams Wm Willett Wm Peebles Robt Powers John Johnston John Sample Robt P Currin Wm Ashlin. Plf recovers agt dft damages $199.85 and costs of suit.

p.91   Jason Hopkins vs Isaac Crow. Appeal. Justices Wm Anthony Archer Jordan Geo Tillman. Jury Edwd Gossage Jos Pollard Burrell McLemore Jas B Thompson Wm Glover Jacob Harden Wm McCandlass John Byrns Wm Gatlin Lazarus Dodson John Johnston John Cox. Plf recovers agt dft.

APRIL 1813

Wm Glover vs Andrew Campbell & James Stewart. Case. Justices Oliver Williams Richd Puckett Geo Tillman. Jury Edwd Gossage Jos Pollard Jas B Thompson Jacob Harder Wm McCandless John Byrns Wm Gatlin John Johnston John Cox Wm Peebles Henry Inman James Thompson say plf sustained damages $388.93¾. Plf recovers damages and costs.

John Newman vs George Hulme. Debt. Justices O Williams Hinchey Pettway R Puckett. Jury Burrell McLemore Robt P Currin John Sample Daniel Williams Geo Slaker Wm Williams Wm Glover Jason Hopkins James Owen John Cox Wm Banke John M Armstrong. Plf recovers his debt, damages, and costs of suit.

Robert Hill vs John Hill. Debt. Justices[above]. Jury Burrell McLemore Robt P Currin Wm Willett Danl Williams Geo Sluker Wm Williams Wm Glover Jason Hopkins Jas Owen John Cox John M Armstrong. Plf recovers agt dft his debt, damages, and costs.

p.92 John Sample surviving Partner &c vs William Shute. Debt. Justices [above]. Jury Burrell McLemore Robert P Currin Wm Willett Daniel Williams Geo Sluker Wm Williams Wm Glover Jason Hopkins Jas Owen John Cox Wm Banks John M Armstrong. Plf recovers agt dft his debt $182.75 & 5 mills, damages, and costs of suit.

John Sample surviving partner &c vs Bennett Shelton & Henry Cook. Debt. Justices [above]. Jury [above]. Plf recovers his debt $195.65, damages, and costs.

Attendance as jurors proven by Wm Williams 5 days Edward Gossage 5 days Henry Inman 5 days James Thompson 5 days.

Campbell & Stewart vs Bennett Shelton & Henry Cook. Debt. Justices [above]. Jury [above]. Plfs recover debt $125, damages, and costs.

p.93 Campbell & Stewart vs Henry Rutherford. Debt. Justices[above]. Jury[above]. Plfs recover debt $129.43¾,damages, and costs.

Campbell & Stewart vs Burrell McLemore. Justices[above]. Jury Robt P Currin Burrell McLemore Wm Willett Daniel Williams Geo Sluker Wm Williams William Glover Jason Hopkins James Owen John Cox Wm Banks John M Armstrong. Plfs recover agt dft debt $116.61⅛, damages, and costs.

Order Hinchey Pettway & Chas McCallister Esqrs take examination of Susanna Reese wife of Beverly Reese relative to her voluntary exn of deed to Herbert Reese for 1400 acres in Dinwiddie County Virginia.

Stephen Cantrell Jr vs William Shute. Debt. Justices[above]. Jury[above]. Plf recovers agt dft his debt $500, damages, and costs.

p.94 John Stealy vs John Bukley[Berkley?]. Debt. Justices[above]. Jury[above]. Plf recovers agt dft his debt $1552.12, damages, and costs of suit.

William Rutledge vs Andrew Campbell & James Stewart. Debt. Justices[above]. Jury [above]. Plf recovers agt dfts his debt $122.35½, damages, and costs.

Joseph Pollard vs Ebenezer Coleman. Attachment. Justices[above]. Jury[above]. Plf

JULY 1813

recovers agt dft his damages $1798.93, and his costs of suit.
Court adjourns until Tomorrow morning nine 0 Clock.
                                    H Pettway J P   G Hulme   R Puckett J P

Saturday 17th April 1813. Present the worshipful H Pettway Geo Hulme R Puckett.
Licence Thos L Robertson to keep an ordinary at his dwelling house in this Town;
bond $2500 with John H Eaton & William P Harrison his securities.

p.95   John Den Lessee of Thomas Haynes vs Richd Fen. Ejectment. Nicholas P
Hardeman admitted defendant in this case in the room of Richd Fen confesses lease
entry and ouster and relies on the title only, pleads not guilty.

John Stealy vs John Berkley. Debt. Dft granted appeal to Circuit Court; gave as his
security Thomas Bradley and Alexander Smith.

Wm Glover vs Campbell & Stewart. Defts granted appeal to Circuit Court; bond with
John Sample and John Hardeman their securities.

Robert Smith vs Thomas McElwee. on Sciri facias. Dft came not. Plf granted judgt
and exn agt dft for $38.19 the debt mentioned, also his interest and costs.
Court adjourned untill Court in Course.
                                           G Hulme   R Puckett   C Boyles

Williamson County Monday 12th July 1813. Court of Please and Quarter Sessions.
Present the Worshipful George Hulme Sion Hunt James Boyd, Esquires.
Jurors summoned: John Morrow (not) Alexr Smith Billington Taylor John Watson (exd)
Abraham North Bernard Richardson William Thomas (not) William Marshall Thos Wilson
Jr Ephriam Andrews Moses Turner Edwd Buford George Mebane Thomas B Walthall(excused
for Thursday) James Neelly (came. exd) Jas Berry George Oliver James Clem Benjamin
Gholston Robert Rogers (excused) Wm Jones (excused) Thomas Cash John Hailey Thomas
Old Daniel Perkins (exd) Alson Edney. Constables Robert Sample & John Carothers.

Grand Jurors Wm Marshall foreman Moses Turner Thos Old John Hailey Bernard Richardson Billington Taylor James Berry Ephriam Andrews Thomas Cash Alson Edney George
Mebane James Clemm Alexr Smith 4th day dismissed.

John Den lessee of John Smith vs James Gault. James Gault admitted deft instead of
casual ejector confesses lease entry and ouster & pleads not guilty on title only.

p.96   Mordecai Pillow vs William Radford. Parties in proper persons agree suit
shall be dismissed, each pays own costs.

James Davis Esqr heretofore apptd Justice/peace in bounds of George Burnes malitia
company sends into open Court his resignation.
Deed Robert Rogers to Benjn Russell 150 acres ackd.

JULY 1813

Deed Henry Walker to Jason Hopkins 1 lot proven by James Walker & Stephen Biles.
Deed Wm Shute to Alson Edney 150 acres ackd.
Deed Christopher Robertson to Lewis Loyd 38 acres proven by Nichs T Perkins & Henry Lysard.
Deed Millington Smith to James Sanford 200½ acres proven by Robert Sanford & John Matthews.
Deed James Price Hannah Price exrs of Samuel McCutchan James Marshall exors of Patrick McCutchen decd to Benjamin Roberts 150 acres ackd.

On petition of Elijah Mayfield ordered that writs/certiorara issue agreeably to prayer of sd petitioner to James Allison bring in the papers that further prosecuting may be had thereon; further proceedings stayed until the matter be farther heard and determined at our next Court.

Settlement with Wm Brown admr/estate of Joseph Roberts decd returned.
Agreement Robert Young & Wm Wilson proven by Moses Hale.
Grant Abraham North liberty to build a water grist mill on his own lands on West Harpeth included in bounds of sd tract.
Thomas E Jones allowed $3 each for killing 4 wolves over age 4 mos and under 6 mos.

Appt Nancy Bugg gdn to Benjn Bugg Polly Bugg Lucy Bugg Sally Bugg Patsey Bugg minor orphans of Benjn Bugg decd; bond $1600, Ephriam M Bugg & John Robinson securities.

p.97   John Adams in open Court gave bond with Thomas Goff and James Boyd his securities $140 condition maintenance of girl child by sd John Adams begotten on body of Anne Shaffer single woman & to keep harmless the County Warden/Poor.

James L Reed in open Court gave bond with Joseph Summers and John Mathews securities sum $140 condition maintenance of child by sd James L Reed begotten on body of Jane McCans[McCaul?] single woman of this County.

William Kidd heretofore apptd Constable resigns as such.
Lettr/atty Jonathan Douglass to Wm Young proven by Joseph Young.
Appt Edith Harris gdn for Patsey Harris minor orphan; bond $500, David McEwen and John House her securities.
Acct/sales of Benjamin Bugg decd returned by Nancy Bugg David Pinkston & Ephriam M Bugg executors.
Division/chattel estate of Jordan Reese decd returned by Hinchey Pettway Edward Swanson Wm Parham & David Dickinson.

Commissioners James Gordon Charles McAlister & John Sample report that on Saturday 15 August 1812 they sold old Jail to Gurdon Squire, highest bidder for $12.37½.

David P Anderson vs Rouelham Poe. Arbitrators Abram Maury & Samuel Moor award in favour of deft Poe. Dft recovers agt plf his costs.

Buckner Harwell Thos & Jesse Westmoreland & William Wells agt Henry Lester. Debt. Geo Hulme Sion Hunt James Boyd justices. Dft in proper person confesses judgt for residue of debt and damages $804.23. Plf recovers debt and damages. Plfs are granted stay of execution untill 20th January next.

JULY 1813

p.98   John Carson vs Joseph Carson. Debt. Geo Hulme Sion Hunt James Boyd. Dft in proper person confesses debt $68.16. Plf recovers debt, damages, and costs.

Wm W Cunningham vs William Maxwell. Appeal. Justices[above]. Parties in proper person; dft dismisses his appeal; each pays own costs.
Court adjourns till tomorrow 9 O Clock.   G Hulme   Wm R Nunn   E Ragsdale

Tuesday 13th July 1841(sic). Present George Hulme Wm R Nunn Edward Ragsdale Esqrs. Order William Bond oversee road from Maury County line ending at Fountain Creek road at Jno Jacksons; hands work thereon in bounds including Mrs Doherty west to Indian boundary line across Col Russels road south including Abhm McCarty Jr.

Ordered everyone who failed to return taxable property come forward and it it in. Order Zachariah Jackson be paid for supporting John Kerr Wilson put on the parish at the rate $46/yr from 28th April 1813.

Order Enoch Galloway be paid what is due him for supporting Bird Taylor put on parish list at rate of $25 from 30th May 1812.

p.99   Order Wm Wilson Jacob Garrett & Saml Shelburne Esqrs settle with Sarah Porter relative to her admn on estate of Dudley Porter decd.

Order Charles McAlister & Hinchey Pettway settle with Sherrod Green gdn of children of Samuel Clark decd.

Elihu S Hale vs Sampson Sawyers. John Smith & Genl L Nolen appearance bail for dft surrender deft.

Wm Bond heretofore apptd constable in Capt Richardsons malitia company resigns.

Elihu S Hale vs Sampson Sawyers. Sd Sampson entitled to prison bounds.

Jackson Wood Jos H Scales Richd W Hyde Saml Perkins & John D Hill report they marked a road beginning at Rutherford County line near Christopher Venattes intersecting Franklin rd that leads to Carrs mill near a pile of rocks on one of which is marked 8 miles to Franklin.

Order William Black oversee road from John Currys to Widow Woods line; those in bounds from plantation where John Curry did live then to Geo Manskers to Frederick Davis to Widow Woods to Jason Wilsons work thereon.

Order William Logan Thomas Wilson & Wm R Nunn Esqrs settle with James Joyce admr/ estate of Littleberry Epperson decd; make return to next Court.

Order Wm Edmiston David Shannon & Wm Wilson Esqrs be Judges of ensuing election for a Senator and Representative to the General Assembly, and as clerks for sd election Genl Lee Nolen & Richd W Hyde; Sheriff to notify them accordingly.

Order John Witherspoon Isham R Trotter Spencer Buford David Dunn Charles Boils and

JULY 1813

Saml Shelburne be judges of the election for members to Genl Assembly, and as Clerks to sd election James Giddens Thos Ridley Wm W Cunningham & Ewen Cameron.

p.100 Nicholas Scales allowed $10.50 for a blank book furnished the Registers Office.

Order Matthew Lee oversee road from John Evans's lane to John Witherspoons; hands from John Eachols & Hy Cook then with Natchez road including Martin Proutham[?] Peter Holliday Bradford Balance & Thos Walton work thereon.

Order David Pinkerton oversee from Natchez road to near Methodist Meeting House; hands up Trace Creek thence East including Robert Hill thence North work thereon.

Release Thomas Simmons from payment of value of two head of cattle by him posted afterwards proved to be property of another person.

Jurors to attend next Circuit Court: George Hulme Thomas Garrett Samuel Shelburne Nichs Scales Edwd Ragsdale Francis Burrows David Dunn Sion Hunt James Black Samuel Wells Tristram Patton John K Campbell Nathan Adams Joseph H Scales David Dickinson Oliver Williams Elisha North Sherwood Green Meredith Helm Cordd Nickerson Wm Parham Richard Hightower Saml Benton Collin McDaniel John Hill Esqr Henry Cook. Constables Green Sent[Scot?] Vincent Greer

Jurors to County Court: Danl German Timothy Shaw Allen Hill Joshua Coleman Michael Kinnard Berry Nolin Joseph Braden Saml Brown Robert Donelson Jno D Hill Johnson Wood Nicholas Perkins D R Benjamin Brown Wm Haley Edwd Warren Wm White Geo H Allen Saml F Glass Jason Hopkins James McCombs Charles Perkins Wm Banks Chas A Dabney Jas Wilson James Bradley Joshua Cutcher. Constables William Williams & Nicholas Branch.

Order Henry Cook Nicholas Perkins (DR) John Witherspoon David Dickinson Joseph Philips Wm Parham Robert McLemore George Parham Matthias B Murfree Jas Wilkinson & Daniel Perkins Esqr any five lay out a road from Bennett Shelton to Big Bridge.

Order John Bond John Williamson Wm Williams Richard Hay Geo Kinnard & James Glover lay off a road from Thomas Mayfields to Glovers Gap.

Order John H Eaton Owen T Watson Garner McConnico Amos Rounsevall Wm Stephens Chas
p.101 Stephens & Lewis Stephens alter the road at Atkinsons Black Smith Shop so as to go round a bad mud hole if they deed same most expedient.

Order George Barnes John L Fielder Nimrod Fielder John Primm John Hamer John Edmintston (B) David Cummins & Gersham Hunt lay off a road from John L Fielders plantation near the bridge near Liberty Meeting House to David Cummins lane.

Order Sheriff summon a jury to allot to Elizabeth Crawford widow of John Crawford decd her dower of perishable property of the estate.

Michael Kinnard Henry Walker Joseph Braden John J Henry William Marshall report they laid off a road from end of bridge to Dr[?] Cash.

Enoch Galloway allowed Certificate on trustee for killing one grown wolf scalp.

Order Hinchey Pettway Chas McAlister & Robt P Currin let to lowest bidder necessary repairs to Court House, and draft some plan to secure windows from falling when hoisted.

JULY 1813

Order James Craig oversee road to John Buchanans between Hays Creek & Commissioners Creek; residents from 5 mile tree at Hays Creek to Harpeth including Aaron Askee to John H Eatons plantation & Frederick Davis work thereon.

Order Thompson Wood oversee road from Franklin to Murfreesboro lying between Wilsons Creek near John D Hills and intersecting at line between Johnson Woods and Hartwell Hydes; all in bounds from Hills Still House including J H Scales to Nelson Creek to Wm Jordans plantation to Wiltshire Jordan Johnson Woods & by Hydes to Arrington Creek to Wilson Creek work thereon.

Order James Billingsley oversee road East of Hydes & Woods lane to Rutherford Cty line near C Vinaths; those from Wm Jordans on Nelsons Creek North to include Docr McClain near Rutherford Cty line down Arringtons Creek to Woods bounds including p.102   Richd W Hyde and Hartwell Hyde work thereon.

Order Thos Patton oversee road from Henry Childress to Natchez road where A M Degraffenreid was overseer and same hands work thereon.
Order Jurors who served at last Circuit Court be allowed 50¢/day for time served.
Order Jurors attending County Court be allowed 50¢ each per day of attendance.
Order Eleazer Hardeman released from appraised value of a cow by him posted and afterwards proven to be property of Richd Ogilvie.

Order Jason Patton oversee road to Murfreesborough lying between Arringtons Creek and Wilsons Creek; those in bounds from Wilsons mill to Nelsons Creek to Arringtons Creek to Wilson Creek work thereon.

Order John H Crockett oversee road to Murfreesborough beginning near Commissioners Creek and ending at Arringtons Creek; hands in Benjn Robersons Dist work thereon.

Order Thomas Carson oversee part of the road from Nashville to Shelbyville; those in bounds where road crosses Harpeth including James Ridley George Parker & Robert Wilson to Franklin road including Nicholas Gentry thence East including Thos Carson & Jas Carson Senr work thereon under his directions.

Order Saml Benton oversee Natchez road from Saml Bentons crossing Big Bridge to fork above Johnstons old place; residents from Samuel Bentons west including Jas Crenshaw to Dunagens to Myatts to Pewitts to Ropers to Edwd Campbell work thereon.

Order George Gentry oversee road from John Walkers to top of Tennessee ridge; hands that formerly worked under Samuel Gentry with addition of J W Manier David Edmiston p.103   Robert Wilson and Thomas Wilson Junr work thereon under his directions.

Order John Moor oversee road from Franklin to Chambers Ferry from the ten mile tree to Maury County line; residents from sd tree up Walkers branch to ridge between Leepers fork & Murfrees fork to Big Carter to include Eli Hope down sd creek including Jos McCollister to Little Carter leaving out Wm Simpson work thereon.

Order Joseph Robinson John Ogilvie James Ridley Moses Ridley John W Manier Thos Wilson & James Reese[Reed?] any five lay off a road from end of road leading from Columbia to intersect fishing ford road near John Walkers to County line.

JULY 1813

Order Perry Underwood oversee road from Sampson Sawyers to Cty line; those from Sawyers to John Burnett to Rutherford line, crossing ridge between Mill & Arringtons Ck west to Saml McBrides including John Matthews & Dens[Diers?] work thereon.

Order Saml Bradshaw Wm Demoss Jas Pewit Thos Alexander Wm Campbell & Jas Thompson any 5 lay out a road from Saml Bradshaws to Malakiah Kirbys running up creek, taking a dry ridge, stem all water & muddy difficulties to head of Lick Creek.

On application of Knacy Andrews surviving executor of Ephriam Andrews decd, sd Knacy having received of sales of personal property of sd decd $1616, the same doth belong by will of sd Ephriam Andrews to Elizabeth Young during her life and after her death to such children as she may have except Rebekah Kile to whom one Dollar is given by sd will, and that sd Elizabeth Young is now desirous to relinquish to her children Howard, Francis, Nancy, William, Elizabeth, Thomas, Michael, Ephriam & Patsey sd property so bequeathed to her by sd Ephriam, and sd executor is desirous to pay over the moneys by him received, therefore he is permitted to pay to Howard Francis Nancy William Thomas and to the guardians of Michael Ephriam and Patsey the
p.104 $1616 collected by him by sales of personal property of testator.

Order Sarah B Shelburne & Samuel Shelburne have ltrs/admn on estate of James Shelburne decd; bond $3000, John Crafton Wm Williams & James Boyd securities.
Inventory/estate of James Shelburne decd returned.
Appoint Wm Williams constable in Williams Company; bond $625, John Hardin & Saml Shelburn security.
Appoint Green Suit[Sent?] constable in Capt Barnes Co; bond $625 with Joel Riggs and John Waters securities.
Appoint Nicholas Branch constable in Richardsons Co; bond $625, Nathaniel Barton & Thomas Ridley securities.
Sales/estate of Wm Ogilvie decd returned by Jas Allison & Richd Ogilvie exrs.
Bill/sale R P Currier to A Johnson for negro woman ackd.
Acct/sales estate of Stephen Elam decd returned by Moses Ridley & Dianna Elam admx.
Settlement with Knacy Andrews surviving exr of Ephriam Andrews decd retd by Jacob Garrett James Allison & Thomas Wilson Esqr.

Deed Andrew Campbell by atty in fact James Stewart to Saml Cummins 332 acres ackd.
Deed Wm Hickman to Wm King & Nathaniel Ray 207 acres ackd.
Deed James Hicks to Henry Cook Lot 124 ackd.
Deed Vineyard Crawford to Thos Berry 137½ acrs proven by Robt Hulme & Robt C Hulme.
Deed Wm Lytle to Saml Cummins 320 acres proven by Hinchey Pettway & Wm Hulme.
Deed Saml McBride to Joel Johnston 127¼ acrs proven by Chas Johnston & Isaac Nance.
Deed Jas Shelburn to Geo Kinnard 91 acres proven by John R Tankersly & Wm Williams.
Deed Stephen Jordan to Nathaniel Warner[Warren?] 100 acres ackd.
p.105   Deed William Wilson to Robert Wilson 122 acres proven by James Allison & David Edmiston.
Deed Turner Pinkston to Henry Cook Lot 138 proven by John Hardeman & John H Eaton.
Deed Henry Cook to Andrew Johnston Lot 138 ackd.
Deed Henry Cook to Andrew Johnston Lot 124 ackd.
Deed Saml Cummins to Andrew Campbell 308 acres ackd.
Deed John Anderson to James Hughes 101 acres proven by Bernard Richardson and Gilbert G Washington.

JULY 1813

Deed Newton Cannon to Prudence Nelson 200 acres proven by A Potter and William Hulme.
Deed Valentine Allen to Newton Cannon 400 acres proven by John Dalton & Wm Wilson.

John K Campbell vs John Gossage. Attacht. Attachment levied on 12 acres on east fork Lick Creek by W Bond constable & returned before John Witherspoon Esqr on 13 April 1813; judgt in fvour of plf for $50 & costs. Order property attached be condemned for use of sd judgt & costs and order/sale issues to Sheriff.
Court adjourns till tomorrow 9 O Clock.   John Witherspoon S Green E Ragsdale

Wednesday 14th July 1813. Present John Witherspoon Sherwood Green Edward Ragsdale. Appoint Charles McAlister & Hinchey Pettway to settle with Joshua Cutchen guardian for Amos Moore & Esther Moore orphans of Moses Moore decd.

Edward Buford assignee vs Edward Ragsdale. Debt. J Witherspoon John J Henry Jacob Garrett Wm Wilson. Jury Abram North Thos Wilson Thos B Walthal Geo Oliver Benjn Gholston Thos Ridley John Pillow Thos Jones Moses Chambers John Mayfield Wm Bond
p.106   John Porter say dft hath paid debt and plf hath sustained damages by reason thereof mistrial.

Edward Buford assee vs Edward Ragsdale. Debt. George Andrews subpoenaed to give testimony behalf deft came not. Forfeit set aside on dft paying costs.

William Logan Esqr collected & paid $2 as one half fines agt Elias Scott for swearing on 5th Feby 1813 and six two & half cts agt Wm Alexander for swearing on 4th day Feby 1813.

Thomas W Stockett reappointed overseer of road from Beach Cr to Davidson Cty line.

Deed Anthony Foster to John Haywood 368 acres proven by Wm Lytle & Thos H Fletcher.

Order John Carothers summponed to attend this Court as a constable be fined $5 unless sufficient cause of absence be shewn.

Deed William Willett & Mary Willett to James Terrell ackd by sd Wm & Mary Willett for 105 acres. Sd Mary wife of William Willett being first privily examined by Jno Witherspoon Esqr.

Daniel Tradewell vs John L Fielder. Certiorara. Jury Athelston Andrews John McSwine Hugh Pinkston Charles Stephens William Goff Angus McPhail John Evans Andrew Cowsart Frederick Davis John Cox Christopher E McEwen Charles Perkins. Plf recovers agt dft his damages $6.66¾.

Daniel Tradewell vs John L Fielder. Benjamin Evans subpoenaed to give testimony behalf dft came not; he forfeits agreeably to act of assembly.

p.107   Isaac Crow vs Francis Gunter. Jury Thos Wilson Geo Oliver Ewen Cameron Benj Gholson Thos B Walthal Thos Ridley Edwd Buford Wm Bond Richd Sampson Thos Jones Abram North Ruffin Brown assess plfs damages to $26.60.

JULY 1813

Thomas Younger vs William Nall[Nale?]. Certiora. Motion to dismiss. O Williams D Mason Jacob Garrett. Motion overruled.

Deed Acquilla Suggs exr will of Noah Suggs decd to John Porter 320 acres proven by James Pinkston and John Douglass.

Order Walter B Owen oversee road to James Allisons spring branch; all in bounds from Charles Cahoons down branch by James Allison to mill, all in Capt Ogilvies company down to Overall Creek to road from Mrs Ogilvies to Wilsons to beginning.

Order Robert Patton oversee road from John Hardemans survey to Wolf pen above McRorys Creek with hands that formerly worked thereon.

Settlement made with Joshua Cutchen guardian to Easther Moore returned by Charles McAlister & Hinchey Pettway.
Settlement with Joshua Cutchen gdn for Amos Moor orphan of Moses Moore returned by Chas McAlister and Hinchey Pettway.
Settlement with Sherwood Green gdn for orphans of Samuel Clark decd retd by Charles McAlister and Hinchey Pettway.

John Tillman Jesse Kennedy John Johnston James Carson & Benjamin Smith report they marked a road from New Columbia road near George Tillmans to near John Hills horse mill intersecting road to Warren Court House.

Order Jesse Kanada oversee road from Columbia road to William Logans; hands in Capt Hookers company to cut out said road.

Order John Johnston oversee road from Logans to Wolf pitt, balance of hands of Hookers Company and part of Capt Ridleys Company beginning at Mr Ridgeways to Mr James and Moses Ridleys to Capt Hills Company line including all hands to Bedford County line to work thereon under his directions.

Order John Hill Esqr oversee road from Wolf pitt to Rutherford County line; hands in Capt Hills Company work thereon under his directions.

Deed Thos Washington & Chapman White exrs/will of Thos Masterson decd to James Gordon lots 80 115 125 in Franklin proven by Archibald Patton & John M Armstrong.

Deed John Mayfield to Thomas Edmondston 150 acres ackd.

Hamilton S Walker vs Abraham Secrest. Certiorara. Plf by his atty no further prosecutes; dft by his attorney assumes all costs.

Robert Moor vs Athelston Andrews. Debt. Jno Witherspoon Jacob Garrett William Wilson. Plf by atty agrees to take a nonsuit & no farther prosecutes.
Court adjourns till tomorrow nine O Clock.   G Hulme John J Henry C H McAlister

Thursday 15th July 1813. Present the Worshipful George Hulme John J Henry Charles McAlister Esqrs.

JULY 1813

State vs James G Jones. Affray. Oliver Williams Chas McAlister Thos Garrett. Jury Abram North George Oliver Thos Wilson Edwd Buford Thos B Walthal Benjn Gholston Moses Chambers Richd Sampson Groves Sharp Geo Andrews Richd Steele Wm Sparkman find defendant is guilty.

p.109 State vs Jas Carroll & Robt Salmon. County solicitor no further prosecutes.

State vs Angus McPhail. Affray. Court: Oliver Williams Chas McAlister Thos Garrett. Jury Athelston Andrews Wm Peebles Newton Cannon Richd Hightower Jas Wilson Beverly Ridley Robt Hill Jas McGavock Jno Cox Jno McSwine Kenneth Morrison Jas B Thompson find defendant not guilty.

James Wilson a juror in State vs A McPhail fined $2 for contempt to Court by not coming in with the Jury. Remitted by the Court.

State vs Jesse White. A&B. O Williams G Hulme Thos Garrett. Jury Abraham North Geo Oliver Thos Wilson Edwd Buford Benjn Gholson Moses Chambers Richd Sampson Groves Sharp Geo Andrews Richd Steele Richd Hightower John Holt say dft is guilty.

William Peebles and Robert Hill fined $1 each for not attending when summoned jurors for this day. Fine on Wm Peebles remitted by Court.

State vs Robert Salmon. Indictment. Court Oliver Williams Geo Hulme Thos Garrett. Dft in proper person pleads guilty; to be imprisoned in common jail for 60 days and further remain there untill the costs of this Indictment be paid.

State vs James Carroll. A&B. G Hulme Richd Puckett Gershom Hunt. Jury Athelston Andrews James Wilson Beverly Ridley John Cox John McSwine Kenneth Morrison James B Thompson Wm McCandlass Edwd Gossage Wm Sparkman Matthias B Murfree Wm Bateman say
p.110 deft is guilty; fined $10 & costs of this prosecution.

Order Robt Sammons delivered out of jail immediately for purpose of giving testimony in case of State vs Jas Carroll; then to return from whence he came.
Order Wm Anthony & Wm Denson settle with Garner McConnico and Richard Puckett Esqr guardians of heirs of Benjamin Collenton deceased.

State vs Edward Gossage. A&B. Richd Puckett Chas McAlister Gersham Hunt. Jury Abraham North George Oliver Thos Wilson Edwd Buford Richd Sampson Grove Sharp Geo Andrews Richard Steele Jonathan Currier James Patton John Parks John M Walker find dft guilty. Gossage to be imprisoned in county jail ten days without bail and fined $10 and pay costs of prosecution and sheriff to carry this judgment into execution. Deft obtained appeal to Circuit Court; bond with Moses Chambers & Isaiah Cotes[Cates?] his securities.

Account/sales of estate of Thomas Ballow produced.

State vs John Cox. Malicious mischief. Court Oliver Williams David Dunn Richd Puckett. Jury Abram North George Oliver Thos Wilson Edward Buford Richard Sampson Grove Sharp Richd Steel Benjn Gholston James Wilson James Patton Jno Parks Beverly Ridley find dft guilty; fined $75. New trial granted; motion to arrest judgment.

JULY 1813

State vs Edward Gossage. A&B. Appearance Bond, Edward Gossage in sum $250; Moses Chambers Kenneth Morrison & Isaiah Cotes in sum $82 each. William Sparkman & Berry Donaldson appearance bond, sum $50 to appear at Circuit Court to testify in behalf
p.111   the state against Edward Gossage.

Order Alexander Smith oversee road from near Collin McDaniels to Bradleys mill; hands in bounds from Bradleys mill down Little Harpeth opposite Jacob Grays then west to include David Johnstons plantation to Widow Reads thence to Capt Thos Bradleys thence to Alexander Smiths work thereon under his directions.

Bill/sale Daniel Carter Senr and Sarah Carter his wife Daniel Carter Junr Margaret Carter Benjamin Carter Sarah Harriet Carter to James Black for two negroes Fillis & Winny proven by Joseph McMun[McMein?].

Deed John Robinson to Thomas Morton 137 acres proven by William Sparkman and Joseph Robinson.
Deed Thomas Haynes to Turner Saunders town lot & half ackd.
Account/sale Sally L R Gray decd retd by Young A Gray admr.
Ltr/atty George H James to John Sample ackd.
Newton Cannon discharged as a juror.
Court adjourned until tomorrow morning 9 OClock.   O Williams Dd Dunn Dd Mason

Friday 16th July 1813. Present George Hulme Oliver Williams David Dunn Esquires. David K McEwen qualified as a Justice of the peace for this County.

Motion of Reuben Nance by his atty; at Jany session 1813 judgt agt Wm Alexander & John Hill & Thomas Simmons his securities in favour of Reuben Nance for sum $71.14
p.112   with costs of suit; sd judgt was omitted to be entered at sd term for debt & costs afsd. Judgt to be entered agt sd William & Jno Hill & Th Simmons his securities as of that term.

William Betts vs Thomas Mastersons exrs. O Williams David Dunn Jacob Garrett. Jury Abram North Geo Oliver Thos B Walthal Richd Samsom Grove Sharp Finch Scruggs Benjn Gholson Thos Wilson Jno S Campbell Robt Ragsdale Jno Evans Thos Wallace. Plf recovers agt dft his damages $502.96½ besides his costs of suuit.

Thomas B Walthal vs Rowland Tankersley. Motion of Thos B Walthal by atty John Hardeman; he paid as security for Rowland Tankersley $20.09 by reason of judgt agt him in behalf exrs of James Thompson vs Rowland Tankerly. Thos B Walthal recovers agt sd Rowland Tankerly $20.09 and costs of this motion.

Ltr/atty David Craig & Alexander Miller to Joseph Hart ackd.
Deed Alexander Campbell to Hendley Stone 149 acres proven by Edward Warren & John T Burnett.

Tapley B Andrews constable to whom was issued a fifa from Jesse White, Justice, to make of chattels of Sampson Prowell the sum of $3 the amount of a judgt recovered agt sd Sampson by Jones Terrill, also 50 cts costs; Tapley B Andrews not finding in this county personal estate whereon to levy exn has levied on 75 acres property of

JULY 1813

sd Sampson on Leepers fork of West Harpeth. Execution issues to Sheriff to expose to sale sd land to satisfy judgt $3 with costs besides costs of sd motion.

Deed William T Lewis to Richard Hightower 750 acres proven by O Williams and G Dudley.
p.113

Order James Barnet oversee road to Harpeth Lick; bounds beginning at Lytles road, running to include Joseph Love Burnet Mayfield Boyd to Bearskin nob work thereon.

Following proved attendance as jurors 5 days at this court: Benjamin Gholston George Oliver Thomas Wilson Abraham North Edward Buford.

Geo H Allen Jno Walker Joseph Robertson David Spain Josiah Wilson report they laid off the road beginning south of Thos Wilsons North boundary leaving sd road to left then intersecting sd road below his south boundary it being fishing ford road. Court adjourns untill tomorrow morning nine OClock. H Pettway C H McAlister Jacob Garrett.

Saturday 17th July 1813. Present Charles McAlister Hinchey Pettway Jacob Garrett.

Jesse Wilson vs Stephen Smith. Debt. Justices[above]. Motion granted to amend plea of dft to plf declaration on dft paying all costs. Bill of exception by plf.

State vs James G Jones. Motion to arrest judgt--affray. C McAlister Jacob Garrett. Judgment arrested.

Wm Cheatham vs William King. Tapley B Andrews constable commanded to make $5.85 the amt of judgt had by Wm Cheatham agt Will King together with $1 cost of suit; not finding personal property, sd Tapley levied on 100 acres on flat Creek. Order issues to Sheriff to expose to sale sd land.

p.114 John McSwine vs Joseph McAlister. McAlister failed to appear; plf has judgt but damages to be determined next term of this Court.

Licence Joel Hobbs to keep an ordinary at his dwelling house in this County; bond $2500 with Thomas H Perkins and Thomas Goff his security.

Thomas McAlister vs Richard R Ballance. David Dunn E Ragsdale Saml Shelburne. Dft came not; Plf recovers agt dft; damages to be inquired of by jury at next Term.

Order Oliver Williams Esqr Thomas Ridley Freeman Walker & James Hardee view estate of James Shelburne decd and set apart a reasonable portion for use of Sarah R Shelburne relict of sd James & the children during one year.

Samuel Andrews constable to whom was issued a fi fa from John Witherspoon commanding him of goods of Sampson Prowell to make $3 the amt of a judgt recovered agt sd Sampson by John McSwine and one dollar costs; not finding personal estate, Samuel levied on 75 acres property of sd Sampson on Leepers fork of West Harpeth. Sheriff to expose to sale sd land to satisfy sd judgt costs and costs of motion.

OCTOBER 1813

Deed Thomas Williamson to Benjamin Williamson 78 acres proven by Thos Walker and Thomas S West.
Deed Thomas Williamson to William Williamson 100 acres proven by Thos Walker and Thos S West.

Isaac Crow vs Francis Gunter. New trial granted dft.

Samuel Shelburne & Richard Puckett report they settled with Michael Kinnard & Lewis Stevens admrs of Michael Kinnard decd.

p.115 William McKey vs Peter Holliday. On motion of Wm McKey by atty John Reed; judgt by John Sample & Co agt Peter Holliday principal & W. McKey security of sd Peter before David Mason JP for $61; sd McKey paid sd judgt; therefore sd Wm McKey recovers agt sd Peter Holliday sd $61, costs of suit, and costs of motion.

Thomas Wells vs William McKey. On motion of Wm McKey by atty John Reed; heretofore before Hinchey Pettway JP Thos Wells recovered judgt agt Peter Holliday for $61.16. Sd Wm McKey recovers agt sd Holliday sd sum $61.16 & costs of suit, & of motion.

Angus McPhail vs James G Jones. Subpoena issues to Marshall of West Tennessee to appear at next County Court bringing certificate of report of Angus McPhail made to him, relative to his being born without the U.S. in Kingdom of Great Britain with all other papers he may have in his possession.

Court adjourned till Court in Course.   Dd Dunn   G Hunt   E Ragsdale

Williamson County, Monday 11th October 1813. At Court of Pleas and Quarter Sessions held at Court House in Franklin when were present the Worshipful Oliver Williams Edward Ragsdale Thomas Garrett Esquires.

Jurors summoned: Danl German Timothy Shaw Allen Hill Joshua Coleman Michael Kinnard Berry Nolen Jos Braden Saml Brown Robt Donelson John D Hill Johnson Wood Nicholas Perkins D R Benjn Brown William Hailey Edward Warren William White George H Allen Saml F Glass Jason Hopkins Jas McCombs Charles Perkins Wm Banks Chas A Dabney James Wilson James Bradley Joshua Cathen. Constables William Williams & Nicholas Branch.

Grand Jurors: Nichs Perkins foreman Chas Perkins Allen Hill Chas A Dabney Jas Wilson James McCombs John D Hill Joshua Coleman Samuel F Glass Samuel Brown William
p.116   White Jos Braden.

Ordered Zachariah Jackson oversee road; hands in bounds from near Robt Johnston to Nortons to Montgomerys to John Grays on Spencers Creek to Joel Stephens to Mr Goff to McConnicos Meeting house thence with Commissioners road leaving John Goff on liberty road work thereon.

Order George Gillaspie oversee road from Franklin to first knob south of Maj

OCTOBER 1813

Porters plantation to a tree marked S G; James Williams George Neelly Thomas Neelly Watson John Hay George Sluker Nathan Bullock Amos Bullock John McKinney Charles Boyles Andrew Cowsart George Bennett James Terrell James House Mr Gillaspie Thomas Duty Balaam Ezell Jesse Tarkington John Tarkington Richard Swanson Robert Dysert Mr Dobson Ephriam Sampson work thereon under his directions.

Order Robert Hogg oversee road from Franklin to Holly Tree Gap from two mile tree to sd Gap; hands from Andrew Goffs up Spencers creek to Commissioners road to ridge between Spencers Cr and Little Harpeth to Holly tree gap between David McEwens and Isaac Mairs work thereon.

James Tremble in Open Court was admitted to practice as an attorney.

Jesse Wilson vs Stephen Smith. Deft to pay the attendance of all the witnesses he summoned previous to the demurrer being filed or this cause set for trial.

Elihu S Hale vs David Shannon. Oliver Williams Charles Boyles Samuel Shelburne. Jury Edwd Warren Berry Nolen Andw Roundtree Alexr McCowan Jas Wilkins Benjn Merritt John Mairs Geo Bennett Wm Parham Jas Swanson Burwell McLemore Andw Cowsart. Plf recovers debt $161.38, costs of suit; dft moved to arrest judgt.

p.117   Elihu S Hale vs George Shannon. Oliver Williams Charles Boyles Samuel Shelburne. Jury Edward Warren Berry Nolen Andw Roundtree Alex McCown James Wilkins Benjn Merritt John Mairs Geo Bennett Wm Parham James Swanson Burwell McLemore Andw Cowsart. Plf recovers agt dft his debt, damages & costs; motion to arrest judgt.

Deed Elisha Dodson to Beverly Reese 360 acres proven by Elisha Madden & Jno Watson.
Deed Jas Hopkins to Thos Prowell 50 acres proven by Sampson Prowell & Thos Duness.
Deed Thomas Shute & Asa Shute to Thomas Prowell 1200 acres proven by Wm Williams & Sampson Prowell.
Deed Michael Kinnard to Josephine Shelburne James Shelburne Elizabeth Shelbourne & Mary Shelbourne minors of James Shelbourne 100 acres ackd.
Deed William Sloan to John Minor & Lanselot Minor 200 acres ackd.
Deed William Hulme as Sheriff to John Mairs 50 acres ackd.
Deed Robert Neelly to Ambrose Hadley 114 acres proven by David Dickinson & William Parham.
Deed Thos Shute to Hugh Love 50 acres proven by Sampson Prowell and Harrison Bond.
Deed Thomas McCrory Senr to Thomas McCrory Junr 100 acres proven by James Campbell & Jacob Gray.
Ltr/atty William Sloan to David McEwen ackd.

Grant David Squire ltrs/admn on estate of Gurdon Squier decd; bond $2000 with Henry Walker and Benjn Gholson securities. Inventory Gurdon Squier decd returned by admr.
p.118   Order David Squire sell chattel estate of Gurdon Squier decd.

Grant Eliza Norton and Saml Anderson ltrs/admn on estate of William Norton decd; bond $500 with Thos Bradley and John McSwine securities.
Inventory/estate William Norton decd returned by admr and admx.

On petition of George Cahoon, order George Tillman surveyor James Allison Wm Wilson

OCTOBER 1813

Thos Wilson Kimbro Ogilvie & John Ogilvie allot to George Cahoon 350 acres, part of 1000 acres granted to Charles Harris on headwaters Harpeth River adj lands of Washington Smith and Joseph Carr; sd Charles Harris is dead and leaves an heir and executor Samuel Harris to whom descended title to sd thousand acres.

Edward Buford assee vs Edward Ragsdale. Debt. Oliver Williams Thos Garrett Charles Boyles. Jury Edward Warren Berry Nolen Andw Roundtree Alexr McCown Jas Wilkins Benjn Merritt John Mairs Geo Bennett Wm Parham Jas Swanson Burwell McLemore Andw Cowsart. Plf recovers agt dft debt $250, damages, and costs.
Court adjourns untill tomorrow morning at 9. James Black Jes White I R Trotter

Tuesday 12th October 1813. Present James Black Jes White Isham R Trotter. William Neelly and Thomas H Benton vs George W Neelly. Parties by their attorney Wm Smith moved to have judgt entered agt George W Neelly; at May Term 1813 Joseph Engleman recovered agt sd plfs as securities of deft $189.16 as damages and costs. p.119   Therefore plfs recover of dft sd sum and costs of this motion.

Grant James Barrington sum for killing 2 wolves over 4 months old in this county.

Appoint Geo Tillman Wm Logan Esqrs to settle with David Riggs relative to his admn on estate of Wright Rigs decd.

George Bennett vs Lewis Stephens & Michael Kinnard exors. Grant permission to amend writ from exors to admrs.

Order Hugh Dobbins Samuel Benton Joel Hobbs Robert McLemore Nathaniel Benton John K Campbell David Dickinson Samuel Cummins Jesse White Charles Robertson Henly Stone Nicholas Perkins Senr Thomas Morton view road from Joel Hobbs to William Bonds on Leepers Fork of West Harpeth and lay off same to advantage of inhabitants.

Order Oliver Williams and Samuel Shelbourne to let to lowest bidder the support of Ezekiel Kavanaugh an object of charity.

Justices of the Peace to receive lists of Taxable property & Polls for 1814: Capt Williams Company of Malitia Jas Boyd; Capt Duberrys George Hulme; Capt Perkins John Witherspoon; Capt Richardsons David Dunn; Capt Simpsons Jesse White; Capt Anglin Robt McMillin; Capt Gideons Isham R Trotter; Capt Patton Tristram Patton; Capt Wells Samuel Wells; Capt Mebane Alexr Mebane; Capt Doltons James Allison; Capt Hooker George Tillman; Capt Hill John Hill; Capt Ridleys Thos Wilson; Capt Garretts Archie Jordan; Capt Hickman Saml Perkins; Capt Shannon David Shannon; Capt Johnston Sherwood Green; Capt Barnes Gersham Hunt; Capt McCrory John Johnston; Capt Edmondston Thos W Stockett; Capt Crockett John J Henry; Capt MacKeys Sion Hunt.

Jurors to ensuing Court: Ephriam Brown Zacheus German William J Boyd Elijah Hamilton Benjn Gholston Athelston Andrews Alexr Smith James Sneed Peter Hardeman Thos B Walthal Martin Standley Henry Walker William O Perkins Thomas E Jones Joseph Love Nathaniel Benton William Simpson Wm Sparkman James Gideon Beverly Reese James S Clem George Brooks Ephriam Andrews George Oliver John Dalton Wm Edmiston.
Constables Robert Sample & John Carothers.

OCTOBER 1813

Appoint Peter Pinkston constable in bounds of Capt Shannons Company; bond $625 with
p.120   Benjamin White and George Shannon his security.
Appoint John G Love constable in bounds of Captain Dilliards Company; bond $2500
with Nicholas Dilliard & Jacob Garrett his securities.
Order Collin McDaniel oversee road from Holly tree Gap to forks of sd road.

John Manier Jas Ridley Jos Robinson John Ogilvie & Moses Ridley report they laid out a road...passing through John Maniers plantation, James Ridleys plantation Moses Ridleys plantation crossing Harpeth below where Ridley is building a mill thence passing near a place called the Gulph to south of John Winroe.

Order Joseph Bell oversee road from Walkers to Big Harpeth; all hands in Ridleys Company east of Harpeth Lick road and North of Shelbyville road work thereon.

Order David Lewis oversee road from Harpeth to a narrow passage between two large rocks that the road passes through; hands in John Hills Company work thereon.

Order John Windrow oversee road from where Lewis stopt to County line; hands in Garretts company work thereon.

Order Wm Logan Thos Wilson Wm R Nunn Esqrs settle with James Joyce relative to his admn on estate of Littleberry Epperson decd.

Order James Giddens David Dickinson Edward Swanson Alexr Clark & Wm Parham or any 3 partition estate of Jordan Rees decd among the legatees agreeably to will of sd Jordan Rees of land on West Harpeth not specially devised by decedent.

Order Moses Turner John Lemmons Saml Lemmons John Scott Guilford Dudley Isham R Trotter Edwd Ragsdale Jas Giddens Allen Hill Edward Buford any five to view the propriety of altering road from Franklin to Flat Creek by Edward Bufords which passes through Glen Owens plantation and make report.

Order Timothy Shaw oversee road from George Hulmes to Betts mill; hands from Widow Hopkins down Little Harpeth to Natchez road up Big Harpeth to Patrick Campbell up
p.121   branch to G Hulme leaving him out, work thereon.

Order Joseph Bell Watson Gentry Jos Dillinder Spencer Reynolds John Dalton Robt Rogers John Walker Philip Maurey Joseph Robinson any five alter road through the lands of Richard Ogilvie where sd road spoils his field.

Order Wm Simpson oversee road from Franklin to Chambers Ferry, from Nicholas Hardemans lane to 10 mile tree; hands east of Murfrees boundary...Wm Simpson to ford of Walkers branch to ridge between Leepers and Murfrees forks... including Joseph Cowan work thereon.

Order Haden Tillman oversee road...to Wm Logans; hands in Capt Hookers Company work thereon.

Order Joseph Sumner oversee road from ridge between Arrington and Mill Creeks to ridge between Arringtons and Wilsons Creeks; hands in bounds from Widow McKnight on

OCTOBER 1813

Arringtons Creek to Benjn Russels old place with ridge that divides Arringtons and Stewarts creeks including Thomas McGaugh work thereon.

Order Wm Thomas oversee road from McConnicos Meeting house to near Hayes Creek; hands from Meeting house including Wm Marshall and Wm Thomas to Pulliams branch and David McEwens plantation up Big Harpeth to Hays Creek to John Richards plantation thence west including Michael Kinnard Charles Herrald Wm Denson work thereon.

John Williamson Geo Kinnard Richard Hay Wm Williams & Jones Glover report they marked a road from Thomas Mayfields to Glovers Gap intersecting road from Little Hurricane to sd Gap.

p.122   Order Wm Glover oversee road as marked from Thos Mayfields to Glovers with the marked trees; hands in bounds from Richard Tankersleys to Thos Mayfield to Wm Glover including Wm Brooks to Arthur Stewart to John Bond work thereon.

Order Saml Crockett Jno Gray Jno West Thos Bradley Alexr Smith Thos West & Wm Pettway mark road from Franklin to Liberty Meeting House where it runs through lands of E W Beasleys should it be no disadvantage to the public.

Isham Matthews released from tax on stud horse for this year.

Grant John Atkinson & Andrew Herrin ltrs/admn on estate of Isaac Crow decd; bond $6000 with George Tillman & Thomas Herron securities, the widow having relinquished her right of administration.

Grant Garner McConnico ltrs/admn on estate of Richard Puckett decd; bond $4000 with Oliver Williams and Andrew Goff his securities. Inventory returned by G McConnico. Order Garner McConnico sell chattel estate of Richard Puckett decd.

Grant Joseph H Bell ltrs/admn on estate of Jas Shoemate decd, widow having relinquished her right; bond $1500 with James Wilson & Richd Ogilvie his securities.

Stephen Bairfield licensed to keep an ordinary at his house; bond $2500 with Enoch Bateman and Benjn Williamson his securities.

Deed Richard Oston to Stephen Childress Lots 163 & 174 ackd.
Deed Turner Saunders to Kemp Holland 50 acres ackd.
Deed Shearwood Green to John Freeman 149½ acres proven by Saunders Freeman and Silas Winset.
Deed John Matthews to John Dyer 150 acres ackd.
Deed Henry Walker to John Sappington Lot 104 ackd.
Deed James Cockrel to John Gray Senr 100 acres ackd.
p.123   Deed James Shumate to Joseph Bell 100 acres proven by Tanner Williams and Thos Shumate.
Deed Jacob Garrett to Thos Hill 160 acres ackd.
Deed Henry Cook to Joseph Dodson 40 acres ackd.
Settlement with Garner McConnico guardian for John Coddington returned by Wm Denson & Wm Anthony.
Rect Jacob Coddington one of legatees of Benjn Coddington decd to Garner McConnico

OCTOBER 1813

admr of Richd Puckett who was his guardian before sd Pucketts death for $413.71. Court adjourns till tomorrow 9 O Clock.

        John Witherspoon HDy Stone Robert McMillin.

Wednesday 13th October 1813. Present John Witherspoon Hendly Stone Robert McMillin. Will of George Reynolds decd produced by Susannah Reynolds and Pryor Reynolds executors therein named, whereupon Richard Hughes & Walter Bennett contested sd will. Ordered Jury be called to inquire whether sd paper be will of sd George Reynolds decd. Jury Berry Nolen John Hardin Henry Hunter Richd Herbert George Shannon Moses Wooten John McSwine Wm Patton Joel Dilliard Nicholas Dilliard Ewen Cameron Archibald Lytle say sd paper is will of George Reynolds decd. Susannah Reynolds & Pryor Reynolds recover of sd Richard Hews and Walter Bennett their costs.
Susannah Reynolds and Pryor Reynolds executors named in will of George Reynolds decd qualified.

David Mason vs George Andrews. Covenant. Geo Hulme Robt McMillin Saml Akins. Jury Edwd Warren Thos Reynolds Robt Guthrie Saml Moore Swanson Johnston Drury Pulliam John T Bennett John Cunningham Isham Cole Archibald Lytle George Oliver Alexander p.124 White say dft hath not kept covenant. Plf recovers damages & costs.

Daniel Carter vs John Johnston. Certiorara Wm McMillin David Mason Samuel Aikins. Jury Berry Nolen Ewen Cameron Dixon Vaughn Geo Shannon Wm Shute Henry Hunter John McSwine Andw Herrin Isaac Bezzel John Harden Finch Scruggs Geo H James find for deft; plf pays all costs of suit.

Deed Michael Kinnard to Henry Secrest 100 acres ackd.
Inventory/estate of James Shumate decd retd by Joseph H Bell admr.
Inventory/estate of Isaac Crow decd retd by John Atkinson & Andw Herrin.
Deed John Gordon to Turner Saunders Lot 112 proven by John Witherspoon and Metcalf Degraffenreid.

State vs David Bate. David Bate now confined in jail for stabbing John Waggoner be brot up; writ directed to Sheriff directing him to do so.

State vs David Bate. David Bate in open Court; solicitor says he will no further prosecute; defendant forthwith discharged from further answering.
Court adjourns till tomorrow nine O Clock.
        John Witherspoon John J Henry O Williams

Thursday 14 October 1813. Present J Witherspoon Jno J Henry Oliver Williams Esqrs. Order Hugh R Orr be committed to Jail and remain there for two hours for swearing in presence of the Court.
Thomas S Adkins records his stock mark.
p.125 Jno Inois[Juvis?] summoned as talisman fined $1 for failing to attend.
State vs Joseph McMins. Indict. Oliver Williams John J Henry Collin McDaniel. Jury John J Bennett Henry Dobson Burwell McLemore Robt Gray Jas Cockrell Hugh Dobbins Elijah Hunter Edwd Warren Berry Nolen Hugh Barr Enoch Bateman John Cunningham say dft is not guilty.

OCTOBER 1813

State vs Thomas Bradley. Presentment. C McDaniel O Williams Samuel Shelburne. Jury John Wilkins Reuben Parks Joseph Braden James McCombs Charles Perkins John D Hill Nichs Dilliard James Wilson Henry Walker Andrew Johnston Nathaniel Benton Samuel F Glass say deft is not guilty.

State vs Henry Hunter. Presentment. Justices[above]. Jury[above]. Solicitor says he will no farther prosecute in behalf of the state.

Order James Miller oversee road from Francis Gidens on fountain creek road to County line; residents in bounds from old Indian boundary east to include Enon Spring settlement down branch to include Amos Denikin[Derrikin?] & Widow Johnston down to the settlement of the Staggs and Ben Curtis work thereon.

Supplemental inventory of Jas Shelburne decd retd. Also the proportion allotted to widow and children for their support for one year as retd by O Williams Thos Ridley Freeman Walker Jas Hardee.
Account/sales of estate of James Shelburne decd returned.

Settlement with Sarah Porter admx/estate of Dudley Porter decd retd by Jacob Garrett Wm Wilson & Saml Shelburne.

p.126 Ordered that Edward Ragsdale Alexr Mebane or either of them with John Miller John Andrews & Ephriam Andrews view estate/Isaac Crow decd to allot each part of the crop stock & provisions as they conceive necessary for support of the widow and family for one year.

Deed John Sweeney to Young A Gray part of Lots 108 & 118 proven by Wm W Cunningham and John Sappington.
Deed Walter McConnell to James Carothers 50 acres proven by Jeremiah Parker and Zachariah Parker.
Deed Wm Perry to Benj Leigh 90 acres proven by Simpson Perry & John Berkley.
Deed Wm Floyd to James Wilkins 227 acres proven by Page Bond & John Branch.
Bill/sale Finch Scruggs exr of Jesse Thomas decd to Jas Cockrell ackd.
Bill/sale Mary Clay to Elisha North proven by Thos W Linster Jno W Henley[Whealey?]

Appt John Thomas gdn to Nathaniel H Thomas minor orphan of Jesse Thomas decd; bond $6000 with Joel Dilliard Nichs Dilliard & Finch Scruggs his securities.

State vs Hugh R Orr. Wm Patton & John B Cunningham surrender him to sheriff.

Hendley Stone vs Daniel Carter Jr & Daniel Carter. Debt. O Williams C McDaniel S Shelburne. Danl Carter Sr says he cannot deny debt. Plf recovers agt dft debt, damages by detention of debt, and costs. Plf stays execution till 25 decr next.

State vs John Sheron. John Sheron now confined in Jail for stabbing Wm Kindrick be brot up; writ directed to Sheriff commanding him to do so.
p.127 State vs John Sheron. John Sheron produced in open Court. Solicitor says he will no further prosecute sd John Sheron.

State vs Jesse White. Affray. Last Court. Jesse White fined $10 and costs.

OCTOBER 1813

State vs Andrew Dorton. A&B. Last Court. Solicitor no farther prosecutes.

William McColpin vs Wm Wooten. Last Court. Plf was security for Wm Wooten in an obligation given by plf and sd Wooten to John Compton for $93 5th Decr 1808; Compton at Octr 1810 Court obtained judgt agt Wm McColpin for $99.04½ & $10.15 costs. Jury Finch Scruggs Archd Lytle Nichs Dilliard Jas Cockrel Berry Nolen Edwd Warren John Cox Henry Cook Wm Banks Jesse Benton Thos Younger Joel Dilliard. Plf recovers of dft amt of judgt interest & costs as also his costs & charges of suit. Court adjourns until tomorrow morning nine O Clock.
              G Hulme Robert McMillin Jes White

p.128 Friday 15th October 1813. Present the Worshipful George Hulme Jesse White Robert McMillin.
James Boyd vs Mary Thomas Phineas Thomas Finch Scruggs John Thomas. Debt. Justices [above]. Jury Edward Warren Chas A Dabney Chas Perkins Saml F Glass Jas McCombs Wm White Wm Bright Nathl Benton Joel Dilliard Nichs Williams Berry Nolen Joseph Braden say dfts have not paid plf. Plf recovers agt dfts debt, damages, and costs.
James Boyd vs Mary Thomas Phineas Thomas Finch Scruggs John Thomas. Debt. Justices [above]. Jury[above]. Plf recovers agt dfts his debts, damages, and costs.

John Den lessee of Thomas Haines vs Nicholas Perkins Hardeman. Ejectment. Jury Edwd Warren Saml F Glass Jas McCombs Wm White Wm Bright Nathl Benton Joel Dilliard Nichs Dilliard Jos Braden Archd Lytle Thos Scott Geo Martin. Plf recovers of deft his term yet to come in premises afsd together with his damates by jury assessed as also his costs of suit. Deft obtained appeal to Circuit Court giving bond with Jno Hardeman and Nichs Perkins his securities.

p.129 Edward Buford vs Edward Ragsdale. Appeal. Dft prays appeal to Circuit Court; bond with Thomas Ridley and Tapley B Andrews his securities. Appeal granted.

State vs Jesse White. R McMullin Geo Hulme E Ragsdale. Dft who was fined on 14 Octr this session for an affray; motion for mitigation of fine; reduced to 50¢ & costs.

David Hogan assee vs Fielder Helm. Appeal. G Hulme Charles Boyles Jesse White. Jury Berry Nolen Charles A Dabney Chas Perkins Thos Ridley Angus McPhail John Harden Jas Neelly Gregory Wilson Geo H James Wm Clark Josiah Knight John P Broadnax [blank].

George Seaton vs James McCracken Benjamin White Harrison Boyd. Debt. C Boyles J White R McMillin. Jury Edwd Warren Nathl Benton Wm Hope Joel Dilliard Jas McCombs Jos Braden Nichs Dilliard Wm White Saml F Glass Archd Lytle Jno Tucker; plf recovers debt, damages & costs, but judgt may be discharged by payment of damages afsd for breach of covenant $26.58 & costs recovered in Circuit Ct & costs of suit.

John McSwine vs Joseph McColister. A&B. C Boyles J White R McMillin. Jury Edwd Warren Nathl Benton Wm Hope Joel Dilliard Jas McCombs Jos Braden Jos Meadows Nichs Dilliard Wm White Saml F Glass Archd Lytle Jno Tucker. Plf recovers of dft his damages $116.66½ besides costs.

Deed Abraham Maury to Commissioners of Franklin Lot 102 ackd.

OCTOBER 1813

p.130 Deed Jesse Tarkington to Jalund Causby[Cansby?] 40 acres ackd.
Deed Jesse Tarkington to John Tarkington 100 acres ackd.
Deed/gift John Nichols Senr to Josiah Wooldridge & wife Keziah 272 acres ackd.
Deed Abraham Maury to Isaac Holmes 600 acres ackd.

John Motherell & Joseph Motherell assee vs Tristram Patton. Debt $500. Chas Boiles Jesse White Robt McMillin. Defendant by his atty withdraws his plea of payment. Plfs recover agt dft debt $500 damages and costs.

Richard Steele vs Jesse Benton. Debt. Justices[above]. Dft cannot deny he owes $132.55. Plf recovers of dft his debt, damages, and costs.

Alexr Bennett vs Julian Nail & Knacy Andrews. Debt. Justices[above]. Dfts withdraw plea. Plf recovers agt dfts debt, damages, and costs.

George Golliday vs Jacob Reader. Justices[above]. Plf no further prosecutes; dft assumes payment of all costs.
Court adjourns untill tomorrow monring nine O Clock.
G Hulme   Robert McMillin   C Boyles

p.131 Saturday 16th October 1813. Present Geo Hulme Chas Boyles Sion Hunt Esqrs. Thomas Younger vs William Nall. Certiorara. Justices[above]. Jury Edwd Warren Jas McCombs Allen Hill Chas Perkins Saml F Glass Jos Braden Jno Harden Nathl Benton Geo H James Wm Clark Nichs Dilliard Chas A Dabney. No jurisdiction; judgt quashed.

Collector for 1812 vs John Armstrong. John Armstrong reputed owner of 128 acres on Leepers Fork & 1 white poll hath not paid taxes due thereon for 1812; Shff could not find goods whereon he could distrain for same; Collector granted judgt agt sd Armstrong; order of sale granted.

[Also the same for] Carey Bibb, Wm C C Claiborne, Archibald Craig, Samuel Jackson, Benjamin McCuiston, George McLain,   p.133   Francis A Ramsey, Sampson Sawyers, Robt Smith, Absalom Tatum,   p.134   Joseph Watkins, John Gray Blount, James Carothers, Jonathan Davis Jr   p.135   John Gillaspie, Thos Jones.

Order Nicholas Scales and Jesse White Esqrs take privy examn of Polly Moor wife of Samuel Moor relative to her relinquishment of dower to deed from Samuel Moor and her to Ambrose Lee lying in Lincoln County Kentucky.

Proved attendance as jurors to this Court Jas McComb 6 days Saml F Glass 6 Allen Hill 6 Jos Braden 6 Chas Perkins 6 Chas A Dabney 6 Berry Nolen 6 John Harden 6 Edwd Warren 6 William White 6.

Alexander Simpson the use of John Sample vs William Shute. Debt $82.86 Dam $50. G Hulme C Boyles S Hunt. Demurrer filed by plf to dfts plea sustained. Deft granted leave to amend his plea; stand trial next Term; dft pays costs of amendment.

p.136 Wilson Cahoon vs Abraham Hill. Appeal. Appellant failing to bring up his appeal in proper time made default. Plf recovers agt dft $5 and costs.

JANUARY 1814

John Sample surviving partner vs William Shute. Debt. G Hulme C Boyles S Hunt. Plf recovers agt dft his debt $82.86, damages, and costs.

State vs John Carruthers. Defendant appearing in Court, sd deft released of fine assessed heretofore agt him, but he pays costs of scire facias.

John S Campbell vs John Johnston. S Hunt Chas McAlister Chas Boyles. Court grants writ of certiorara to plf.

Nicholas Scales and Jesse White report that Polly Moor wife of Saml Moor voluntarily relinquished her right/dower in land sold to Ambrose Lee in Lincoln Co KY.

Collector for 1812 vs John Hopkins. Shff has judgt agt John Hopkins; order/sale.
p.137   Court adjourns until Court in Course.   G Hulme S Hunt C H M Alister

Williamson County Monday 3d January 1814. Court of pleas and Quarter Sessions. Present the Worshipful George Hulme James Boyd and Edward Ragsdale Esquires. Jurors summoned: Ephriam Brown Wm J Boyd Elijah Hamilton Benjn Gholston Athelston Andrews Alexander Smith Peter Hardeman Thos B Walthal Martin Standley Henry Walker Wm O Perkins Thos E Jones Joseph Love Nathaniel Benton William Simpson Wm Sparkman James Gideon Beverly Reese James S C Clemm George Brooks Ephriam Andrews John Dalton Wm Edmonston. Constables Robert Sample & John Carothers.

Grand jurors: William J Boyd Martin Stanley Henry Walker Ephriam Brown George Brooks Ephriam Andrews James Giddens Peter Hardeman Thomas E Jones foreman Beverly Rees Athelston Andrews William Edmonston. Discharged 5th day.

Order Charles McAlister & Hinchey Pettway settle with Lidia Hewston admx of Samuel Hewston decd.
James S Clemm Thos B Walthal Benjamin Gholston excused as jurors this Court.
Release John Carothers from serving as a constable at this Court.
Order Nicholas Perkins (DR) Daniel Perkins Robert McLemore Edward Warren settle with Hendley Stone and heirs of John Pryor decd.

Order Isaac Williams oversee road; hands from John Witherspoons to Saml Williams to Hugh Dobbins to Richard Steele incl Hendley Stone & Wm Bonds hands work thereon.

Order Ezekiel Puryear oversee road whereon Beverly Rees was overseer; hands of Sally Rees Thos Old Beverly Rees & Ezekiel Puryear work thereon.

p.138   Order John Nunn oversee part of road from Nashville to Shelbyville; bounds from James Ridleys & Geo Parkers incl Robt Wilson Nicholas Gentry Thos Carson & James Carson Senr work thereon.

Bill/sale Martin Adams to Wm Hope five negroes ackd.
William Parham guardian in acct with orphans of William C Hill decd produced.

JANUARY 1814

Inventory/estate of George Reynolds decd returned.
Bill/sale William Hope to Daniel German negro woman & three children ackd.
Deed Joseph Farrier to John Brantley 155 acres ackd.
Deed Thomas Henry to Robert White 90 acres proven by Adam Miller & George White.
Deed Richard Hay to John Gibson 50 acres ackd.
Deed William Hope to Martin Adams 100 acres ackd.
Deed Wm Price to Joseph Mason 36 acres proven by Rebecca H Mason & Isaac Mason.
Deed John McDaniel to John Damind[Durnins?] 103 acres ackd.

Berry Nolen William Banks Samuel Merritt & Eleazer Hardeman who were commissioned as Justices/peace took the necessary oaths for qualification.
Additional inventory/estate of Wm Norton decd returned.
Court adjourned until tomorrow morning 9 0 Clock.
         G Hulme John Witherspoon Nichs Scales.

p.139 Tuesday 4th January 1814. Present Geo Hulme John Witherspoon Nichs Scales.
Deed John Moody to Amos Roundsevall 8 acres proven by Berry Nolen & Stephen Nolen.
Alexr Smith excused as Juror this Court.
Order Edward Ragsdale & Nicholas Scales Esqrs examine Nancy McPhail wife of Angus McPhail relative to her relinquishment/dower to fifty acres sold to Saml Winstead.

Wm S G L Nolen vs Bartholomew Stovall. Archibald Brown and Edward Chitwood surrender Bartholomew Stovall in discharge of themselves; sheriff notifyed.

Order Lawrence Fly have order on County Treasurer for support of Wm Deacon.
Order Elisha Hood let to lowest bidder for support by Wm Banks & Jno J Henry Esqrs.
Order Berry Nolen & Frederick Davis admitted as bail in suit wherein W S G L Nolen is plf and Bartholomew Stovall deft.
Order John H Eaton allowed $50 for exofficio services as County Solicitor for 1813.
Wm Hamilton vs Barthw Stovall. Wm Anthony & Gersham Hunt special bail for deft.
Settlement with Lidia Hewston admx of Samuel Hewston decd returned.

Order Charles McAlister Hinchey Petway & Charles Boyles Esqrs settle with Joel Dyer & Sherwood Green exrs of William Christman decd.
Order Robert Bates oversee road; hands in bounds David Dickinson to David Davies [Davis?Dumes?] to Elijah Hunter to Nathaniel Benton incl Wiley Myatt & John Belcher [Belden?] to John Andrews to Andrew Roundtree work thereon.
p.140 Order George Hulme & John Witherspoon settle with Lawrence Bass admr of John Patton.
Order Archer Jordan Esq take tax list of those in Capt Gaults Company of malitia.
Ltr/atty David Crockett to George Calhoun proven.
Acct/sale of James Shumate decd.
List of hire of negroes, estate of Benjn Bugg decd returned.

Edward Ragsdale and Nicholas Scales return that Nancy McPhail wife of Angus McPhail was examined apart from her husband, and signed deed to Samuel Winstead for 50 acres freely of her own will and accord.

Order Thos Hendrix Matthew McGaugh Samuel Butler Joseph Lamb & David Lamb lay off

JANUARY 1814

part of the road from Columbia to Warren Court House from Thos Hendricks plantation near Francis Jacksons land supposed about half a mile.
Charles McAlister sends his resignation as Justice of the peace.

Order Robert McLemore James Giddens James Black George Nally Spencer Buford Alexander Mebane Samuel Eakin Daniel Perkins and Nicholas D R Perkins & Berry Nolen view road from Joel Hobs to Wm Bonds on Leepers fork and lay off same with greatest ease and advantage of the inhabitants & as little prejudice to enclosures as may be.

Allotment made to widow Crane for one year.

Order James Giddens Francis Giddens James Black Ezekiel Penspar and Beverly Reece partition 349 acres on Duck River between legatees of Elisha Hunt[Hurt?] Senr, to
p.141   wit Milly Hurt Moses Hurt Henry Hurt Bird S Hurt Sally P Hurt William Hurt James S Hurt John Hurt Is[Jo?] Hurt Elisha Hurt.

Order Andrew Craig Jacob Halfacre Robt Crafton Michael Kinnard James Price Mordecai Pillow & Wm J Watkins lay off a road from Wm Marshalls fence to Commissioners Crk.

Inventory/estate of John Hodge decd returned.
Additional inventory/estate of Richard Puckett decd returned.
Acct/sales estate of Richard Pucket decd returned.
Ltr/atty Thomas G Watkins to Oliver Williams proven by Roger B Sappington and O B Hays.
Appoint Richard Jackson constable in Capt John Hills Company; bond $600 with Francis Jackson and John Hill his securities.
Admit William Hodge admr/estate of John Hodge decd; bond $1000 with Francis Hodge and John Hail his securities.
Admit William Smith to keep an ordinary; bond $2500 with James Gordon and Nicholas Perkins his securities.
Order Ann Harrison be guardian of Allen Harrison; bond $1000, George Kinnard and Murrell Brady her securities.
Order Hinchey Pettway guardian to minor orphans of Samuel Hewston decd; bond $3000 with Jesse Benton and Charles Boyles his securities.

Court elected William Hulme sheriff; bond $10,000 with David Mason John Sample Jacob Garrett Sion Hunt John H Eaton Jacob Gray and John J Henry his securities; gave bond $3,000 for collection/public taxes for 1814 with John H Eaton David Mason John Sample Jacob Gray John J Henry Jacob Garrett and Sion Hunt, securities. Took oath.

p.142   Deed Michael Kinnard to Charles Harrell 150 acres ackd.
Deed George Kinnard to Murrell Bresere 91 acres ackd.
Deed Joseph Jarmain to Daniel Jerman 126½ acres proven by S Hunt & Martin Adams.
Deed John Wells to William Wells 60 acres proven by Samuel Wells & John W Pinder.
Deed Peter Hardeman to John Crafton 100 acres ackd.
Deed Angus McPhail & wife to Samuel Winstead 50 acres ackd.
Deed Thos G Watkins by Oliver Williams his atty/fact to Harden P Holt 143 ac ackd.
Deed Uriah Bass to Oliver Williams 640 acres proven by Drury Pulliam & Wm Thomas.
Deed Thos G Watkins by Oliver Williams his atty/fact to Wm P Harrison 224 ac ackd.
Deed John Hill to Francis Jackson 100 acres ackd.

JANUARY 1814

Deed John Hill to Francis Jackson 135 acres ackd.
Deed John Moody to Amos Rounsevall 8 acres proven by Stephen Nolen & Berry Nolen.
Deed Henry R Ballance to Jacob T Rivers Town Lot proven by James Crenshaw & Joseph Crenshaw.
Deed Joel T Rivers to Robert P Currin 1 Town Lot ackd.
Deed Robert T Currin to Joseph Crenshaw 1 Town Lot ackd.
Deed Benjamin Kidd to Wm Kidd 300 acres proven by S Green & N Fields.
Deed Sterling Brown to Benjamin Kidd 125 acres proven by Wm Anthony & Wm Kidd.
Court adjourns until tomorrow morning 9 OClock.
John Witherspoon John Hill Jes White

p.143 Wednesday 5th January 1814. Present John Witherspoon John Hill Jes White.
Acct/sale estate of Isaac Crow decd returned.
Acct/sale estate of Gurdon Squier decd returned.

Order Ruffin Brown Amos Roundsevall Alexr Wood Owen T Watkins Turner Pinkston Michael Kinnard & Joel Stephens mark that part of road from Franklin to Howells mill beginning at a hill near Chambers shop so as to shun a bad hill & mud hole.

Deed Nicholas T Hardeman to Thomas McCrory 265 acres ackd.
Deed James Hill to Solomon Bennet 50 acres ackd.
Deed James Hill to David O Bryant 50 acres ackd.
Deed James Hill to Absalom Taylor 50 acres ackd.
Deed John Hill to Benagy Cartton 50 acres ackd.

Reuben Huggins vs Jacob Harder. Motion by security. John Witherspoon John Hill John J Henry. Plf by atty Nicholas Perkins; plf was security for Jacob Harder the dft for an appeal in suit brot by Asa Shute vs him 15 Jany 1812. judgt agt Jacob Harder Simon Bateman & Reuben Huggins for $112.25 & costs. Reuben Huggins paid. Plf Reuben Huggins recovers of Jacob Harder sd sum, costs, and costs of this suit.
Court adjourns until tomorrow 9 OClock.   O Williams   HLY Stone   David Dunn

p.144 Thursday 6 January 1814. Present Oliver Williams Hendley Stone David Dunn.
State vs Benjamin Bedford. Sherwood Green Hendley Stone Thos Garrett. Jury Richd Steele Jos Crenshaw Thos Wilson Ruffin Brown Francis Burrows John Kirtcher Gnl L Nolen Wm P Harrison Chas A Dabney Armstead Boyd James Cavender James Swanson find defendant not guilty.

Isaac Crow admr vs Grove Sharp. H Stone S Green T Garrett. Jury Thos Ridley Wm J Boyd Martin Stanley Henry Walker Ephriam Brown Geo Brooks Ephm Andrews Peter Hardeman Thos E Jones Beverly Rees Athelstone Andrews Wm Edmonston find for deft.

Order George Hulme & John Witherspoon to settle with Henry Cook gdn for Henry John & George E Cook minor orphans of Edward Cook decd.

Inventory/estate of Richd Smith decd returned.

Order David Spain oversee road; hands in bounds from Thomas Wilson Jr & Thomas

JANUARY 1814

Wilson Esqr to James Allison to Philip Maniers incl Drury Burnett to John Ogilvie to David Spain work thereon under his directions.

Deed/gift Walter Bennett to John Bennett & others proven by William P Harrison & Robert McLemore.
Division/estate of Hardy Murfree decd returned.
Just Claim deed George Hulme to legatees of Anthony Sharp decd ackd.
Account/sales property of Peter Perkins decd returned.
p.145   Order Berry Nolen take list/taxable property in Capt Shannons Company.
Admit Young A Gray guardian to Jackey G Jones; bond $2000 with William Banks and Robert McLemore his securities.
Division/estate of Harris or an allotment made to George Cahoon 350 acres retd.
Deed Arnsey[Amsey?] Jones to Joseph Ledbetter part Town Lot 153 ackd.
Deed/gift David Evens to his daughter Martha Gilaspie Evens ackd.
Deed Elizabeth Spencer to John Mallory 150 acres proven by John Littleton & William Spencer.
Deed John Thompson to Joseph Berk 62 acres proven by Saml Carson & James McCutchen.

Order James Reed John Cahoon Wm Logan Wm Nunn Thos Wilson Esqrs divide between Josiah Wilson Thomas Wilson and Margaret his wife Polly Betsey Anita[Arissa?] and Sally Wilson land which Samuel Wilson decd lived on at time of his death.

Admit John Childress & William Smith to admr on estate of Henry Childress decd; bond $2000 with Oliver Williams & Hinchey Pettway their securities.
Admit Oliver Williams as admr/estate of Richard Smith; bond $5000 with John H Eaton & N Perkins his securities.
Admit Elizabeth Jones guardian to Abigail S Jones; bond $2000 with William Banks and Young A Gray her securities.
Bond for letting out Elisha Hood for one year at $49.87½ to Allen Hill returned by John J Henry and William Banks.
Allow Garner McConnico $3/day for dividing estate of Hardy Murfree decd, 35 days.
Allow Oliver Williams $3/day for dividing estate of Hardy Murfree decd, 30 days.
p.146   Allow David Dunn $3/day for dividing estate of Hardy Murfree decd, 49 days.
Court adjourns until tomorrow morning 9 OClock.   S Green William Banks E Ragsdale.

Friday 7th January 1814. Present S Green William Banks, Edward Ragsdale.
Inventory/estate of Henry Childress decd returned. Order/sale issued.
Supplemental inventory & acct/sales estate of John Allison decd returned.
Hinchey Pettway resigns his commission of Justice of the peace in open Court.

Alexander Simpson use of John Sample & Co vs William Shute. Debt. H Stone E Ragsdale Jas Boyd. Jury Wm J Boyd Martin Stanley Henry Walker Ephriam Brown Geo Brooks Ephriam Andrews Jas Giddens Peter Hardeman Thos E Jones Beverly Rees Athelstone Andrews Wm Edmonston. Plf recovers his debt and damages and costs.

John Sample surving partner &c vs William Shute. Debt. Justices[above]. Jury[above] find for plf; plf recovers debt damages & costs.

p.147   William Parham vs Henry Lyon. Debt. G Hulme E Ragsdale B Nolen. Jury[above]

JANUARY 1814

say there remains of debt $103.40 & damages. Plf recovers debt, damages, & costs.

Order Berry Nolen & Geo Hulme Esqrs settle with admrs/estate of John Atkinson decd. Elijah Hamilton proved attendance as a juror 5 days.

Order Turner Saunders Abram Maury Senr Daniel Perkins Andw Goff & David McEwen partition to legatees of Anthony Sharp decd land which fell to Widow Sharp now wife of George Hulme which they the sd Peggy Hulme & George Hulme have sold to legatees John J Henry & his wife Sarah James G Jones & his wife Elizabeth to John P Broadnax & his wife Jane to Angus McPhail & his wife Anne & to Sala N Sharp Searcey D Sharp Sumner M Sharp & Peggy N Sharp the four last of whom are infants under age of twenty one.

Deed Harrison Boyd to Pleasant Russell Town lot 109 ackd.
Settlement with Lydia Hewston admx/estate of Samuel Houston decd returned.
Order Collin McDaniel Esqr take list of taxable property & persons in bounds of Capt McCrorys company and make return.

Order John Harden oversee road; residents east of Joseph Love to fork of Neellys crk to James Neellys work thereon.

Jurors to next Circuit Court: George Hulme John Witherspoon Jacob Garrett George Gillaspie George Kinnard Sherwood Green Archibald Lytle Nathaniel Stancil Ephriam Brown Thomas E Jones Wm Logan Saml Perkins Zachariah Drake Berry Nolen Genl L Nolen Alexr Johnston Hendley Stone Nathl Benton Andw Craig Drury Pulliam Thos Bradley Thos W Stockett Nichs Perkins (DR) Wm Denson Wm Bond (near Giddens) and John Watson. Constables Nicholas Branch & Nelson Chapman.

p.148 Benjamin White & Harrison Boyd vs James & John McCracken. On motion as security. G Hulme E Ragsdale B Nolen. Plfs by atty Nicholas Perkins. Plfs were security for dfts; 15 Octr 1813 judgt agt James McCracken, Benjn White & Harrison Boyd; fieri facias issued in name of George Senter agt sd plfs & sd dfts. White & Boyd paid to Geo Senter through hands of Sheriff the sum afsd. Plfs White & Boyd recover of dfts James & John McCracken $259 and costs.

Wm & Genl L Nolen vs Bartholomew Stovall. Debt. G Hulme E Ragsdale B Nolen. Dft in proper person cannot deny debt. Plfs recover debt & damages; stay execution.

Wm C Hicks for use of Thomas Brandon vs Nicholas Branch. Debt. Justices[above]. Dft in proper person cannot deny balance of debt. Plf recovers debt damages & costs.

Mark Harden vs James Hill. Debt. H Stone E Ragsdale Jas Boyd. Jury Wm J Boyd Martin Stanley Henry Walker Ephriam Brown Geo Brooks Ephm Andrews Jas Giddens Peter Hardeman Thos E Jones Beverly Rees Athelston Andrews Wm Edmondston assess plfs damages; plf recovers $640 and costs.

John McSwine vs Kenneth Morrison. Certiorara. Jury Elijah Hamilton Jno Evans Francis M Dean Jno Cox Burrell McLemore Andrew Goff Jacob Tillman Thomas Bell David Houston William Grimes Richard Simpson Milton Gamble . Plaintiff recovers debt $50 damages $3.08 & costs.

JANUARY 1814

p.149   William & Genl L Nolen vs Walter Kinnard. Debt. Dft came not. Plf recovers agt dft his debt, damage, and costs.

Jno Den lessee of Jno Smith vs James Garrett. Hdy Stone Ed Ragsdale Jas Boyd. Eject. Jury J Bond H Walker Martin Stanley Ephriam Brown Ephm Andrews Geo Brooks James Gidden Peter Hardeman Thos Jones Beverly Reese Athelston Andrews Wm Edmonston. Plf recovers agt dft his term yet to come to the premises besides his damages and costs.

Charles McAlister vs Richard Ballance. Trespass. Jury Will J Boyd Martin Stanley Henry Walker Ephm Brown Geo Brooks Ephm Andrews Jas Giddens Peter Hardeman Thos E Jones Beverly Reese Athelston Andrews Wm Edmonston. Plf recovers agt dft damages $200 and his costs in this behalf expended.

Thos S Adkins vs Burwell Temple. Debt. Dft came not. Plf recovers agt dft $1351 the balance of the debt, his damages, and costs.
Court adjourns until tomorrow morning 9 OClock G Hulme John Witherspoon Berry Nolen

p.150   Saturday 8th January 1814. Present G Hulme John Witherspoon Berry Nolen. Jurors to next County Court: John T Burnett Benjamin Brown Alexr Clark John Miller Andw Herron Isaac Bizzel Benjn White Alexr McCown Thos Hendrix John Crockett Daniel Hill Burwell Temple Joel Stephens Thos Merritt Saml Edmonston Geo Strambler Thomas Wells Alexr Moore Benjn Mitchell David Nolen Ewen Cameron Robert Rogers Geo Oliver James Turner Richd Polk Abram Mason. Constables Caleb Manley William Wells.

On petition of Andrew Dorton, he is granted writs/certiorara in a case wherein George W Glasscock is plf and sd Dorton is dft.

Order John Williams oversee road; hands from near Andrew Cowsar to gap between Moses Oldhams & John Hewston to Bufords ford to Pattons road work thereon.

John Childress & Wm Smith admrs vs Daniel A Dunham. On petition of sd John Childress & Wm Smith admrs of Henry Childress decd, order writs of certiorara issue.

Order Sion Hunt & John Witherspoon Esqrs take privy examn of Peggy Hulme touching her execution of a deed given by her and her husband George Hulme to heirs of Anthony Sharp decd for land lying in Bedford and Sumner Counties.

James S Young vs Adonijah Edwards. Dft came not; plf granted writ/enquiry.

William Hulme Esqr Sheriff reported a list of taxable property and polls which appear not to have been returned for taxation for year 1813.

Deed/partition between heirs and legatees of Robert E Beasley decd was produced and ackd by Phillip Beasley John W Beasley Ephraim W Beasley & James Hicks and signature of Ann Beasley also subscribed thereto was proven by Isham Coles & John Gray Senr subscribing witnesses thereto.

p.151   Deed William Shute to Samuel Mairs 25 acres ackd.
Court adjourns till Court in Course.   Jno Witherspoon B Nolen Geo Hulme

APRIL 1814

Williamson County. Monday 4th April 1814 at court of Pleas and quarter Sessions at the Court House in Franklin. Present the Worshipful George Hulme John Witherspoon and Berry Nolen Esquires.

Jurors summoned: John T Burnett[Bennett?] Benjamin Brown Alexr Clark John Miller Andw Herrin Isaac Bizzle Benjn White Alexander McCown Thomas Hendrix John Crockett Dann Hill Burwell Temple Joel Stephens Thos Merritt Saml Edmiston George Strambler Thos Bell Alexr Wood Benjn Mitchell David Nolen Ewen Cameron Robert Rogers George Oliver James Turner Richd Polk Abram Mason. Constables Caleb Manley William Wells.

Grand jurors: Ewen Cameron foreman Richard Polk Dann Hill George Strambler Benjamin White Alexander Clark Benjamin Brown Abram Mason George Oliver Alexander McCown Thomas Merritt Alexander Wood. Discharged 5th day.

Deed Jonathan Wood to John Wood 20 acres ackd.
Deed Edward Gossage to Thomas Cox 30 acres ackd.
List/taxable property in Capt Fitzpatricks company returned by Samuel Perkins.
List/taxable property in Capt Williams company returned by James Boyd.
Settlement with Baalam Hay admr/estate of John Atkinson decd returned by Geo Hulme and Berry Nolen Esqrs.
Ltrs/admn granted to Oliver Crenshaw on estate of John C Crenshaw decd; bond $1000 with Joseph Crenshaw and Samuel Cummins his securities; qualified.
Garner McConnico released from appraised value of estray horse posted by him.

Order Edward Stephens oversee from Wilsons road beginning at fork of Arringtons Crk p.152 leaving Wm Denson Michl Kinnard Chas Harrell John Richardson then up Hayes cr to Fredk Davis north to Alexr Simpson west to Dann Hill incl Lewis Stephens.

Michael Kinnard Owen T Watkins Joel Stephens Amos Rounsevall Ruffin Brown apptd to amend road to Howels mill to avoid a bad hill and mud hole near Chamberses shop are of opinion that the old way be continued.
Court adjourns until tomorrow morning nine OClock.   G Hulme A Jordan Geo Tilman

Present George Hulme Archer Jordan George Tillman Thomas Wilson Esquires.
Ltr/atty William K Stuart to James Stewart ackd.
Bill/sale David Johnston to Robert Johnston ackd.
Deed Richard Orton to William Banks 2 town Lots ackd.
Deed Isaac Patton to Jacob Patton 70 acres ackd.
Bill/sale David Johnston to Robert Johnston ackd.
Deed David Johnston to Robert Johnston ackd.
Deed John Gary to Moses B Francis 178 acres ackd.
Deed James Davis to Nicholas Scales 29 acres proven by Geo Hulme.
Deed George Shannon to Alexander McClaran 140 acres ackd.
Deed Richard Fowler to Alexander Johnston 10 acres proven by Franklin McClaran & Jacob Adams.
Deed Oliver Williams atty/fact for Thomas G Watkins to John W Crunk 200 acres proven by Eleazer Hardeman and Yancey Powers.
p.153   Deed Minos Cannon to Jacob Adams 100 acres proven by George Oliver and Alexander Johnson.

APRIL 1814

Deed David Craig to James Craig 200 acres ackd.
Deed Nicholas Perkins to Turner Saunders 6 acres ackd.
Deed David McGavock atty/fact for James McGavock to William Perkins 400 acres proven by Daniel Perkins and James Walker.
Deed Benjamin Henderson to David Holliday 12 acres proven by Ewen B Ormes and John McCalpan.
Deed Richard Ogilvie to William Phillips Senr 60 acres ackd.
Deed Richard Ogilvie to William Phillips Junr 39 acres ackd.
Deed Patrick Gibson to Mark Wilson 75 acres ackd.
Deed Alexander Simpson to Thomas Wilson 10 acres ackd.
Deed Thomas Garrett to John Webb 160 acres ackd.
Deed John Anderson to William Bond 130 acres proven by Henry Hunter & Archer Butt.
Deed William Perry to Sarah Slater and Henry Slater 100 acres proven by Saml McCutchen & John Porter.
Deed James Billingsly to Benjamin Bass 100 acres ackd.
Deed Henry Barrow Wm Barrow Susan Barrow Milly Barrow Charity Barrow Rebecca Barrow to Edwin H Childress proven by Matthew Barrow.
Deed Edwin H Childress to Matthew Barrow 640 acres ackd.
Assignment/plat & certificate from Joshua Burnham to William Hutchinson 20 acres proven by John White & James Burnham.
Deed William Henderson to William McCalpan 110 acres with sundry certifates(sic) thereon are ordered by the Court to be registered.
Deed Moses J Edmiston to Moses Thompson 100 acres proven by Thos Wilson & James Allison.
p.154 Order Daniel Perkins Thos Berry Sion Hunt Francis Burrows & Alson Edney lay off a road from the bridge to intersect the Nashville road near Patrick Devlins.

Justices made returns of Taxable property for 1814: Gersham Hunt in Capt Barnes Co, Archer Jordan in Capt Gaults Co, Alexander Mebane in Capt Mebanes Co, Thomas Wilson in Capt Ridleys Co, John Witherspoon in Capt Perkins Co, Thomas W Stockett in Capt Edmistons Co, Isham R Trotter in Capt Giddens Co, Jesse White in Capt Simpsons Co, George Tillman in Capt Hookers Co.

Report/division of land of Anthony Sharp decd returned.
Elect David Edmiston constable in Capt Ridleys company; bond $625 with Wm R Nunn and Thomas Wilson his securities.
Appoint Garner McConnico guardian of Sally Puckett orphan of Richd Puckett decd; bond $600 with Thomas Merritt and James Cavender his securities.
Appoint William Walker guardian of Elizabeth Puckett orphan of Richard Puckett decd; bond $600 with Daniel German & Henry Puckett his securities.
Appoint Harvey Puckett guardian of Richard Puckett orphan of Richard Puckett decd; bond $600 with William Walker & Daniel German his securities.

License Francis Giddens to keep an ordinary at his dwelling house in this County; bond $2500 with James Black his security.
License John D Hill to keep an ordinary at his dwelling house in this County; bond $2500 with Daniel Perkins & John Bostick his securities.

Elect William Bond Jr constable in Capt Richardsons company; bond $625 with Wm Bond Senr Hendley Stone & Robert McLemore his securities.

APRIL 1814

Order William Fives[Fwer?] be bound apprentice unto George H Allen until age 21 to be taught the art mystery or occupation of a cabinet maker & teach him to rule of three in arithmetic, give him $60 in tools or a horse of that value and a suit of homespun clothes at expiration of his time of apprenticeship.

Appt Daniel German guardian of Zacheus German Elizabeth A German Michael D German p.155 & Matilda A German; bond $600, Wm Walker & Harvey Puckett his securities.

Order John Wheat oversee part of road from Franklin to 5 mile tree on Hayes creek as far as McConnicos meeting house; hands in bounds from Big Harpeth to Drury Pulliams to David McElwees plantation including Wm Marshall including hands that heretofore worked under Henry Ingram as overseer work thereon.

Order Robert Johnston oversee road whereof John White was formerly overseer; hands on flat rock branch, and at Smiths lower mill on Little Harpeth work thereon.

Order Henry Cook and Robert McLemore value estate of John Tapley decd.

Jurors to ensuing County Court: Thomas Atkins John Lemmons Joel Dilliard Jas Neelly (Laine) Lewis Stephens Saml Brown Bernard Richardson Wm Bond Robt Guthrie Nicholas Gentry Isaac Patton Thomas Terry Chas Brown Alson Edney Luke Pryor Jr John Blackman Wm Shute Joseph Hassell Thomas Cash Felix Staggs Moses Chambers Wm Denson William Read Wm Ashlin John Swinney Joshua Farrington. Constables Wm Bond & David Edmiston.

Order Moses James[?] John Lemmons Samuel Lemmons John Scott Guilford Dudley Isham R Trotter Edward Ragsdale James Giddens Allen Hill & Edward Buford any 5 view propriety of altering road to Flat Creek leading by Edward Bufords which passes through Glen Owens plantation and lay off same.

Order Joseph Bell Warren Gentry Joseph Dillinder Spencer Reynolds John Dalton Robt Rogers John Walker Philip Manier Joseph Robinson any five view or alter road Nashville to Fishing ford on Duck River where sd road spoils Richard Ogilvies field.

Account/sale estate of Richd Willett decd returned.

Order William Legate David Riggs Senr Jesse Canaday John Tillman Francis Tillman John Smith Haden Tillman James Stephens George H Allen Thomas Wilson Joseph Moore any five lay off the fishing ford road leading to County line near William Legate.

p.156 Settlement with Hendley Stone gdn/heirs of John Pryor decd returned.

Order Hugh Bell Wm Bell Saml McCutchan John McCutchan Samuel Edmiston Thomas Berry Wm Hope Daniel Perkins & Thos W Stockett any five alter road through land of William Neelly and Thomas McCrory if they same most expedient.

Order Thomas Old James Hicks John Dabney Senr David Dickinson John Watson Isham R Trotter Wm Parham & Edward Swanson any five lay off a road from James Terrells mill to near plantation of John Swinney.

Order George Andrews John Andrews David Gillaspie George Neelly Archibald Lytle

APRIL 1814

James House James Neelly (Cane) Finch Scruggs Wm Banks Thomas Hiter Turner Saunders David Squier & Samuel Winstead any five lay off a road to intersect road from Flat Creek to Gillaspies in Maury County.

Order James Ridley Moses Ridley John Hail Minos Cannon Newton Cannon Wm Phillips Senr Alexander Ralston Thomas Hendrix Matthew McGaugh Daniel Patmore Wm H Ballow and William Phillips Sr any five lay out a road from County line where John Clarks north boundary crosses same to near William Wilsons mill on Harpeth.

Order Nathan Adams oversee road from Nelsons crk to Big Harpeth; hands from sd crk incl Alexander Ralston down to Wilsons mill work thereon.

Order Samuel Shelburn George Kinnard Richard Hay Nathaniel Smithson Jacob Garrett John W Crunk David Lancaster & Wm Williams any five alter road to Harpeth Lick from Saml Shelburns dwelling leaving present road to right going easterly to intersect present road where road leads to George Kinnards still house.

Order Gabriel Buford oversee road from John Clicks or his former residence to Bufords ford; hands from Herrons incl Giddens rd west to Cornelius Wilson to ridge
p.157   north of Mark Andrews to James Hurrons incl James Boyd & Edward Ragsdale with ridge to West Harpeth incl Mebanes hands.

On petition of Eliza C Childress order James Gordon Robert P Currin William Banks allot to Elizabeth C Childress widow of Henry Childress decd so much of crop and provisions now on hand as may be necessary for the support of her and her family for one year from the time of his death.

Thomas W Stockett resigns his commission as a Justice of the peace for this County.
Account/sales estate of John Hodge decd returned.
William Logan Esqr paid to Clerk $1.25 a fine imposed on Benjamin Welch for profane swearing on 17th Nov last.
Appt Thomas Wilson Wm R Nunn & Wm Logan Esqrs to settle with James Joyce admr of estate of Littleberry Epperson decd.
George Barnes qualified as a Justice of the peace for this County.
Allow Wm Hulme $50 for exofficio services as Sheriff for last year.
Allow jurors summoned to this Court and to Circuit Court 50¢ each per day.
Allow Edmund Weathers $3 for wolf scalp he killed in this County over 4 mos old.

Order Spencer Buford oversee road whereof Francis Giddens was formerly overseer; with same hands also those of Beverly Reese Clement Owens & Edward Hood.
David Dunn is elected Coroner for this county for two ensuing years.
Order Wm R Nunn Esqr take lists/taxable property in bounds of Capt Carsons Co.
Order Samuel Edmiston oversee road whereof Henry Slater was overseer; same hands.
p.158   Order James Owen oversee road whereof John L Fielder was overseer.
Order William Simmons oversee road whereof David Lewis was overseer; same hands.
Order Obadiah Wade oversee road whereof John Windrow was overseer; same hands.

Matthew McGaugh Samuel Butler Joseph Lamb Thomas Hendrix and David Lamb report they laid off a road from Thomas Hendricks plantation running with line of Francis Dickson to county line near north of John Clarks line.

APRIL 1814

Order George Haynes Edward Elam John D Hill Richard W Hyde Joseph H Scales Thomas Almond & Stephen Jordan any five alter the road by Johnson Woods.
Order old road from Rutherford County line to Carrs Mill be discontinued.
Award writ of certiorara to James Carothers in case adjudged before Eleazer Hardeman wherein Wm Saunders was plf & Carothers deft.

Order Johnson Wood oversee road from Wilsons Creek near John D Hills still house to to sd Woods lane; hands in bounds incl Mrs Flemings Richd W Hyde, Taylors & Thomas Jordans thence to Nelsons Crk incl Hartwell Hyde Archer Jordan Fredk Browns down to Wm Jordans plantation thence to Absalom Bosticks plantation work thereon.

Order Christopher Vanatta oversee road from Johnson Woods lane to Rutherford County line; hands from sd line to Nelsons Crk near John Coffees incl Doct McClarans to Archer Jordans plantation incl Edward Lawrence Salmons &c to Rutherford county line near Thomas Jordans work thereon.

p.159 Order Stephen Jordan oversee road from John D Hills lane to Nelsons Creek; hands from Hills lane to crk where Wilson Mill road crosses including Stephen Jordan and up to Wm Jordans incl Absalom Bostick work thereon.
Court adjourns until tomorrow morning 9 OClock.
                                Robert McMillin C McDaniel John Witherspoon.

Wednesday 6th April 1814. Present Robert McMillin Collin McDaniel John Witherspoon.
Order Lawrence Bass admr/estate of John Patton decd sell Amy Bob & Mariah, slaves.

Jesse Wilson vs Stephen Smith. Debt. Justices John Witherspoon Robt McMillin Jacob Garrett. Jury Saml Edmiston John Miller Knacy Andrews Archd Lytle Kemp Holland Michl Kinnard Oliver Crenshaw John Evens David Pinkston Jacob Gray Ebenezer Darby Wm Hill. Dft recovers agt plf his costs in this behalf expended.

Returns/taxable property for 1814 made by James Allison in Capt Daltons Co, Sherwood Green in Capt Chs Johnsons Co, Sion Hunt in Capt McKeys Co, David Dunn in Capt Richardsons Co, Collin McDaniel in Capt McCrorys Co.

Licence Collin McDaniel to keep an ordinary at his dwelling house in this County; bond $2500 with Wm Hulme & Wm P Harrison his securities.
Deed Thomas W Stockett to Nathl Smithson 200 acres proven by Saml Edmiston & Joseph H Stockett.
Ltrs/admn granted Susannah Crouch on estate of John Crouch decd; bond with Nicholas
p.160 Perkins Senr John Witherspoon & George A Shelton securities.
Order Sion Hunt Hendly Stone & John Witherspoon Esqrs settle with admrs/estate of Anthony Sharp decd.
Deed Garner McConnico to John Parks & Abel Garrett ackd.
Settlement with Henry Cook gdn of John Cook George E Cook & Henry Cook minor orphans of Edward Cook decd returned.
Inventory/estate of John Crouch decd returned.
Order Henry Cook Edward Warren & Wm Bond Sr allot to Solomon(sic) Crouch widow of John Crouch decd one years provisions of the estate.
Order James Hughes oversee road from Joel Hobbs to McDaniels ford of West Harpeth;

APRIL 1814

hands of James Gee Thos Blair Richd Hughes Robt Guthrie Francis McDaniel Wm McDaniel John McDaniel Turner Saunders David Dunn Moore Bragg on those on Leepers lease work thereon under his directions.
Order Paisley Dodson oversee road from Isaac Pattons to near Andrew Cowsarts; hands from Thomas Aydelottes thence on Murfrees boundary to cross West Harpeth to include Andrew Nolls old place to Devers branch to Robert Reeds leaving out Thomas G Caldwell & incl James Giddens work thereon.
Order admrs/estate of Anthony Sharp decd pay David McEwen Andrew Goff & Turner Saunders $10 each for services in allotting the dower of Mrs Hulme formerly widow of Anthy Sharp decd among the heirs of sd Sharp decd.
Order Sheriff summon Jury to divide perishable property/estate of John Crawford decd among widow and children of sd Crawford decd.

Harvy[Hany?] Lyon vs Wm W Cunningham & Wm Smith. On Motion of Harvy Lyon by atty; 20 March 1813 by Wm Dooley J P for Maury County sd Hany recovered judgt agt Wm W Cunningham for $10.70 & costs. Sion Hunt J P directed execution; on 11 Decr 1813 constable Samuel Cox took Wm C Cunningham into custody; Cunningham for purpose of obtaining prison rules on 11 Decr 1813 made bond with Wm Smith his security in sum $25 to be void if sd Cunningham should kekep bounds of Williamson County until discharged therefrom. Cunningham hath departed; execution awarded agt Wm W Cunningham & Wm Smith for $11.50 and costs of former suit and this motion.

John Taylor admr/Henry Taylor decd vs James Jackson. Justices David Dunn Robert McMillin Jas Allison. Jury Joseph Ledbetter Wm Walker Joel Dilliard Wm Edmiston Michael Kinnard Lewis Stephens Jas McCombs Thos S Adkins Henry Stephens Spencer Reynolds Jacob Gray Robt Sayers. Plf recovers agt dft damages $80 & costs. Burwell Temple dfts bail summoned dft in open Court & dft is ordered in custody of shff.

David Hogan assee vs Fielder Helms. Appeal. Justices D Dunn Jas Allison Thos Garrett. Jury[above]. Plf recovers agt dft damages $57.78 & costs.
Elisha Perkins vs Nicholas Scales & Nicholas Perkins exr of Peter Perkins decd. Appeal. Dft confesses judgt for $96.18. Plf recovers sd sum & costs to be levied on goods and chattels of sd deceased in hands of defts.
Court adjourns until tomorrow morning nine OClock.   S Green Ed Ragsdale A Jordan

Thursday 7th April 1814. Present Sherwood Green Edward Ragsdale and Archer Jordan.
Inventory & acct/sale estate of Richard Smith decd returned.
List/taxable property for 1814 in Capt Pattons Co retd by Tristram Patton Esq.
Deed John Mitchell to Joseph & Lawrence Thompson Town Lot in Franklin proven by Samuel F Glass & George Stephens.
Deed Thomas Cox to Wm McGilvery Lot in Franklin proven by Thos Hiter & Henry Lyon.
Deed David Squier & Sarah his wife to John White town Lot ackd. Oliver Williams & Wm Banks Esqrs to take private examn of sd Sarah.
Deed Hendley Stone to Newell Gracy 69 acres ackd.
Deed Wm Parham & Sarah his wife & James Wilkins & Martha his wife to Sarah Trower 512 acres in Halifax County North Carolina ackd by sd Wm & James. Order Oliver Williams & Wm Banks Esqrs take private examn of sd Sarah & Martha.

Spencer Reynolds vs Valentine Allen & John Dalton. Debt. Justices Shd Green Edward

APRIL 1814

Ragsdale Archer Jordan. Jury John Miller Saml Edmiston Wm Bond Sr Burwell McLemore Robt P Currin Thos T Maury John Williamson Joshua Tarkington Thos Herron Moses Oldham John Mairs Page Bond. Plf recovers agt dft debt $100, damages, costs.

p.163

Carey Bibb vs Richard Herbert. Debt. Justices[above]. Jury[above]. Plf recovers agt dft debt $100, damages, and costs of suit.
Currin & Mason vs Daniel Carter. Debt. Justices[above]. Jury[above]. Plfs recover agt dft debt $62.19½, damages, costs.
Deadrick & Somerville vs Mary Thomas. Debt. Justices[above]. Jury[above]. Plfs recover agt dft $93.75 debt, damages, & costs.
John Sample vs John Witherspoon. Debt. Justices[above]. Jury[above]. Plf recovers agt dft $100.66 debt, damages, costs.

p.164

Wm Bradshaw vs Samuel Long & Edwd Ragsdale. Debt. Justices[above]. Jury[above]. Plf recovers agt dft $106.32 debt, damages, costs.
John Sample surviving partner vs Wm Betts. Debt. Justices[above]. Jury[above]. Plf recovers agt dft $95.63 debt, damages, costs.
Robert Moore vs Athelstone Andrews. Debt. Justices Oliver Williams Edwd Ragsdale Sherwood Green. Jury[above]. Plf recovers agt dft his debt, damages, costs.

p.165

John McKinney vs Wm Russell. Appeal. Deft not appearing, plf recovers agt dft $40 the judgt obtained before the Justice/peace & his costs.
Samuel Bell vs Richard Orton. Debt. Justices[above]. Jury[above]. Plf recovers agt dft $138.54 debt, damages, costs.
James & Young vs Adonijah Edwards. Trespass. Justices[above]. Plfs recover agt dft damages $101.75, and costs.
Samuel H Williams vs Wm Campbell. Debt. Justices[above]. Jury[above]. Plf recovers agt dft $75 debt, damages, & costs.

p.166 Henry Lyon vs Wm W Cunningham & Wm Smith. Appeal granted defts to Circuit Court; gave bond with Thomas Hulme & Oliver Williams security.
William Perkins assee vs Jordan Solomon. Sciri facias. Dft came not; plf granted execution agt dft for $85.89 amt of judgt & costs.
Buckner Howell vs Henry Ingram. Debt. Justices[above]. Jury[above]. Plf recovers agt dft debt $202 and costs.
Jacob Gray vs Joseph C McDowell. Trespass. Justices[above]. Plf dismisses suit.
John Den lessee vs John Bostick. Ejectment. Deft came not. Plf recovers agt dft his unexpired term in tract/land on Arringtons Creek beginning in line of McGaughs preemption...boundary of Genl Jethro Sumners tract...to Robert Nelson it being land on which Nicholas Scales now lives...with Scales line formerly Nelsons to boundary line of land granted to Robt Nelson to oak in David Shelbys line....

p.167 David Craig vs Josiah Wooldridge. Debt. Justices[above]. Dft came not; plf recovers agt dft $111 debt, damages & costs.
Court adjourns until tomorrow morning 10 OClock.
            Wm Anthony Berry Nolen John Witherspoon.

Friday 8th April 1814. Present William Anthony Berry Nolen John Witherspoon Esqrs. Order Wm Banks & Geo Hulme Esqrs take private examn of Eliza Jones wife of James G

APRIL 1814

Jones touching a deed from sd James & Eliza to Wm Manning.
Acct/sales estate of Henry Childress decd returned on oath of Wm Smith.

Report of commrs apptd to set apart crop & provisions of estate of Henry Childress to Elizabeth C Childress his widow: provisions from time of sd Henrys death 20 Sept 1813, 50 barrels corn $50, 1000 lbs pork $30, 300 lbs beef $9, stack fodder 30 dozen of oats $7.50 20 bushels rye $10. R P Currin Wm Banks James Gordon.

License Bernard Richardson to keep an ordinary at his dwelling in this County; bond $2500 with Henry Lyon and Anderson Berryman his securities.
License Thomas L Robinson to keep an ordinary at his house in Franklin; bond $2500 with James Gordon and William P Harrison his securities.

William Shaw vs James Gentry[Gurley?]. Dft to take deposition of witnesses in State of Louisiana at the Court House in Saint Francisville.
Appt Berry Nolen & Wm Banks Esqrs to settle with admrs/estate of Joseph Potts decd.

p.168   Harrison Boyd vs John Johnston. Ceritorara. Justices John Witherspoon Berry Nolen Wm Anthony. Dft not appearing, plf recovers his debt $30 & costs.
John Miller proves attendance as a juror 4 days.
Deed Benja Gholson to Wm Banks part of lot in Franklin ackd.
Deed Jonathan Bateman to William Bateman 102 acres proven by Joseph Hassell and Samuel Bradford.
Deed Jonathan Bateman to Simon Bateman 79 ac proven by Jos Hassell & Saml Bradford.
Deed Jonathan Bateman to Bimah[Beniah?] Bateman 45 acres proven by [above].
Deed David McEwen atty in fact for Wm Sloan to Hugh F Bell 260 acres proven by James Gordon and Metcalf Degraffenreid.
List/taxable property in Capt Jones Co returned by John J Henry Esqr.
List/taxable property for 1814 returned by George Hulme Esqr in Capt Dabneys Co.
Acct/sales estate of Joseph Potts decd returned.
List/taxable property in Capt James Anglins Co retd by Robert McMillin Esqr.
Order William Dowdy oversee road lately laid off from Davidson Co line near Shannons pond to Dickson line; hands on Brush Crk & Turnbull work thereon.

Order Thomas Simmons oversee road; hands from Widow McClarans path to Esqr Green to Squire Goode, on north side Mill creek except hands of Samuel Morton Benjamin Kidd John P Irion work thereon.
Hugh Dobbins John K Campbell Samuel Cummins Hendley Stone & Charles Robinson report they laid off a road from Joel Hobbs to Wm Bonds on Leepers fork...a way already opened to Baileys pond along to Kemp Holland near his barn.... Jas Hughes and Henry Hunter apptd to oversee clearing out sd road & divide hands.
Order orphan Rebecca Hill bound to Francis B Dudley until age 21 years to be taught to read, write, and the common parts of needlework.

Anderson Berryman vs Stephen Smith. Appeal. Justices John Witherspoon Wm Anthony Berry Nolen. Jury Ewen Cameron Richd Polk Dann Hill Geo Strambler Benjn White Alexr Clark Abraham Mason Geo Oliver Alexr McCown Thos Merritt Alexr Wood. Plf recovers agt dft $21.50 and his costs of suit.

Bradley & Berkley vs James S Neelly Harrison Boyd & Jason Hopkins. Certiorara. Jus-

JULY 1814

tices[above]. Execution issued agt dfts was illegally issued; original exn quashed; dfts recover agt plf their costs in defence expended.
Bradley & Berkley vs James S Neelly Jason Hopkins & Harrison Boyd. Justices Wm Banks Berry Nolen Wm Anthony. Order sd certiorara dismissed; plf recovers agt dft
p.170   costs about this suit expended, to be levied on chattels of dft.

State vs James Hicks. Presentment O/road. Justices[above]. Dft in proper person pleads guilty; fine one cent & costs of prosecution.
David Hogan vs Fielder Helm. Motion. Appeal granted dft to circuit Court; bond with John Witherspoon and Kemp Holland his securities.
Robert Moore vs Athelstone Andrews. Appeal granted dft to Circuit Court; bond with Benjamin Gholson & Henry Lyon his securities.
Order commrs apptd to divide estate of Jordan Reese decd to divide sd estate.
Deed James Gordon to John Berkley ackd.
Power/atty Abram Maury to Lewis Bullock ackd.

Metcalf Degraffenreid vs Francis Carter. Certiorara. Justices John Witherspoon Wm Anthony Berry Nolen. Plf granted benefit of his judgt recovered agt dft & costs.

Order to lay off dower of Lovey Page wife of Wm Stephens revived.
Court adjourns untill Court in Course. John Witherspoon Wm Anthony Berry Nolen.

Williamson County, Monday 4th July 1814. Court of Pleas & quarter Sessions, Court House in Franklin. Present the Worshipful George Hulme David Mason Thomas Garrett.
p.171   Jurors summoned: Thomas Atkins John Lemmons Joel Dilliard Jas Neelly(Cane) Lewis Stephens Samuel Brown Bernard Richardson William Bond Robert Guthrie Nicholas Gentry Isaac Patton Thos Terry(issued certif) Charles Brown Alson Edney Luke Pryor Jr John Blackman Wm Shute Joseph Hassell Thomas Cash Felix Staggs Moses Chambers William Denson excused William Reed William Ashlin John Swinney(certificate issd) Joshua Tarkington. Constables William Bond (not executed) and David Edmiston.

Grand Jurors Joseph Lemmons Thomas Atkins Robert Guthrie Joseph Hassell Joel Dilliard John Blackman Lewis Stephens Samuel Brown Bernard Richardson William Shute foreman Isaac Patton James Neelly Junr Luke Pryor Junr.

Thomas Garrett resigns his commission as a Justice of the peace.

Order Peter Hardeman oversee road to Lytles road; bounds from 3 mile tree to Joseph Love Thomas Barnet Elias Mayfield James Boyd to bear skin knob work thereon.

Ambros Hilbourn granted certificate on Treasury for killing six wolves under age six months and one over age of four.
James Pritchett granted certificate on Treasury for killing one old wolf.
Lettrs/admn granted Jason Hopkins; bond $300 with Saml Cox his security.
Hugh Fox certified to Treasury for killing 3 wolves 1 over six mos, 2 under four.
John Ray certified to Treasury for killing 8 wolves under four months.

JULY 1814

Lettr/atty Benjamin Gholson to James J Hill ackd.
Deed George Strambler to Francis Gunter one Town Lot ackd.
Deed John Hill to Matthew McGaugh 148 acres ackd.
Schedule of property/estate of Jane Wheaton decd returned by Thomas T Maury admr.

George Kinnard William Williams Richd Hay Nathaniel Smithson & David Lancaster apptd April 1814 to lay off a road from Franklin to George Kinnards report: begin west of Samuel Shelburns house, leaving old road, intersecting old road between a
p.172   quarter and a half mile at a marked beech.

Deed John McKinney to John House 130 acres ackd.
Plat and certificate to Albert Higgins for 6 acres proven by John Higgins and Philemon Higgins.
Deed Hartwell Miles to Robert Sharp 51 acres proven by Nicholas Scales and William G Boyd.
Deed Merryman Landrum to John Clark 19 acres ackd.

Order George Shannon oversee road from John Curry to Widow Woods following the marked trees; hands from plantation where John Curry did live to George Manscars to Frederick Davises to widow Woods to Jason Wilsons work thereon.

Order Josiah Wilson oversee road; hands west of Franklin road opposite head of Rutherfords Creek incl Richard Sampson to Fishing Ford road work thereon.

Deed John Hill to Merryman Landrum 52 acres ackd.
Deed Charles Boyles to John Sweeney 200 acres proven by Robert Sample Jr & David Anderson.
Deed Wm Dooley to Francis Gunter Lott 52 proven by Wm Hulme & John C Hulme.
Ltr/atty David Lamb to Merryman Landrum ackd.

Order James Smith oversee road from Ephriam Brown to Natchez road near Hoges old place; hands from McCutchens crk...to Lytles Knob...to Thomas H Perkins horse mill leaving out his hands...to Newsoms mill to Donalsons Crk to Harpeth River leaving out Ephriam Browns plantation work thereon.

p.173   Deed Samuel B McKnight to Robert Sharp 72½ acres ackd.
Deed John Moody to James Wood 25 acres ackd.
Order David Gillaspie oversee road; hands on waters of Flat Crk except David Christman work thereon.
Bill/sale William Glover to John Bond proven by William W Bond.
Deed William P Harrison to Angus McPhail Town Lot 35 ackd.

Order James Southall oversee road from Saml Bentons old place to Leepers fork up to Jonas Meadows to Elijah Hunter to Baleys ford on West Harpeth work thereon.
Court adjourns until tomorrow morning 9 OClock. G Hulme Berry Nolen Robert McMillin

Tuesday 5th July 1814. Present George Hulme Berry Nolen & Robert McMillin Esquires.
Deed Obadiah Wade to Stephen Smith 30 acres ackd.
Deed Abraham Walker to Andrew McCrady 40 acres ackd.

JULY 1814

License Samuel Winstead to keep an ordinary at his dwelling house; gave bond with John Sweeny and Nicholas Perkins securities.
Deed John P Irion to Sarah Irion 90 acres ackd.
Deed Caleb Willis to Thomas White 100 acres proven by John P Irion & Nelson Fields.
Deed William C Prewitt to Joseph H Scales 243 acres proven by Stephen Jordan and John Bostick.
Deed Samuel Blair to Samuel Wilson 160 acres ackd.
Deed John Stephens to Elisha Davis 25 acres ackd.
p.174 Bill/sale Joshua Cutchin to Sheadwood Green proven by James Turner.
Deed Nelson Fields to John P Irion 95 acres ackd.
Deed William C Prewitt to Stephen Wood and Johnston Wood Junr 100 acres proven by Johnston Wood and Joseph H Scales.
Deed James McCarrell to Pleasant Russell 179 acres proven by Wm Smith & Jno Sweeny.
Deed Jno Hill Matthew McGaugh & Joseph Lamb to James Ray 50 acres ackd by Jno Hill.
Will of David Lewis decd proven by John Hill & Francis Jackson; Francis Jackson qualified as executor.
Account/sales estate of John Crouch decd returned.
Deed Thos Anderson to John D Hill 23 acres proven by Nichs Scales & John W Cradock.
Deed John C Prewitt to Stephen Jordan 100 acres proven by Wm Wilson & John Bostick.
Bill/sale Henry Walker to Job Mayberry ackd.
Deed Samuel Walkup & Nancy Walkup to Robert Guthrie Senr 256 acres on motion and examination of certificates thereon endorsed ordered to be registered.

Order Barnet Dololdson[?] oversee road from John Andrews to half mile west of where David Dobbins formerly lived; hands that formerly worked under Thomas Morton late overseer of sd road work thereon under his direction.

Order Abram Ballance oversee road from John Evans to John Witherspoon; hands down West Harpeth incl John Achols and Henry Cook thence with Natchez rd incl Martin Trantham J Lee Peter Holliday Bradford Balance Jr & Thos Walthall work thereon.

Order David Spain oversee road from James Allisons to Duck River ridge; hands up Allisons branch to school house thence to Zacheus Wilsons to Thos Wilson Junr to
p.175 Thos Wilson Esqr with Franklin rd work thereon.

Order James Martin oversee road from Natchez road to county line near Methodist meeting house; hands from trace creek incl Robert Hill work thereon.

Order Henry Baley oversee road from James Allisons to ford of Harpeth at Robert Rogers; hands from Charles Calhouns to grove creek to Overalls creek to old path crossing Francis Younger to Kimbro Ogilvies work thereon.

Order James Mayfield have hands in bounds from John Walkers to county line incl Robert Wilson and Charles Cahoon to James Ridgway & Wm Owen incl Nicholas Gentry to Benjamin Watts & Christopher Erwin & George Gentry, all those in the bounds work under his direction.

Order John Nunn oversee road to Shelbyville; bounds from Harpeth incl John Everett to James Buckley & James Gentry & Elias Mayfield & Francis Nunn thence incl Willis Williams Samuel & James Carson to beginning work thereon.

JULY 1814

Order Harden Tillman oversee road to Warren Court house beginning at intersection with road from Columbia to Murfreesborough including all Tillmans Caswell Philip James Joseph and Ephriam Mairs the Stephensons John Smith Jesse Canady and David Riggs work thereon as far as Wm Logans.

Order Tignal Martin oversee road from Wm Logans to wolf pit incl Mark Brak[?] Henry Brees[?]...to Joseph Bond to Wm Allen John Johnston to Tignal Martin & Anderson Epperson to the beginning work thereon.

Thos Hardin Minos Cannon John Hail Mattw McGaugh Wm Philips Moses Ridley Danl Pittman & Wm Philips apptd to lay out a road from county line near John Clarks to near Wm Wilsons mill on Harpeth joining Franklin rd report they marked same.

p.176   Order David Nolen Elisha Fly John Edmiston(Ken) Joshua Cannon John L Fielder David Cummins Wm Stone & John Cochan any 5 mark a road from John L Fielders near Barneses shop by Liberty mtg house along road near John Edmistons lane then north to John Edmiston [illeg] lane to David Cummins to Davidson line and make report.

List/taxable property for 1814 returned by John Hill Esqr.

Order Henry Walker John J Henry Andw Goff David McEwen Thos Walker Martin Adams Martin Stanley James McEwen any 5 alter road from Franklin to Liberty Meeting House which lies between the Town & Henry Walkers if they deed necessary.

Jurors to Circuit Court: Thomas Wilson Esqr George Tillman John D Hill Richard Reynolds Sion Hunt Finch Scuggs William Wilson Esqr Moses Ridley Hinchey Pettway Jonathan Currier John Witherspoon Daniel Perkins James McGavock Stephen Childress Robert McMillin Dempsey Nash Elisha Davis Thomas Wells James Caperton Jordan Fipps James Pugh Wm Anthony Richard Hightower Samuel Crockett gunsmith William Hope Hue Bell. Constables David Edmiston & Nichs Branch.

Jurors to next County Court. William Neely Senr Martin Adams John P Broadnax John Mairs John Porter Junr Thomas A Pope Thomas Black Benjamin May Thomas Moton John Robertson Joseph Philips Edward Warren Jacob Gray Ambrose Hadley Wm Parham Christopher McEwen Joel Riggs Thomas Merritt Andrew Johnston Angus McPhail Alexr McClaran Benjn J Bass Jacob Halfacre Samuel Moton Junr Ephriam Andrews Senr Edward Buford. Constables Wm H Downing & Richard W Hide.

Order Nathaniel Alexander oversee road from Capt Alexanders plantation up South Harpeth to ridge; hands on South Harpeth & Hunting Camp Creek work thereon.
Thomas Blair released from payment of appraised value of eleven hogs posted by him and afterwards proved away.
Order Collin McDaniel & John J Henry let to lowest bidder for 12 months John Wilson an object of charity.
Zachariah Jackson allowed 10/6 for phisic besides what his bond calls for in maintenance of sd object.
Order William Logan Wm R Nunn and Wm Wilson let to lowest bidder Betsey Epperson an object of charity.
p.177   Deed George Shannon to Edward Lawrance 300 acres ackd.
Order Richard Reynolds oversee the road to fishing ford beginning at Duck River

JULY 1814

ridge to Bedford county line; hands from William Moody Spencer Reynolds Charles & William Legate John Tapley and Thomas Wilson work thereon.

Court lay County tax: on each 100 acres 12½ cents, on each white poll 11 cents, on each slave 24 cents, on each town lot 24 cents, on each stud horse the price of the seasonof one mare, on each merchant $5, for the poor tax on each white poll 2 cts 5 mills, on each slave 5 cts, on each town lot 6¼ cents, on each 100 acres 5 cents.

James Turner released from payment of appraised value of a steer taken up by him.
Order James Hughes oversee the road from near Joel Hobbs to Baileys ford on West Harpeth; hands that worked under Francis McDaniel work thereon.
Order Absalom Bostick Thomas Jordan Newell Sammon Stephen Jordan Thomas Almon Thos Allman Edward Laurance George Hanes[Harris?] Frederick Browder alter the road by Johnston Woods if they deem it necessary.
Obadiah Wade released from payment of appraised value of mare proven away.
Order Benjamin Roberts oversee road to Murfreesborough from where road crosses Commissioners crk, ending at Arringtons Crk; hands in Benjn Roberts dist work thereon.

Order Joshua Cutchen oversee road from Sampson Sawyers; all in bounds from Sawyers to John Bennetts to Rutherford County line incl P Underwood, crossing ridge between Mill & Arringtons Crk then West to Samuel McBrides incl John Mathis & Dyers then from McBrides to beginning work thereon.
Order that the road formerly laid out from Fishing ford road near John Walkers to Rutherford County line near John Windrow be discontinued.
Order Hue Bell oversee road from John Evans fence to ford of Little Harpeth; hands
p.178 that worked under Dempsey Nash work thereon.

Hue F Bell W R Bell Samuel Edmiston Samuel McCutchen Thos Berry & Wm Hope apptd to alter road through land of William Neelly and Thos McCrory report; begin at Ephriam Browns mill thence down McCutchens creek to Big Harpeth to Motheralls and McCrorys line to Bells old road.
Dann Hill released from appraised value of a stray horse.
Will of Joseph Brown decd proven by Alexander Martin & Matthew Morgan; extrx Anna Brown qualified.
Order bounds of hands to work under Robert H Warren begin at end of Main Street, & end at two mile post, from Hinchey Pettway, to fork near Alexander Lesters to North of George Hulmes improvement south to John Minter & Robert H Warren north to Alexr Lesters to beginning work thereon.
Hands to work under James Hicks, overseer, from two mile post to John Blackmans South to sd Blackman James Hicks and John McCorlins East to Joel Hobbs Samuel Estes & John Dabney to beginning work thereon.
Deed John Stephens to Greory Wilson & Daniel Wilson 75 acres ackd.
Order Benjamin Russell oversee road from Berry ford on Harpeth to Russels on Nashville rd; those between sd road, Big Harpeth & Nelsons Crk incl William Wilson work thereon.
Order Wm Philips oversee road from Shelby road to Murfreesborough rd; hands east of Nashville rd to Nelsons Crk to Harpeth incl Rogerses & Hugheses work thereon.
Order Samuel Butler oversee road from Murfreesborough rd to County line; all Capt Carsons Company south of sd road work thereon.
Grant Andrew Hunter ltrs/admn on estate of Walter Orech[Breck?] decd; bond $50 with

JULY 1814

John McSwine & Elijah Hunter his securities.
Ephriam Brown proves attendance as juror at Octr session 1813 six days.
p.179   Order Enoch Galloway have certificate on Treasury for $12 for killing six wolves under six months within bounds of this county.
Jurors to last Circuit Court and last County Court allowed 50¢ each per day.
Caleb Manley released from payment of tax on Negro woman Dorcas.
Revive order for dividing estate of Samuel Wilson decd.

On application of Joel Dilliard, order Abram Maury Turner Saunders & Wm Banks examine John Donelson relative to beginning corner of land granted to John McNeal for 640 acres; subpoena to issue to Sheriff of Davidson County requiring attendance of John Donalson 5 & 6 Septr next.

State vs Thomas Mayfield. Judgt agt dft for costs; bond Thos Mayfield with William Alexander Steven Dyer Joseph Stringer & William Tucker his securities acknowledged condition Thomas Mayfield keep the peace towards Roberta Garner and her children.
Court adjourns till tomorrow 9 O Clock.   G Hulme   Berry Nolen   Robert McMillin.

Wednesday 6th July 1814. Present George Hulme Berry Nolen & Robert McMillin Esqrs.
Court adjourned until Twelve OClock
Court met. Present George Hulme Berry Nolen & Robt McMillin.

At a call Court wherein the State vs Gilbert a negro man slave property of Andrew Goff charged with killing a negro man Bob the property of Joseph Braden whereon a Court of Oyer and Terminer having convened for his trial composed of David Mason John Witherspoon and William Banks Justices and Archibald Lytle Saml Crockett John Watson and James Pugh freeholders and owners of slaves say slave Gilbert from evidence is guilty of wilful murder.
Marginal note: This court is not to be considered as a part of the record of the County Court, but the proceeding of a special Court. N P Hardeman.
p.180   Court again met having considered verdict; Gilbert to be remanded to prison to be taken on last Saturday and hanged untill he is dead.

Isaac Crows admrs vs Francis Gunter. Justices George Hulme Robert McMillin David Mason. Jury James Neelly Wm Bond Thos Terry John Swinney Michael Kinnard Ruffin Brown Jordan Fipps John House Joel Hobbs Arthur Fulgham Joel Stephens Wm Goff. Dft recovers agt plf his costs, and to have execution for the same.

Samuel Andrews vs James G Green. Appeal. Justices[above]. Jury[above]. Dft recovers agt plf his costs. Plf obtained appeal to Circuit Court; bond $100, John Andrews & Barnet Donelson his security.

Settlement/estate of Joseph Potts decd returned by Wm Banks & Berry Nolen.
Deed Henry Phenix to Thos Simmons 149½ acres proven by Wm Anthony & Lewis Stephens.
Deed John Pope to Charles Mason 91¾ acres ackd.
Bill/sale Willliam Shute to Charles McAlister negro girl Jenny proven by Henry R W Hill and Maurice L Bond.
Division/estate of John Crawford returned.
p.181   Grant Charles Brown ltrs/admn on estate of Nathaniel Brown decd with

JULY 1814

noncupative will annexed which was proven by Saml Edmiston & Chas Brown.
Order Joseph Pollard oversee road from N P Hardemans on Murfrees fork to Natchez road near Joel Hobbs, hands from Frederick Issels to Robert Smiths on West Harpeth up creek to Joel Hobbs old place work thereon.
Order James Swanson oversee road to James Terrells mill with hands from Cowsers to Edward Swansons to Terrills mill to Grays to Huggins to Swinneys.
Deed James G Jones & Elizabeth Jones to Wm Manning 25 acres ackd by Jones; examn of Elizabeth Jones taken by George Hulme & Wm Banks.
Order Luke Pryor oversee road from near Nolens shop to Liberty meeting house; hands that worked under Willis work thereon.
Order James Black & Isham R Trotter examine Betsey Old & Jane Watson respecting their relinquishment right of dower to 326 acres conveyed to Hezekiah Puryear and Matilda his wife formerly Matilda Reese.
Deed Beverly Reese Thomas Old Betsey Old John Watson Jane Watson to Hezekiah Puryear and Matilda for 326 acres ackd by Beverly Reese Thos Old & John Watson.
Deed N P Hardeman to William & Mary M Neelly 875 acres ackd.
Court then adjourned until tomorrow morning 9 OClock.
                                        Berry Nolen David Mason Robert McMillin.

Thursday 7th July 1814. Present Berry Nolen David Mason Robert McMillin Esquires.
John Doe lessee of John Sample & others vs John Alford. Ejectment. Justices Berry Nolen David Mason Robert McMillin. Jury Felix Staggs Joshua Tarkington Thomas Terry Jordan Phipps James Gentry Archibald Lytle David Robertson Kinchen P Bass Jonathan Currin Metcalf Degraffenreid Benjamin Gholson William Bright find dft not guilty; recovers agt plf.
John Sample Surv Part &c vs Abram Maury. Debt. Justices[above]. Dft confesses judgt for $187.21. Plf recovers debt, damages, costs. Fire facias not to issue untill directed by Thomas Mastersons executors.
On application of Joel Dilliard, order Abram Maury Turner Saunders and William Banks take examination of Jno Donelson relative to beginning and specialties of 2560 acres granted to James Skirlock by Grant 912; subpoena to issue to Sheriff of Davidson County requiring attendance of sd Donelson on 6 & 7 September next.

Deed Elisha Dodson to Reuben Dodson 43[73?13?] acres proven by Ewen Cameron and Morrison L Bond.
Deed Henry Childress to John Shute 18¼ acres proven by Jas Clemm and Hinchey Pettway.
Division of lands of Jordan Rees decd agreeable to his will returned with the plat annexed by James Giddins A Clark and Edward Swanson commrs.
Court adjourns for half an hour. Court met according to adjournment.

State vs William Bright. Justices Wm Banks Berry Nolen Robt McMillin. Jury John Swincy Wm Bond John Mallory Matthias B Murfree Robert P Currin Edward Warren John McSwine John Parks James Boland Henry Hunter Athelston Andrews Moses Chambers. Dft fined one dollar and costs of suit.

p.183 State vs William Bright & Joel Parrish. Affray. Justices[above]. Jury: Ewen Cameron Joshua Tarkington David Robertson Benjn Gholston Thomas Terry John Mallory Robt Warren Jonathan Currin Jordan Fipps Wm Bright Moses Chambers Kemp Holland find

JULY 1814

the defendant not guilty.

State vs Micajah Hilliard. Riot. Justices George Hulme Wm Banks Robt McMillin. Jury Kinchen P Bass Wm Bond John Swiney Henry Walker Martin Stanley Josiah Knight James Steward James C Jones Thomas Hiter Erastus Collins Ewen Cameron Jordan Phipps find deft guilty; fined $10 and pay costs of prosecution.

Joseph Stricklin age 16 bound unto John Mallory until age 21 to learn the house carpenter and joiner business; sd Mallory is to give sd apprentice six months schooling all at one time, also a horse saddle and bridle worth $50, a set of bench plains and a plane suit of clothes when free.

David C McCutchen age 11 bound unto John Mallory until age 21 to learn the house carpenter and joiner business, sd Mallory to give sd apprentice schooling as far as rule of three, a suit of clothes with $40, $30 worth of joiners tools when free.

John Dabney John Watson Thomas Old William Parham & Edward Swanson report they laid off a road from James Terrills mill to John Swinny's plantation.

Isham R Trotter Edward Ragsdale Guilford Dudley Moses Turner John Simmons Allen Hill report they altered road from Franklin to Flat creek to Glen Owens fence.

Supplemental inventory of William Norton decd returned by Samuel Andrews and Eliza Norton admrs.

Thomas Fullerton vs John Hill. Certiorara. Justices Geo Hulme Wm Banks Robt McMillin. Deft in proper person says he cannot deny plfs debt $94.08 which was rendered agt him before William R Nunn on 4 Decr 1813. Plf recovers agt dft his debt and p.184 costs; execution stayed nine months.

State vs John Cox. Justices: Berry Nolen Wm Banks Robt McMillin. Deft discharged.

State vs Joseph McAlister. Justices[above]. Dft came not; State to recover of dft $250 and of David Robinson and John Moore his securities $125 unless sd Joseph appear at next Court and show sufficient cause to the contrary.
Court adjourned till Tomorrow 9 OClock.
Jno Branch vs Nicholas Dilliard. Justices as before. Plf and dft in proper person. Plf no further prosecutes; dft pays all costs.
Court adjourns until tomorrow morning 9 OClock. G Hulme Robert McMillin Wm Banks

Friday 8th July 1814. Present George Hulme Robert McMillin and William Banks Esqrs. Order Sheriff summon again (persuant to order at last term) George Andrews John Andrews David Gillaspie George Neelly Archibald Lytle James House James Neelly (Cane) Finch Scruggs Wm Banks Thomas Hiter Turner Saunders David Squire and Saml Winstead any 5 to lay off a road from Franklin to intersect road from flat creek to Gillaspies in Maury County.

John House vs Nicholas House & Caleb Manley. Justices Berry Nolen R McMillin Wm p.185 Banks. Jury Felix Staggs John Swiney Thomas Terry Joshua Tarkington Geo

JULY 1814

Shannon Moses Chambers Thos Berry Jordan Fipps Jonathan Cooper Andrew Craig John McKinny Metcalf Degraffenreid. Plf recovers agt dft his damages and costs.

John Den lessee of Kenneth Morrison vs Eliza Norton. Ejectment. Justices B Nolen R McMillin Jesse White. Jury Thos Cash Burwell McLemore Edwd McNeal John House Wm Parham Joseph Leadbetter Saml Winstead James Wilkins Levy Oliver Martin Stanley Isaac McNeely Robt P Currin find dft not guilty; she recovers her costs agt plf.

Samuel F Glass vs Archibald Potter. Appeal. Justices[above]. Jury Felix Staggs Thos Terry John Swiney Moses Chambers Joshua Tarkington Ewen Cameron George Shannon Thos Haynes James Pugh John McSwine Jordan Fipps Sander Russell. Plf recovers agt dft $10.50 and costs of suit.

Samuel Perkins assee vs Henry Rutherford. Debt. Justices G Hulme R McMillin Wm Banks. Jury Thos Cash Burwell McLemore Edwd H McNeal John House Joseph Leadbetter Saml Winstead Martin Stanley Thos Berry Andw Craig John McSwine Robt P Currin Geo Shannon. Plf recovers agt dft his debt $210, damages and costs.

Samuel Perkins assee vs Henry Rutherford. Debt. Justices[above]. Jury[above]. Plf
p.186   recovers agt dft his debt $120 and damages $5.38.

Henry Rutherford vs David Mason. Debt. Justices[above]. Jury Thos Cash Burwell McLemore Edwd H McNeal John House Joseph Ledbetter Saml Winstead Martin Stanley Thomas Berry Andrew Craig John McSwine Jonathan Cooper George Shannon. Plf recovers agt deft $420.21 debt and $33.54 damages.

James Jackson vs Harrison Boyd. Present[above]. Jury above except Robert P Currin for Jonathan Cooper. Plf recovers agt dft his debt, damages, and costs.

Bradley & Berkley vs Charles Boyles. Justices[above]. Jury above except Jonathan Cooper for Robt P Currin. Plfs recover agt dft damages $191.80.

Isaac Lays admr vs Richard Orton. Debt. Justices[above]. Jury Thos Cash Burwell Mc-Lemore Edwd H McNeal John Hohn Joseph Leadbetter Saml Winstead Martin Standley Thos Berry Andw Craig John McSwine Jonathan Cooper Geo Shannon. Plf recovers agt dft his
p.187   debt $133.25 and damages $81.61.

James Gordon & Co vs Thomas H Perkins. Debt. Justices[above]. Jury above but John House for John Hohn. Plf recovers agt dft debt $149.89 and $2.48 damages.
James Gordon vs James McGavock. Debt. Justices[above]. Dft came not; Judgt by default for $173.16½ and interest $5.19 & 4 mills. Execution granted.
Francis Gunter vs Felix Staggs. Justices[above]. Plf no further prosecutes; dft pays costs except plfs attorney fees.

James Gordon vs Abram Maury Chapman White admrs of Joel Parrish decd. Justices[above]. C White and A Maury confess judgt as admrs of Joel Parrish for $63.36; execution not to issue until directed by Mastersons executors in person.

p.188   Matthias B Murfree apptd guardian of Martha Ann L C Murfree; bond $50,000 with David Dickinson and Robert P Currin his securities.

JULY 1814

Andrew Craig apptd gdn of Aveline David Craig; bond $1,000 with David Craig and John McKinney his securities.
License Samuel Moton to keep an ordinary at his house in this County; bond with Samuel Moton Junr his security.
Deed Young A Gray to Thomas Haynes 41 acres 121 poles ackd.
Order Wm Parham Isaac McNealy James Wilkins fined $1 each for nonattendance as jurors at this Term.
Appoint David Dickinson & Isham R Trotter Esqrs to take private exmn of Martha Wilkins & Sally Parham relative to execution of a conveyance for 554 acres.
Deed/gift John Minter to Robert Warren ackd.
Claiborne Pillow vs Robert Crafton Senr. Depositions of Owen Smith & others to be taken at house of Owen Smith in Prince Edward County [VA].
Will of Elizabeth Holstead decd proven by Robert Davis & Wm Manning; exta Julia Jones qualified.
Deed Anthony Foster to Joseph Meadow 306 acres proven by Henry Coleman and Patsey Robertson.
Aaron Wells vs George Glasscock. Justices Berry Nolen Jesse White Robt McMillin. Cause continued.
Bill/sale Thomas J Martin to George H James proven by John Berkley.

Order George Hulme David Dunn Wm Banks Esqrs & Garner McConnico & Jno Watson settle the accounts of David Dickinson actg admr of Hardy Murfree decd, also to divide the Negroes belonging to sd estate among the legatees.
p.189   Court adjourns until tomorrow morning 9 OClock.
                                                            Robert McMillin Jes White Berry Nolen.

Saturday 9th July 1814. Present George Hulme William Banks Berry Nolen Esquires.
Claiborne Pillow vs Robert Crafton Senr. Justices[above]. Plf came not; dft recovers agt plf his costs in this behalf expended.

Thomas Younger vs William Neell[Nall?] Justices[above]. Jury John Lemmons John Ackins Robert Guthrie Joseph Hassell Lewis Stephens Saml Brown Luke Pryor Jr John Swiney Joshua Tarkington Isaac Patton James Neelly Joel Dilliard. Plf recovers of dft his damages $60.50 and costs.
Deed Jacob Jacoby to Pleasant Russell one lot proven by Eli McGan & Thomas L Robertson.
John Sample Surv part vs George Strambler. Justices[above]. Dft came not. Judgt recovered by plf agt dft on 14 Oct 1812 $156.04 debt $2.24 damages, & costs revived; plf granted execution of sd judgment & recover costs of sciri facias.

Order James M Gray oversee road to Henry Childress; hands that worked sd road under Thomas Patton except hands on plantation of Geo Hulme south of road work thereon.

p.190   License Benjamin White to keep an ordinary at his house in this County; bond with Geo Strambler and William Stephens Senr his securities.
Commrs to take deposition of Daniel Holman in case State vs Stephen Barfield one day notice to be given.
John Sample vs John Williamson. Attachment. Dft came not. Writ/inquiry next Term.

JULY 1814

Thos Reed & Gilbert G Washington vs Kinchen P Bass & Charles Slater. Debt. Dfts came not. Plfs recover agt dfts $478.78½ the debt, $$4.78 damages and costs.

Metcalf Degraffenreid vs Francis Carter. Certiorara. At last Term, plf recovered judgt agt deft Francis Carter; judgt not entered agt Branch H Anderson dfts security; judgt now entered for them agt sd Branch H Anderson for amt of judgt.

Stephen Smith vs Anderson Berryman. Certiorara. Last Term plf recovered judgt agt dft Stephen Smith for $21.50; judgt not entered agt Wm Peebles his security; judgt now entered for them agt Wm Peeples for amt of sd judgt agt Stephen Smith.

Settlement with Henry Cook admr of Anthony Sharp decd returned by John Witherspoon Hendley Stone & Sion Hunt, commissioners.
Settlement with Margaret Hulme late Margaret Sharp returned into Court by John Witherspoon Hendley Stone & Sion Hunt.
Order Francis Burrows oversee road near McCandlasses field to near Patrick Devlins; p.191   hands Spencers Crk incl James Standleys...down Hurricane incl Sion Hunt and Daniel Perkins...Parrishes branch...work thereon.

E S Hale vs Sampson Sawyers. Plf came not; dft recovers agt plf his costs.
Thos Reese & Gilbert G Washington vs Kinchen P Bass & Charles Staler. Debt. Dft came not. Plfs recover agt deft $478.78¼ debt, $11.95 damages, & costs.
Thomas Terry as a Juror proves 6 days.
Jno Sample Surv partner vs Sampson Sawyers. Plf came not; deft recovers his costs.

State vs John Hilliard & Samuel Graham. Defts assumed payment of costs; solicitor therefore entered a nolle prosequi.
Thomas Reid & Gilbert G Washington vs Kinchen P Bass & Charles Staler. Debt. Defts came not. Plfs recover of defts $578.78¾ debt, damages and costs; plfs release to defts all sd debt except $184.14¾ and 1 cent damages.
p.192   James T Green & Jesse White vs Isaiah Kutes. Plfs in proper person no further prosecute; dft recovers of plfs his costs of suit.
John Smith vs Matthew McGaugh Andrew Lapp & John Hill. Debt. Dfts came not. Plf recovers agt dfts $799.20 which may be discharged by payment of $349.60 with $16.25 damages together with his costs.
Thomas Younger vs William Nall. Appeal granted; bond and security given.
Court adjourns till Court in Course.   George Hulme William Banks Berry Nolen.

Monday 3d October 1814. Court of Pleas and quarter Sessions. Present the Worshipful John Witherspoon Collin McDaniel and Nicholas Scales Esquires.
Jurors summoned Wm Neelly Sr Martin Adams John P Broadnax(excused) John Mairs(issd) John Porter Jr Thomas A Pope Thomas Black(exd) Benjamin May Thos Moton John Robinson(issd) Joseph Philips Edward Warren Jacob Gray Ambrose Hadley Wm Parham(issd) Christopher McEwen Joel Riggs(exd) Thos Merritt Andrew Johnston Angus McPhail(exd) Alexr McLarin(exd) Benjn J Bass(issd) Jacob Halfacre(excd) Saml Moton Jr(excd) Ephm An- drews Jr Edwd Buford. Constables Wm H Downing & Richard W Hyde.

OCTOBER 1814

Grand jurors: Jacob Gray foreman Benjn May Thomas A Pope Chrisr McEwen Andrew Johnston Jasper Phillips Edward Warren Ambrose Hadley Martin Adams Thomas Moton Thomas Merritt Ephriam Andrews John Porter Jr discharged 5 days & petit Jury the same day.

p.193   Order John Robinson oversee road from Kinnards Still House; all in bounds from John Bidges[Bridges?] to Wm Bolins to Stephen Hails to Charles Cahoons work thereon.
Addl inventory/Jesse Gulley decd returned by Labon Benson admr.
Wm Parham released from fine for nonattendance as a Juror at last Court.
List of Commrs of roads returned by Wm Hulme Shff.
Green Scot sends his reqisnation as a constable.
Orphan Morgan Smith age one year bound unto Martha Mason until age 21 years to learn art & misteries of a farmer, one years schooling & a suit of clothes.

Order Wm Armstrong oversee road from Geo Hulme to Bates[Betts?] mill; hands from Widow Hopkins down Little Harpeth to Natchez road to big Harpeth to Patrick Crawford to Geo Hulme leaving him out to beginning work thereon.

Order John Witherspoon Sion Hunt & John J Henry any two take deposition of William McGaugh relative to boundaries & specialties called for in grant to Charles Brown for 640 acres on Buck Creek of Little Harpeth.
Order John Witherspoon Nichs Scales & James Black Esqrs settle with Susannah Crouch relative to her admn/estate of John Crouch decd.
Order Mordecai Pillow oversee road from Franklin to Buchannons, the part between Haleys Creek & Commrs crk crossing Hayes crk to Harpeth river incl Aaaron Askew Jno H Eaton & Frederick Davis to beginning work thereon.
Addl inventory/chattel estate of Benj Bugg decd retd by David Pinkston Nancy Bugg &
p.194   Ephm M Bugg admrs & admx.

Order John Witherspoon Hendley Stone & David Dickinson settle with Henry Cook relative to his guardianship for John N Sharp Searcy D Sharp Sumner M Sharp & Peggy N Sharp minor orphans of Anthony Sharp decd.
Bond of Eliza Norton and Zachariah Jackson for support of John C Wilson a lunatic for twelve months from 30 July for $60 returned.
Fine of James Wilkins for nonattendance as a juror at July Court remitted.
Grant Saml Williams ltrs/admn on estate of John Benson decd; bond $200 with John Harding his security.
Inventory/estate of Nathaniel Brown decd returned by Chas Brown admr.
Order David Houston oversee road from McGavocks branch, all in bounds from Harpeth Lick rd west to incl John Bridges north to Moses Davis East to Jno H Nichols & widow Marshal to beginning work thereon.

Order Rebecca Berry Bazil Berry & Alexr Johnston have ltrs/admn on estate of James Berry decd; bond $4000 with Thos Berry Wm Wilson Wm G Boyd Geo Hulme John Witherspoon W Gentry O Williams Nichs Scales & John Bostick securities. Inventory retd; order admrs & admx sell chattel estate retd in this inventory.
Order Nicholas Scales Watson Gentry & Wm Wilson set apart to Rebecca Berry widow of James Berry such part of estate sufficient for her & families support for one year.

Inventory/estate of John Benson decd retd by Saml Williams admr.

OCTOBER 1814

Order Gersham Hunt oversee road from John L Fielders lane at Barnes shop to county
p.195   line by Edmistons lane; hands from Jeremiah Primm Jno W Primm Green Primm
Nimrod Fielder Jno Hamer Sr John Hamer Jr Danl Hamer Wm Hamer Jno Depriest Wm Stone
David Cummins Jno Edmiston Jno Edmiston Richard Herbert Wm Alford Wm Edmiston & Jos
Perryman work thereon under his directions.
Deed John T Bennett to Henry Cook 203 acres proven by Jno Atkinson and John Cook.
Deed Maximilian Reading to David Houston 70 acres proven by Josh Love & James Love.
Deed Wm McGee to Elijah Williams 203 acres proven by James Giddens & Alex Mebane.
Deed Saml Shelburn to Jas Williams 103 acres ackd.
Deed Jas Pugh to Alexr Shaw 134 acres proven by Eleazer Andrews & Bryant Huss.
Deed James Robertson by his atty in fact John Davis to Thomas Atkins 100 acres
proven by Isaac Blount & James Gilliam.
Deed John Porter Jr to Abel Garrett 7 acres ackd.
Deed Demsey Nash to Henry Slater 100 ac proven by Timothy Shaw & A Keeling.
Deed John McClellan to Jno Bostick 51 acres ackd.
Deed quit claim Thomas Stewart to John Mairs 148 ac proven by Jno Douglass & Jno
Stewart.
Deed David Gillaspie to Saml Henderson 207 ac proven by Alexr Mebane & Taply B
Andrews.
Deed Newton Cannon to Wm S Webb 350 acres proven by Nathan Adams & Alexr McClaran.
Bill of Sale Sarah W Reeve to James Owen proven by G Hunt.
Deed John R Tankersly & Richard Tankersly to Elizabeth Cordell 100 ac proven by
Knacy Andrews & George Andrews.
Deed William Parham & Sarah Parham and James Wilkins and Martha Wilkins to Sarah
Thrower 554 acres severally ackd, the Court having first apptd O Williams & John
Witherspoon to take privy examn of sd Sarah & Martha ackd they signed deed volun-
tarily; Court certify deed to Halifax County N Carolina where the land is situated.

p.196   Deed Thomas H Meredith and Jane his wife ackd by sd Thos; Geo Hulme & Sion
Hunt took privy examn of sd Jane.
Power/atty John Williamson to Ann Williamson proven by Nancy Sammons & Harry[Hany?]
Sledge.
Deed Lewis Roberts to Jesse Roberts 514 acres proven by James Buford and Samuel
Dobtson.
Deed William Nolen to Stephen Nolen 112 ackd.
Deed James M Gray to Abel Garrett 22½ acres ackd.
Deed Jno & Robt Graham to William Bradshaw 195½ acres executed by Alexander Mebane
atty for sd Jno & Robt and proven by James Giddens and Edward Buford.
Deed William Bradshaw to Jno & Robt Graham 363 acres proven by James Giddens &
Edward Buford.

Robert Scales vs James Gentry. Watson Gentry summoned as garnishee saith he owes
James Gentry nothing but says there is a small trunk of wearing apparel at his
house.
Court adjourns till tomorrow 9 OClock.   John Witherspoon C McDaniel Samuel Wells

Tuesday 4th Octr 1814.   Present John Witherspoon Collin McDaniel Samuel Wells.
Andrew Kaylan records his stock mark.
David Pinkston records his stock mark.

OCTOBER 1814

p.197 Order John B Gibson oversee Harpeth Lick road from 9 mile fork to Glovers Gap; Patrick Gibson Richd Hay Wm Williams John Sledge [blank] Sammons Jones Glover Jno Williamson Joseph Tanner D Tanner Ja Roberts Fred Taylor H Sledge work thereon.

Appt James T Sanford guardian to Polly Crow Bryant Crow Isaac Crow & Thomas Crow minor orphans of Isaac Crow decd; bond $8000 with Oliver Williams and Thomas Wallace his securities.
Release Wm Willett from payment of value of mare by him posted but proven away.
Settlement with Susannah Crouch relative to her admn on estate of John Crouch decd retd by N Scales J Witherspoon & Jas Black.
Order John Miller Cornelius Wilson Peter Edwards Elijah Williams Jeremiah Freeman John Harley & Elisha North lay out a road from Gabriel Bufords shop to intersect road from Hawes Ford to county line.
Order Jacob Gray Thos Bradley Jno White John Carothers Terry Badley[Bradley?] & Robt Carothers any 5 alter fork of road to Nashville by way of Holly tree Gap where it leaves sd road by Carothers.
Inventory/estate of Joseph Brown decd returned by exor.
Appt Peter Pinkston constable; bond $1250, Nicholas Perkins & Wm Bond securities.
John Carothers resigns his appointment as constable.
William Webb resigns his appointment as constable.
Inventory/estate of David Lewis decd returned by Fran Jackson.
Order James Carson oversee road to Shelbyville beginning at Harpeth R west to Moses Ridley south to Saml Gentry east to Francis Nunn & Willis Carson north to river.

Order Turner Saunders Thomas Helve Young A Gray James S Clem Benj Gholson Saml Crockett & James G Jones any five view the convenience that would result from opening a road from North Eastern Franklin eastwardly upon line between Sharp & Ervin to intersect road to McConnicos.
p.198 Order David Spain oversee road from James Allisons branch to Duck River ridge; hands in bounds from sd branch to schoolhouse then to Zacheus Wilson...to Thos Wilson Jr to T Wilson Esqr incl James Allisons to beginning work thereon.

Inventory/estate of Clement Smithson decd returned by Nancy Smithson.
Grant Wm Wilson ltrs/admn on estate of William C Darnay decd; bond $300 with Genl Lee Nolen & Nicholas Scales securities.
Appoint Jeremiah Trantham constable; bond $1250, Cornelius Wilson and Samuel Wells his securities.
Order Anderson Epperson oversee road from Wm Logans to Wolf pit incl Mark Buck & Henry Bress Joseph Brand William Allen & John Johnson, Tignal Martin & Anderson Epperson to the beginning work thereon.
Appt Andrew Carothers constable; bond $1250, John Carothers & Caleb Manley secs.
Grant ltrs/admn to Nancy Smithson and Horatio Pettus on estate of Clement Smithson decd; bond $4000, Nathl Smithson & Saml Shelburn securities.

Order Elijah Blackshere age 14 last June be bound unto Benjamin White to age 21 to learn art & mysteries of a blacksmith, be taught to & including rule of three, and to give him $30 cash & suit of clothes at expiration of his services.

Inventory/chattel estate of William C Devereaux retd by Wm Nelson.
Inventory/estate of Isam Evans decd retd by Jason Hopkins.

OCTOBER 1814

Jurors to next Court: Edward Lawrence Edwd Elam Jacob Gray Henry Walker Drury Pulliam Michael Kinnard Joseph Braden Spencer Buford Edward Hood John W Crunk Elijah Williams Andw Herrin James S Clemm William Manning Wm G Boyd Robt Sharp Thomas Hite Saml Moore Danl German Burwell Temple Charles A Dabney Wm J Boyd Chas Brown Harden p.199 Perkins Jr. Constables Jas G Jones & Andw Carothers.

Following apptd to take list of Taxable property for 1815: Collin McDaniel in Capt McCrorys Company; Geo Hulme, Capt Edmondsons; Sion Hunt in Capt McKeys; Wm Banks in Capt Dabneys; Robt McMillin in Capt Anglins; John Witherspoon in Capt Perkins; Geo Barnes in Capt Barnes Co; Wm Anthony in Capt Johnsons; Oliver Williams in Capt Shannons; Nicholas Scales in Capt Fitzpatricks; Archer Jordan in Capt Gaults Co; Francis Jackson in Capt Harold[?]; Thomas Wilson in Capt Ridleys; Wm Wilson in Capt Dobbins; Geo Tillman in Capt Hookers; Alexr Mebane in Capt Mebanes; Eleazer Hardeman in Capt Dilliards; Isham A Trotter in Capt Mannings; Saml Wells in Capt Wells; Jesse White in Capt Simpsons; John J Henry in Capt Jones; Hendley Stone in Capt Richardsons Company.

Revoke order of July Term apptg a jury to lay off a road from John L Fielders near Barns shop by Liberty mtg house to John Edmistons to John Edmiston Jr to David Cummins.

Order Wm Nolen Spencer Hill Elisha Fly Genl L Nolen Wm Kid Nathl Barnes John Winstead John Depriest Wm Brown & Thos Guch any five lay off a road from John L Fielders interfering least with inclosures to Davidson County line between David Cummins farm and Nathl Herberts farm.

Deed Nathan Scruggs to Josiah Wooldridge 92 acres proven by John Roper & Sarah Roper.
Deed Isaac Bateman to Enoch Bateman 183¾ acres proven by William Peebles & Stephen Barfield.
Deed Matthias B Murfree to John Atkinson 168 acres ackd.
Deed Sampson Williams to Tristram Patton 250 acres proven by Saml Overton & Matthew Patton.
Deed William Wart[Wait?] to Jacob Critz 26 acres proven by Joshua Farmington & William S Watson.
Deed David Gee to Charles A Dabney 46½ acres proven by John House & Wm Bond.
p.200 Deed James Waldruff to Jesse White 30 acres proven by Wm Thompson & Cornelius D White.
Bill/sale Nathan Scruggs to Josiah Wooldridge proven by John Roper & Sarah Roper.
Deed Benjamin Beshan to J & L Thompson part of Lot 93 proven by Saml F Glass & Geo Stephens.
Deed Robt Wart to Jacob Critz 250 acres proven by Joshua Farrington & Wm L Watson.
Deed Sarah Lowry & David Lowry to John Staly 110 acres proven by Jacob Adams & Robt Price.
Deed Wm Spencer to Peter Potts 92 acres ackd.
Deed Joseph Dillender to James Neel 110 acres proven by Robt Elam & Wm Wilson.
Deed Peter Potts to John Mairs 80 acres ackd.
Deed Kenneth Morrison to Jno McSwine 30 acres proven by Jesse White & Isaiah Kates.
Deed Samuel Chapman to Wm Hulme Lot 96 proven by Henry Lyon & Thos W Cerby.
Deed David Squire to John White 50 square poles ackd.
Deed Henry Cook to Nicholas Perkins Sr 464 6/10 acres ackd.
Allow David Lunn $8.56 for keeping Polly Ayres object/charity one year.

OCTOBER 1814

Allow Zachariah Jackson $75 for keeping & $1.75 for medicine for 15 months for John C Wilson.
Order Edward Ragsdale & Isham R Trotter let out widow Shoup[Sharp?] on the Parrish to lowest bidder.
Order lists of taxable property to be returned.
p.201   Allow James Kavenaugh $5 for keeping Hezekiah Kavenaugh object/Charity from 2d Novr 1813 to 2d Novr 1814.
Order Oliver Williams & Berry Nolen let to lowest bidder Hezekiah Kavenaugh object/ charity for 12 mos from 2d Novr 1814.
Order Andrew Ewing oversee road from Hollow Tree Gap to 2 mile tree.
Order Hany Allen oversee road from 2 mile tree to bridge at Franklin.
Order George Kinnard James Williams & Thomas B Walthal lay off to Nancy Smithson widow to Clement Smithson one years provisions.
Order Sion Hunt & John Witherspoon take private examn of Sally Henry relative to exn of deed to Henry Cook for 68 acres.
Order Sion Hunt & John Witherspoon take private examn of Jane Broadnax as to her exn of a deed for 72 acres to Henry Cook.
Order Sion Hunt & John Witherspoon take private examn of Nancy McPhail as to her exn of a deed to Henry Cook for 130 acres.
Order Saml Perkins & Geo Hulme settle with Sherwood Green relative to his guardianship for orphan children of Saml Clark decd.

Matthew Duncan vs Eli Harriss. Jury John Robinson John Mairs Saml Barton George Bennett Jas Terrill Daniel McMahon Wm White Chapman White Jesse Benton Thos Berry Daniel Pinkston. Plf recovers agt dft residue of debt $48.85.

p.202   Appt David Riggs constable; bond $1250, Wm Moody & Richd Reynolds security. Court adjourns till tomorrow 9 OClock.   John Witherspoon Saml Shelburne O Williams

Wednesday 5th Octr. Present John Witherspoon Saml Shelburne Oliver Williams Esqrs.
Appt Wm Williams guardian to minor orphan John McCall; bond $1000, Saml Shelburne security.
Deed James Sneed to Geo Mayfield 60 acres proven by John McCalpin & Moses Wooton.
Deed David Holliday & Mary Holliday to Evan B Ormes 50 acres proven by John McCalpin & Moses Brown.
Francis Gunter vs Isaac Crows admrs. Covenant. Justices[above]. Jury Wm J Boyd Wm Hope Thos Berry John Mairs Wm Parham Edwd Buford Benj J Bass Peter Hardeman John Dillen Geo Burnett Jno K Campbell Robt Sharp. Plf recovers of deft debt & costs.

Appt Wm Ryburne constable in Capt Anglins company.
David McEwen John J Henry Martin Standley Martin Adams & Thomas Walker report they marked a road from intersection of Liberty meeting House rd with Nashville Rd to be used instead of the present road beginning opposite Henry Walkers house running between John P Broadnax & Jas G Jones and between C H McCalister & sd Jones & Jno J Henry.
Order Stephen Barfield oversee road to Liberty Meeting House to forks near Wm Manning and to include the new road, all who worked under Bearfield work thereon.

p.203   Frederick Browder Stephen Jordan Thos Jordan Newett Sammons & Thos Almond

OCTOBER 1814

apptd to alter road at Johnston Woods report sd road be turned at sd plantation and Hartwell Hydes to intersect Franklin rd 200 yds west of Woods horse mill.

James Gray Jones apptd constable yesterday gave bond $1200, John J Henry & George Hulme securities.
George Stramblar fined $1 for nonattendance as a juror & he paid.
Appt John J Henry guardian to Mary Henry & Lavenia Henry; bond $10,000, James Gray Jones & Henry Cook securities.
Settlement with Shearwood Green relative to his guardianship to heirs of Samuel Clark decd returned by Geo Hulme & Saml Perkins.
On petition of Wm Hickman, order writs issue agreeably to sd petition.
On petition of John Hamer & Susannah Hamer his wife formerly widow of Joseph Roberts decd for dower of 200 acres in Maury County on Leepers Lick Crk incl a place known as Walnut flat, Beginning at Crawfords corner....Writ issues to Sheriff of Maury County to lay off for John Hamer & Susannah one third of sd tract; it appearing that Brown admr/estate of Jos Roberts & guardian for his children had 10 days notice of filing of this petition.
Deed Charles McAlister & wife Elizabeth to William Hulme one lot ackd by C H McAlister in open Court; Oliver Williams & John J Henry, apptd to take privy examn of Elisabeth, returned she had signed voluntarily.
p.204 Deed John J Henry & wife Sally to Henry Cook 60 acres ackd; John Witherspoon & Sion Hunt report Sally had signed voluntarily.
Deed John P Broadnax & wife Jane to Henry Cook 72 acres ackd; John Witherspoon & Sion Hunt report Jane had signed voluntarily.
Deed Angus McPhail & wife Nancy to Henry Cook 130 acres ackd; John Witherspoon & Sion Hunt report Nancy had signed voluntarily.
Division of negroes, estate of Hardy Murfree decd amongst legatees; also settlement with David Dickinson acting admr returned.
Order James Black & Tristram Patton take privy examn of Elizabeth Old & Jane Watson touching execution of deed to Hezekiah Puryear.

Robert Sharp vs James Boland. Certiorara. Jury Wm J Boyd Wm Hope Thos Berry Jno Mairs Wm Parham Edwd Buford Benj J Bass Peter Hardeman Geo Burnett John K Campbell Geo Sluker Fielder Helms. Plf recovers agt dft & David Shannon his security $9 with legal interest from 1 Feby 1814 and costs.

Wm Manning vs James Gentry. Debt. Jury[above]. Plf recovers agt dft his debt $200
p.205 damages $48.33½ & costs.
David Frierson vs Henry Dobson. Debt. Jury[above]. Plf recovers of dft debt $197.22 damages $20.71 and costs.
John Taylor admr of H Taylor vs James Jackson Daniel Perkins Daniel A Dunham Burwell Temple & Robt McMillin. Plf by atty Wm Smith moved judgt be entered agt dfts for $121.04 the amt of judgt sd plf recovered 6 April 1814 agt sd Jas Jackson. Jas Jackson on sd day by Sheriff committed to jail till he should pay sd debt & costs, gave bond with sd dfts his securities. Plf recovers agt dfts sd debt & costs, also costs of this motion.
John Den lessee of Richard Pucketts heirs vs Henry Ingram. Eject. Parties in proper person; dft confesses judgt. Plf recovers his term yet to come in the premises & costs.
p.206 Court adjourned util tomorrow morning at nine of the Clock. G Hulme David

OCTOBER 1814

Shannon C McDaniel.

Thursday 6th October 1814. Present George Hulme David Shannon Collin McDaniel Esq.
State vs Joseph McCollister. A&B. O Williams D Shannon R McMillin. Dft saith he is
guilty; fined $10; committed till fine & costs be paid.
Deed Wm Hulme Sheriff to Elihu S Hall 250 acres ackd.
Deed John Park and Moses Park to Jas Southall 104 ac proven by John McCaslin & Joel
Hobbs.
Deed Thos Anderson to Isaac Ledbetter 135 ac proven by Nichs Scales & Jno Bostick.

Deed Joseph Cathey McDowell to George Stratar 1500 acres proven by Wm White; John
Sample in open court proved that subscribing witness Thos Masterson is dead and
that it was the handwriting of sd Masterson decd.
Order Robert Gray fined $2 for nonattendance as a Juror.

George Glasscock vs Andrew Dorton. Certiorara. O Williams Geo Hulme Robt McMillin.
Jury Benjn May Ephriam Andrews John Robinson Ambros Hadley James B Thompson Saml F
Glass Jason Hopkins Robt Gray Thos Hiter Wm Shute Fielder Helms Henry Stater. Dft
recovers agt plf his costs.

Peace Bond of John Gillaspie towards Jane McElwee, David Gillaspie and Wm Hooker
p.207   his securities.
Deed Isaac Williams to Richd Haley 6 acres proven by Hendley Stone & Wm Harrison.

Appt Edmund Hickman Childress guardian to Thomas Madison Childress and Sally Critz
Childress orphans of Henry Childress decd; bond $10,000 with Oliver Williams sec.

State vs Stephen Barfield. Appeal. Solicitor obtained appeal to Circuit Court.

John K Campbell vs Wm Thompson. Plf in proper person no further prosecutes; plf
recovers his cost of suit except attorneys fee.
Douglass J Puckett vs Stephen Thompson. Certiorara. Depositions to be taken of
witnesses in Logan County Kentucky for plf.
Robt Scales vs James Gentry. Attachment. Dismissed; dft recovers of plf his costs.

Wm Hamilton vs Bartholomew Stovall. Jury Benjn J Bass John Marrs Wm Neelly Wm Parham Edwd Buford Geo Burnett Eli McGan Sam Guthrie Thos Cash Swanson Johnson Richd
Graham John McSwine. Plf recovers damages one cent; further, 500 pds NC currency is
value of $1000. Therefore plf recovers of deft his debt $1000 and damages by jury
p.208   assessed and his costs.
Court adjourned until tomorrow morning nine O Clock.   G Hulme S Hunt C McDaniel

Friday 7th October 1814. Present George Hulme Sion Hunt Collin McDaniel Esquires.
Milton Gambill vs Jesse Wharton. John Witherspoon Hendley Stone C McDaniel. Jury
Peter Hardeman Geo Andrews Jason Hopkins Ezekiel Blackshire Wm Neelly Jno Mairs Jno
Robinson Wm Parham Benjn J Bass Edward Buford Fielder Helm Langhorn T Walton cannot
agree.
William McCamney vs Geo Hulme. Debt. Justices[above]. Jury[above]. Plf recovers agt

OCTOBER 1814

dft his debt, damages & costs.
George Gentry vs Wm Allen & Thos Hinson. Certiorara. O Williams J Witherspoon Thos W Stockett. Jury John Cox Ewen Cameron Wm Willett Geo Strambler Wm Shute John K Campbell John McSwine Geo Burnett James McCombs Thos McCrory James Cox Josiah Knight. Plf recovers agt dfts & their security Benj Welch his debt $50 damages $2.37 and costs.
Thomas Mastersons executors vs George Burnett & Nichs P Hardeman. Debt. Jury[above except John Mairs for James McCombs]. Dfts recover of plfs their costs. Plfs obtain p.209 appeal to Circuit Court.
John Sample surviving partner &c vs Geo Hulme & Ephm Brown. Debt. Jury Peter Hardeman Geo Andrews Jason Hopkins Benjn Brown Wm Neelly John Robinson Wm Parham Edwd Buford Wm McCandlass Stephen Spain Matthias B Murfree Joseph Crenshaw. Plf recovers agt dft his debt $273.25 and damages $42.31.
Felix Staggs vs Josiah Wooldridge. Debt. C McDaniel O Williams J Witherspoon. Jury [above]. Plf recovers agt dft his debt $130 damages $6.15 & costs.
John L Young vs John L Fielder. C.McDaniel O Williams G Hulme. Jury[above]. Plf recovers agt dft his damages $136.53 and costs.
p.210   John Sample vs John J Henry. Debt. G Hulme O Williams C McDaniel. Jury[above]. Plf recovers agt dft debt, damages, costs.
Lancaster Glover vs Nicholas Dilliard. Debt. O Williams G Hulme C McDaniel. Jury[above]. Plf recovers agt dft residue of debt, damages, costs.
Hendley Stone assignee vs Wm J Boyd. Debt. C McDaniel G Hulme O Williams. Jury [above]. Plf recovers agt plf his debt, damages, costs.

Will of Sherwood Mills proven by Nathl Benton.
Thomas J Martin admitted to take oath of Insolvent debtors, discharged from imprisonment. Tomorrow sd Thomas to be brought into Court for sd purpose together with the executors under which he is in custody.
p.211   Acct/sales estate of Thomas G Caldwell returned.
Ltrs/atty Elijah Montgomery to Samuel Edmiston the execution of which was taken in the Notary Republic for city of New Orleans, Louisiana.
List of taxable property & polls returned by Wm Hulme Shff.

Settlement with Isaac Mairs guardian to Ezekiel Blackshire Luke Blackshire David Blackshire Elijah Blackshire Jacob Blackshire Jesse Blackshire heirs of Jesse Blackshire decd returned by Geo Hulme & Sion Hunt.
Deed William Spencer to George Strambler land in Miami County Ohio ackd.
Deed William Spencer to George Strambler land in Miami County Ohio ackd.
Bill/sale Thomas Blair to Harpeth T Blair & Thomas S Blair proven by Henry Cook.
Deed Nicholas T Perkins to Wm J Boyd 76 acres ackd.
Deed Henry Cook to Nicholas T Perkins 200 acres ackd.

David Shannon vs Wm Hickman. Plf no further prosecutes. Deft recovers his costs.
Joel Lewis Chas Davidson vs Samuel Winstead. Plf will no farther prosecute his suit. Deft recovers agt plf his cost of defence.

Deed Beverly Reese Thomas Old & Betsey his wife John Watson & Jane Watson his wife to Hezekiah Puryear & Matilda his wife 326 acres ackd last Court by Beverly Reese Thomas Old & John Watson; James Black & Tristram Patton took privy examn of Betsey Old & Jane Watson; deed returned with privy examn annexed.

OCTOBER 1814

Court adjourns till tomorrow morning nine O Clock.
David Shannon O Williams Robert McMillin.

Saturday 8th October 1814. Present Oliver Williams David Shannon Robert McMillin. Ltr/atty David Gee to Charles A Dabney proven by James Hicks & John McCaslin.

Petition of Susannah Crouch praying writs in a cause adjudged before Wm Anthony wherein Peter Wilson plf & Susannah Crouch admx of John Crouch decd dft.

Bradley & James vs Nathan Scruggs. Debt. O Williams D Shannon R McMillin. Dft came not; plf recovers of dft his debt and 1cent damages; plf released all sd debt and damages except $322.67.
Bradley & James vs Nathan Scruggs. Dft came not; plf recovers of dft debt and 1 ct damages; plf releases all sd debt & damages except $370.22.
John Taylor admr of Henry Taylor vs James Jackson & others. One of dfts was in army of U.S. Judgt set aside.
Deed William M Marr to George Mansker Sr 54 acres proven by Daniel Perkins & Harden Perkins.
Deed William M Marr to George Mansker Sr 52½ acres proven by Danl Perkins & Harden Perkins.
John Den lessee of Sherwood Green vs James Gault. Ejectment. Dft came not. Plf releases damages he has sustained by reason of sd tresspass. Plf recovers his costs p.213 and his time yet to come in sd premises.

Bradley & James vs Nathan Scruggs. Dft came not. Plf recovers of deft debt. Plf releases all sd debt & damages except $462.42.

This day Thomas J Martin who had been in confinement in the Jail for 10 days by virtue of two executions at suit of Thomas McGhee agt him was brought to take oath for relief of insolvent debtors, together with sd execution under which he was in custody. Sd Thomas McGhee had been notified by sd Thomas J Martin of sd Martins intention to take sd oath. Ordered discharged from Custody.
Court adjourned till Court in Course.   O Williams David Shannon Robert McMillin.

Williamson County, Monday 28th November 1814.
This day met at the Court House in Franklin a called Court of Oyer and terminer to try a negro man slave named Alfred the property of John Porter having been charged with breaking open the house of Hannah McCutchen with design of committing a rape on her pleads not guilty. After having been convened for his trial, they consisted of Berry Nolen Hendley Stone and Samuel Merritt Esqrs Justices Zachariah Drake Thos Old Robt Guthrie & Owen T Watkins freeholders all owners of slaves in Williamson County find sd Alfred guilty as charged and that he be remanded to prison and be taken thence fourth Saturday in Decr next to be hanged by the neck till he be dead.
Court met according to adjournment. Present Hendley Stone Berry Nolen Saml Merritt Justices Owen Watkins Robert Guthrie Thos Old Zachariah Drake freeholders.

JANUARY 1815

p.214   Williamson County. Court of Pleas and Quarter Sessions, Monday 2d January 1815. Present the Worshipful George Hulme James Boyd William Banks, Esquires. Jurors summoned: Edward Lawrence Edward Elam Jacob Gray Henry Walker Drury Pulliam Michl Kinnard Joseph Braden Spencer Buford Edward Hood John W Crunk Elijah Williams Andw Herrin James S Clemm Wm Manning Wm G Boyd Robert Sharp Thos Hiter Samuel Moore Burwell Temple Charles A Dabney Wm J Boyd Chas Brown Harden Perkins Jr. Constables Jas G Jones Andw Carothers.

Grand Jurors: Spencer Buford foreman Thomas Hiter Joseph Braden Edwd Elam Drury Pulliam Burwell Temple Andrew Herron James S Clemm Charles A Dabney William G Boyd Henry Walker Edwd Hood Saml Moore discharged on 5th day.

Deed Edward Gore to Christopher Aclin 40 acres proven by Peyton Smith & Wm B Ervin.
Deed Joseph Winslow to John Fitzgerald 50 acres proven by Tristram Patton & Clement Farrar.
Will of Sherwood Mills proven by Nathaniel Benton & Andrew Hunter; Thomas Smith executor qualified. Inventory returned by Thomas Smith.
Deed Christopher Aclin to Joseph Hollansworth 40 acres ackd.
p.215   Deed Nicholas Gentry to James Mayfield 100 acres ackd.
Deed Samuel Gentry & Nicholas Gentry to George Gentry 378 acres ackd.
Moses Gordon vs Thomas Stephens & Thomas Neelly. Fountain M Parrish & Henry B Jackson appearance bail for Thos Stephens surrendered him in open court; James Herron Amos Bullock & Thomas Herron special bail.
Daniel Perkins Nichs Perkins Robt McLemore & Edwd Warren apptd to settle with Hendley Stone guardian for Green Pryor & Peter Pryor minor orphans of John Pryor decd.

Deed Samuel Gentry & George Gentry to Nicholas Gentry 348 acres ackd.
Deed Ann Williamson Lazarus Dotson & Burwell McLemore to Wm Williams 60 acres ackd.
Deed George Gentry & Nicholas Gentry to Saml Gentry 395¾ acres ackd.
Deed John Porter to Armistead Boyd 117 acres proven by John Witherspoon & Hendley Stone.
Deed Daniel German to Josiah Walton 126½ acres ackd.
Deed Thomas S West to William Hope 112 acres ackd.
Deed Thomas Harden to John Harden 102 acres proven by Yancy Powers & Benjn Merritt.
Acct/sales estate of John Benson decd retd by Samuel Williams Admr.
Deed/gift David Riggs to Miriam Kennedy ackd.
Deed/gift David Riggs to Sarah Depriest ackd.
Deed/gift David Riggs to David Riggs ackd.
Deed/gift David Riggs to Rebecca Boyd ackd.
Deed/gift David Riggs to Elizabeth Fielder ackd.

p.216   John Den lessee of William Wilson vs Matthias Rosenburn. Ejectment. John Witherspoon Wm Anthony Geo Hulme. Dft came not. Plf releases damages; plf recovers costs of suit and his time yet to come in sd premises.
State vs John R Biddix. A&B. Dft in proper person. Nolle prosequi entered. Dft assumes cost.
State vs John Fitz. A&B. Dft in proper person. Nolle prosequi entered; dft assumes costs.
State vs Thomas S Adkins. A&B. Dft in proper person. Nolle prosequi entered; dft assumes costs.

JANUARY 1815

State vs Jesse Jones. A&B. Defendant in proper person. Nolle prosequi entered; dft assumes costs.
Court adjourns until tomorrow nine O Clock.　　　　G Hulme William Banks Jas Boyd.

Tuesday 3d January 1815. Present George Hulme William Banks Berry Nolen Esquires.
Deed Eli Hope to William Dodson 133 acres proven by James Patton & Andw McCrady. Appoint James Black and Samuel Wells Esqr return private examination of Frances
p.217　　Bond touching her consent to signing a deed 521 acres to David Yarborough & Helen Yarborough.

Order Jas McEwen Martin Stanley John P Broadnax Andw Goff Danl McMahon Abram Maury Sr David Squire Sion Hunt any 5 lay off part of road to Nashville beginning at 1-mile tree to Holly Tree Gap.
Order Thos Hardeman John Thomas Thos Bennett Thos Merritt Langhorn T Walton Joseph Love Yancy Powers any five alter part of road to the Heron Settlement which passes through James Boyds land so as not to pass between house and spring if they think proper.
Order Commrs of Franklin remove & rebuild the market house on the public square at NE end of Court House at their own expence and that of inhabitants of sd town; condition that it be kept neat; when two thirds of the magistrates shall deem necessary it shall be removed.
Order Nicholas Perkins Sr Samuel Moore John Witherspoon Wm J Boyd Robert McMillin Esqr John Porter Elijah Hamilton Joseph Phillips any 5 lay off a road from South Harpeth ridge to Franklin.
Order John Moore oversee road to Chambers Ferry beginning at 10-mi tree to Maury County line; hands in bounds to Walkers branch to ridge between Leepers fork & Murfrees Fk to Big Carter incl Eli Hope Jos McAlister leaving out Wm --pson work thereon.
Order Michael Kinnard oversee road to Murfreesborough beginning at McConnicos Mtg House and ending near Hayes Crk; hands incl Wm Marshall Wm Thomas as far as Pulliams branch at upper end of David McEwens plantation...to John Richards plantation Michael Kinnard Chas Herold & Wm Denson work thereon.

p.218　　Order John Robinson oversee road from Kinnards Still House to rd from Fishing ford; residents from Buggs to Finleys to Knacy Andrews to Wm Borens to Stephen Hales to Chas Calhoons work thereon.
Order Colin McDaniel Sion Hunt & Gersham Hunt Esqrs apptd to settle with Henry Rutherford guardian of Washington P Crawford James J Crawford and Henry R Crawford minors.
Petition of Rebecca Berry widow of James Berry decd for dower 240 acres, tract on which sd decd formerly resided being Lot 2 of 640 acres deeded to sd James Berry decd Basil Berry & Wm Berry decd by Thomas Berry, sd lot bounded [omitted]...down Harpeth...adj Wm Berrys Lot 1.
Release Joseph Farrar from payment of double tax for 1814.
Order Hendley Stone & Jesse White Esqr let to lowest bidder the keeping for 12 mos of William Dacon a pauper.
Order James Boyd & Alexr Maben Esqrs let to lowest bidder Solomon Porch a pauper for term of 12 mos.
Order John J Henry & Oliver Williams Esqrs let to lowest bidder Ruth Beddix a

JANUARY 1815

pauper for term of 12 mos.
Order Isham R Trotter & Tristram Patton Esqrs let to lowest bidder for 12 mos the keeping of Elisha Hood a pauper.
Order Nicholas Branch allowed on bond of $37.50 for keeping Wm Deacon in 1814.
Order Allen Hill allowed sum in bond for keeping Elisha Hood last year.

p.219   Order Moses B Francis oversee road to Shelbyville beginning at James Boyds fence and end at Hurricane Crk; hands in bounds by Horatio Pettis Aron Job James Gibson to Thomas B Walthal to Reuben Parks & James Wilson work thereon.

Order Oliver Williams & John J Henry Esqrs take private examination of Jane Bright touching her voluntary consent to execution of a deed to James Davis.

Court lay County & poor tax for 1815: on each white poll 10 cts for the poor 2½ each 100 acres 12½ County poor 5 cts each slave 25 cts for poor 6 cts each town lot 25 for County poor 6¼ cts stud horse season of mare Merchants 5 Dollars [illegible] carriage ½ amount of State tax for County tax Jack the price of the season of one mare for County.
Order James Hopkins have certificate for killing a wolf over 4 months of age.
Order Wm Simmons have a certificate for killing a wolf over 4 months old.
Order Sherriff refund to Beverly Ridley excess of money collected as tax on stud horse for 1814.
Receipt Joseph Coddington to Garner McConnico admr proven by Nicholas P Hardeman.
Order Philip Beasley released from tax on 156 acres for 1814 charged by mistake.

Account/sales estate of Wm Deveroux decd returned by Wm Wilson admr.
Addl inventory/estate of Wm Deveroux decd returned by Wm Wilson admr.
John H Eaton solicitor allowed $50 for exofficio service for 1814.
William Hulme Sheriff allowed $50 for exofficio services for 1814.
Nicholas P Hardeman Clerk allowed $50 for exofficio services for 1814.

p.220   Order County Trustee pay Susanna McClem half valuation of a steer posted by David Nolen 7 August 1813 appraised to 12 dollars.
William S Garner Thomas Washington Ephriam H Foster & Elijah Roberts Esqrs severally produced licences to practice law and qualified.
Nicholas Scales Register allowed $10 for books furnished Registers office.
Order Isham R Trotter Hendley Stone & David Dunn Esqrs settle with Matthias B Murfree guardian of Martha Ann C Murfree a minor.

Allotment of one years provisions for support of Nancy Smithson widow of Clement Smithson returned by commrs.
Allotment of one years provision for support of Rebecca Berry widow of James Berry decd returned.
William Halbert released from appraised value of two stray mares posted in 1811 or 1812 proven & taken away by the owner.
Account/sales estate of Clement Smithson decd returned by Nancy Smithson & Horatio Pettus admx & admr.
Will of George H Jones decd proven by Robert Bradley & Robert Davis.
Account/sales of estate of James Berry decd retd by Rebecca Berry admx & Basil Berry and Alexander Johnson admrs.

JANUARY 1815

Order John Wilkins an orphan age 13 bound unto John H Hall to age twenty to be instructed in art & mystery of a farmer.
Richard W Hyde apptd constable in Capt Fitzpatricks company; bond $1250, William G Boyd and Nicholas Scales security.
Samuel Cox apptd constable; bond $1250 with John J Henry & Wm Banks securities.
William H Downing apptd constable; bond $1250, Philip Beasley & John Coffee sec.
James Skelly apptd constable; bond $1250, Wm Banks & Stephen Pig securities.

p.221 Appoint William Willson guardian to William Berry a minor; bond $4000, John Bostick & Richard W Hyde securities.
Appoint William Edmondson guardian to Poley Berry a minor, bond $4000, Richard W Hyde & Thomas Berry securities.
Ltr/atty Jackey T Blount to Thos E Sumner proven by John N Nale[H Hals?] & Nathan Stavell[Stovall?].
Deed Henry Brown to Benjn Brown 320 acres ackd.
Deed Michael Kinnard to James Stanley 100 acres ackd.
Deed John Bostick to Horatio Burns 4 acres ackd.
Deed John Davis to John K Cambell 9 acres proven by Samuel Cummins and Edward Gossage.
Deed Saml McBride to Jno Smith 200 acres ackd.
Deed James Henderson to Wm Bradshaw 562[542?] acres proven by Peter R Booker and Thomas T Maury.
Deed Elihu S Hall to David Cummins 260 acres proven by John White and Gilbert G Washington.
Deed O Williams to John H Hall 150 acres ackd.
Deed George Manscoe to John Evans 100 acres ackd.
Deed W Wilson to James Wilson 47 acres ackd.
Deed James Davis to Jno S Williams 109 acres ackd.
Deed Wm Hulme Shff to Robert P Currin 1 Lot ackd.
Deed Joshua Cutchen to George Stephenson 34 acres ackd.
Deed Thomas Simmons to Benj Kid 1/4 acre ackd.
Deed Martin Stanley to Right Stanley 55 acres ackd.
Deed James Davis to Stephen Barefield 20 acres ackd.
Deed James Davis to John Depriest 40 acres ackd.
Deed Andrew Steel to Robt Carothers 125 acres proven by Richd W Hyde & Jno Bostick.
p.222 Deed Conway Oldham to Thos Ridley 280 acres proven by Thos Hardeman & Constant Hardeman.
Court then adjourned until tomorrow morning nine O Clock.
G Hulme John J Henry Robert McMillin.

Wednesday 4th January 1815. Present George Hulme John J Henry Robert McMillin Esq.
Deed Joseph German to Benjamin White 1 Lot proven by John H Eaton & Stephen Nolen.
Deed John Pope to Lemuel Pope 215 acres ackd.
Deed Richard Orton to Samuel Word one lot ackd.

Aaron Wells vs George Glascock. David Dunn Jesse White Robert McMillin. Jury Michael Kinnard Wm Manning Alexr Smith Wm Goff Jason Hopkins Wilkins Harper Robt Carter Richd Hughes Benjn Merritt Abraham North Stephen Spencer Leonard Wood. Plf recovers agt dft damages $20 and costs of suit.

JANUARY 1815

Deed Henry Cook to Henry Lester one town Lot ackd.

Jurors to next Circuit Court: George Hulme John Witherspoon Daniel Perkins Nichs Scales Wm Logan Thos Wilson Saml Perkins Sherwood Green Robt McMillin Nicholas Perkins(D R) Stephen Childress Hendley Stone Berry Nolen Wm Bond Sr Thomas Bradley Richard Hightower Thos Berry Wm Edmondson John Bostick John Watson Beverly Reese Samuel Benton Hezekiah Puryear Eleazer Hardeman Nathan Stansill Isaac Ledbetter. Constables Saml Cox & Thomas Terry.

Jurors to next County Court: Hugh F Bell Samuel McCutchen Joseph Love George Shannon Thos Old Wm Shute John T Broadnax George Kinnard Samuel Cummins Freeman Walker p.223   Lewis Stephens Edward Warren James Price John Nichols Bernard Richardson James Wilkins James McEwen David Squire Jordan Fips Thomas Alexander Jesse Benton Hugh Dobbins John Sweeney Jason Hopkins Richard Hughs William Hope. Constables James Skelly & Richard W Hyde.

Deed Samuel Goodwin John Hogg Catlet[?] Campbell Dancan[?] Cameron by their attorney in fact Abram Maury to Edward Swanson 28 acres ackd.
Order David Dickinson & Isham R Trotter Esqrs take privy examn of Mary Swanson as to her execution of deed, Edward & Mary Swanson to Joseph Philip.
Deed Pleasant Russell to Turner Saunders 1 Lot ackd.
Deed Garner McConnico to Alex White 102 acres ackd.
Appt Thomas Terry constable; bond $1250, Wm Sampson & Geo Glasscock securities.

Andrew Roundtree vs Meredith Helm & Fielder Helm. Debt. Jas Boyd Robt McMillin Jesse White. Jury George Stramler Wm Bond Thos Berry Robt Guthrie Ewen Cameron Richard Graham Ephriam Sampson Jacob Tilman Wm Neelly Elijah Williams Wm Simpson Thos Herron. Plf recovers of dft debt $240 damages & costs.

James Burger vs John Bostick. Covenant. Jas Boyd Robt McMillin Jesse White. Parties in proper persons. Plf no further prosecutes; dft assumes all costs.

Order Charles Gunter oversee road from John Witherspoons to Wm Bonds at Leepers fork; hands that worked under Sterling Gunter work thereon.

p.224   Jacob Gray Thomas Bradley Terry Bradley John White Robert Carothers John Carothers report they moved road.

Turner Saunders Thomas Hiter James S Clemm Benjamin Gholson Young A Gray apptd to lay off a road on line between Sharp & Ewing to intersect road to McConnicos make report.
Grant Thomas Bradley ltrs/admn on estate of George H James decd with will annexed; executors therein named refused to qualify; sd Thomas Bradley gave bond $10,000 with Alexander Smith & James Smith, securities.
Inventory/personal estate of George H James decd returned by Thomas Bradley admr.
Court adjourns until tomorrow nine O Clock.
                                        John Witherspoon William Banks Robert McMillin.

Thursday 5 January 1815. Present William Banks Robert McMillin John Witherspoon.

JANUARY 1815

Deed David Gee to Charles A Dabney 71½ acres proven by James Gee & James Hicks.

Appt John Witherspoon & Wm Banks Esqrs to take privy examn of Peggy Hulme touching her consent to deed to Henry Cook.
Appt John Witherspoon Hendley Stone Wm Banks to settle with Henry Cook guardian of Sala Nelson Sharp Searcy D Sharp Sumner M Sharp & Peggy N Sharp minor orphans of Anthony Sharp decd.

Deed Jason Hopkins to James McCombs 1 Town lot ackd.

p.225   State vs Joseph McAlister. Assault. J Witherspoon Robt McMillin Wm Banks. Jury Wm Manning Michael Kinnard Joel Hobbs Benjn Merritt Wm Peebles John Sweeny Jacob Tillman Ephriam W Beasley Jason Hopkins Michael Layton Thos Berry Henry Dobson. Fined $1 and costs.

Grant Ltrs/admn to Ann E Henderson & Jno H Eaton on estate of Hugh Henderson decd; bond $15,000, Archd Lytle & Will B Eaton securities.
Deed Ephriam Brown to George Brown 60 acres ackd.
Deed Ephriam Brown to Thomas Brown 250 acres ackd.
Deed George Strambler to Wm Spencer 250 acres ackd.
Deed Andw Patton to Thos Berry 127 acres proven by Geo Hulme & Peggy Hulme.
Ltr/atty Isaac Hilliard to Matthias B Murfree proven by John Hardeman.
Bill/sale M F Degraffenreid McD G Reid and Abram Maury to Thomas Stuart ackd.

Will of Lucy Davis Kearney proven by James Hicks and James M Gray; Peter R Booker executor therein named qualified.
Stephen Barfield vs George Strambler. Appeal. J Witherspoon R McMillin W Banks. Plf came not; dft in proper person assumes all costs.

George Hulme chmn vs Philip Maury & Abram Maury. Debt. J Witherspoon R McMillin W
p.226   Banks. Plf came not; dft assumes all costs.
Deed Alexander White to Samuel Swain certified to County Court of Jefferson County Virginia.

Daniel Hamer & Susanna Hamer claim of Dower, Maury County. [plat & description of land omitted]...belonging to heirs of Joseph Roberts decd. Jurors summoned by Sheriff of Maury County, Ephriam McLean Charles Shannon George Hanks William Crawford Jehosophat Ladd Wm Gray James Ashley John Fly Jeremiah Fly John Mitchell Wm Fly Harrison Blagran surveyor John Mitchell & Wm Fly chain carriers. Samuel W Williams D C.
Court adjourned until tomorrow ten 0 Clock. G Hulme HDL Stone John Witherspoon.

Friday January 6th 1815. Present George Hulme Hendley Stone John Witherspoon Esqrs. Order made second day this Term apptg Isham R Trotter Hendley Stone & David Dunn to settle with M B Murfree gdn of Martha A C Murfree a minor, be rescinded, George
p.227   Hulme & Oliver Williams apptd for that purpose.
Settlement of above order returned by George Hulme and Oliver Williams.
Appt Nicholas Scales Saml Shelburne Jacob Garrett Esqrs to settle with Curtis Hooks guardian of Betsey Jane Norman a minor.

JANUARY 1815

Henry B Jackson vs Abraham North. Appl. G Hulme J Witherspoon R McMillin. Jury Robt Carter Jason Hopkins Michael Kinnard Benjn Trotter Thos Reynolds Dickson Vaughn Wm Manning Wm Walker Jacob Tillman Fountain Parrish Wm Shute Thos Walker. Plf recovers of dft $31.25 with costs of suit.

Hinchey Petway gdn vs Jacob Tilman. Debt. G Hulme J Witherspoon R McMillin. Jury Alson Edney Abraham Walker Wm Bright Wm Porter Angus McFail Martin Standly John P Broadnax Stephen Spain John Dunham Jesse Tarkington Geo Strambler Jones[James?] Tomlin. Plf recovers of dft $164.76 debt, damages & costs.

License William Smith to keep an ordinary in Franklin; bond $2500 with William Hulme and John H Eaton securities.
Deed George Hulme & Peggy Hulme to Henry Cook 370 acres ackd.
Grand Jury returned presentment of children of Francis M Dean; order Shff require him to have the children at next Court.
Grand Jury discharged.
Deed Angus McPhail to Samuel F Glass 1 Lot ackd.
p.228 Ltr/atty John Reid to John H Eaton & Robert P Currin proven by Edward Brenthall & Wm Smith.
Jacob Blackshare orphan between age 12 & 14 bound to Henry Allen until age 21 to learn art & mystery of a waggon wright; at expiration of term sd Allen to give apprentice a good suit of clothes and $30 & shall school him 9 months.

Jacob Tilman vs Thomas Bell. Motion. Jacob Tilman by William Smith his atty moved to have judgt agt sd Thos because sd Jacob was security of sd Thomas to Hinchey Pettway for $164.76. To enquire whether sd Jacob was security for sd Thomas came Jury[above]. Plf recovers of dft sd sum, charges, and costs.

Abraham North vs Henry B Jackson. Appeal. G Hulme J Witherspoon R McMillin. Plf came not; dft recovers of plf his costs of defence.
Abram North vs Henry B Jackson. Appeal. G Hulme J Witherspoon R McMillin. Plf came not; Dft recovers of plf his costs of defence.
Bradley & Berkley vs Nathaniel Benton. G Hulme J Witherspoon R McMillin. Death of John Berkley is suggested. Plf survivor by atty dismisses suit; dft assumes costs.

p.229 Richard Orton vs John Movelier. Certiorara. G Hulme J Witherspoon R McMillin. Jury[above]. Plf recovers agt dft debt $59, damages & costs. On motion of plf atty sd judgt is affirmed agt Benjamin White the dfts security; execution accordingly.

John Jackson vs Susanna Crouch admx of John Crouch decd. Plf recovers agt dft his debt $23.31, damages of detention, and costs, to be levied of the goods which belonged to sd intestate at time of his death which shall hereafter come to hands of the deft to be administered.

Peter Wilson vs Susanna Crouch admx of John Crouch decd. Plf recovers agt dft his debt $55, damages of detention, and costs to be levied on goods which belonged to intestate at time of his detah which shall hereafter come to hands of dft to be
p.230   administered.
Court adjourns until tomorrow morning nine O Clock. G Hulme J J Henry Berry Nolen.

JANUARY 1815

Saturday January 7th 1815. Present George Hulme John J Henry Berry Nolen Esquires.

Deed from John H Eaton and Myra E Eaton to William B Eaton 1431 acres 1/3 produced in open Court. George Hulme Berry Nolen & Jno J Henry took privy examination of sd Myra E Eaton as to her free execution of sd deed signed by her and her husband John H Eaton for sd land lying in Giles County on Richland Creek; sd Myra stated she voluntarily signed sd deed.

Order John Witherspoon and Geo Hulme take privy examn of Frances Bond as to her voluntary execution of deed signed by her and her husband William Bond for 2038 acres and 118 square poles to David Yarborough & Helen M Yarborough; afterward sd G Hulme and J Witherspoon report sd Frances had freely signed sd deed; sd William Bond and Frances Bond ackd exn of sd deed.

Deed/gift John West to Lucy Walker proven by John Williamson & Andrew Ewing.

Order John Sweeny oversee road from Franklin to first knob south of Majr Porters plantation to a tree marked S G; hands in bounds south of Andrew Cowsarts to John Thompsons to George Neellys to John Hayes to Mr Ezzels work thereon.

p.231   William Hulme Collector for the year 1814 vs John Alford. The Sheriff and Collector of the public and County taxes for year 1814 made report to January session 1815 that sd John Alford reputed owner of 100 acres lying on Mill Creek hath not paid taxes due thereon. Collector have judgt and order of sale agt sd John Alford of 35 cts eight & third mills & costs.
Collector for 1814 vs John G Blount [worded as above]

William Bond and Frances Bond his wife produced deed/conveyance to them by David Yarborough & Helen M Yarborough his wife for 2241½ acres land lying in Williamson County, same proven in Court of Pleas and quarter Sessions for Orange County NC, it being represented that Helen M Yarborough wife of sd David Yarborough is an inhabitant of Orange County and cannot come into our Court to be privily examined. Order James Webb & Wm Norwood of Orange County NC apptd to take private examination of sd Helen M Yarborough as to her free consent to execution of sd conveyance deed.

Bill/sale John Mentor to George Neelly ackd.
Deed John Davis to Thomas Cox 30 acres proven by Thomas Hiter & Jason Hopkins.
Wm Hulme Shff/Collector for 1814 granted credit on his settlement with treasury for sixty white polls insolvent in sd year.

Collector for 1814 vs Bennett Curry. Wm Hulme Sheriff/collector reported Bennett Curry reputed owner of 640 acres situation not known hath not paid taxes due thereon. Order of sale issued.

p.232   [Orders of sale granted to Collector for 1814 on properties owned by Jacob Crytz, Francis M Dean, Jesse Evans, Zebulon Hassell, James Hopes heirs, William B
p.233   Hart, Nancy Key, Thomas Loal, Joseph Loals heirs, Wm Sargent, Alexr Steel,
p.234   Robert Sconce, James Bruff, Abimelich Cole, Archibald Craigs heirs, Joseph
p.235   Eason, George Swin, Wm Hurst, James G Reed, John H Eaton, John H Eaton].

APRIL 1815

Order Riley Slocum oversee road from Franklin to McConnicos road; hands in bounds including those living on lands of McGavock and Ewin[Ervin?] to Joseph Bradens to McConnicos Mtg House to John J Henry Mrs Stacy & Dixon Vaughan to Liberty Mtg House incl Jas G Jones & Wm Manning work thereon.
Court adjourns until Court in Course.   O Williams J P Berry Nolen G Hulme.

p.236   Williamson County, Court of Pleas and Quarter Sessions, 3rd April 1815. Present the Worshipful Collin McDaniel William Banks Berry Nolen.

Jurors summoned: Hugh F Bell excused Saml McCutchen Joseph Love George Shannon Thomas Old William Shute John P Broadnax George Kinnard Samuel Cummins Freeman Walker Lewis Stephens Edward Warren James Price John Nichols Barnard Richardson excused James Wilkins James McEwen David Squire excused Jordan Phipps not summoned Thomas Alexander Jesse Benton Hugh Dobbins John Sweeny Jason Hopkins Richard Hughes Wm Hope. Constables James Skelly & Richd W Hyde.
Grand Jurors: Samuel mcCutchen foreman Hugh Dobbins Thos Alexander Wm Hassel Freeman Walker James Wilkins Edward Warren Jno P Broadnax James McEwen Richard Hughes Lewis Stephens Saml Cummins James Price James Skelly constable.
Petit Jurors discharged 5th day. J Love.

Deed Thomas P Covey[Carey?] to George Burns 142 acres proven by David Nolen & Joseph Nolen.
Bill/sale Moore Bragg to Henry Hunter proven by James Wilkins.
Deed Francis McDaniel to John Dunham 40¾ acres proven by Richard Steele and William Dunham.
Deed Joseph McDowell to Sherwood Green 120 acres proven by George Glimp[?] and James Turner.
Deed Joseph Hollinsworth to Christopher Aclin 40 acres ackd.
Deed William Span to Thos Jordan 25 acres proven by Archer Jordan & Stephan Jordan.
Deed James Gray to John Lovett 13¾ acres ackd.
Deed Robert Price to Nicholas Lanier 100 acres proven by Jas Burgess & Wm Jackson.
Deed John McCord to William Price 54¼ acres proven by Robert Byer & James Burgess.
p.237   Deed William Jackson to Nicholas Lanier 40½ acres ackd.
Deed John Steely to George Oliver 110 acres proven by Alexr Johnston & Jesse Pate.
Deed William Hulme Sheriff to William Banks 140 acres ackd.
Deed Henry Lyon to Thomas McNutt 182½ acres 26 poles ackd.
Deed James Burgess to Robert Biger 8 acres ackd.
Deed Nicholas Lanier to Stephen Hall 19¾ acres ackd.
Deed Richard Fowler to Jesse Pate 107½ acres proven by Alexr Johnston & Geo Oliver.
Acct/sales estate of George H James decd returned by Thos Bradly admr.
Inventory/ estate of James Norris decd returned by Elizabeth Norris. Order/sale of chattel estate issued.
Inventory/estate of Kinchin Dial decd retd by Joshua Dial admr.
Plat & certificate of Wm Hill 30 acres ackd by Samuel Bell Deputy surveyor.
Bond William Berry to Charles McCord 50 acres proven by Newton Cannon & Wm Wilson; assignment of sd bond by Charles McCord to James Berry proven by Wm Wilson.

105

APRIL 1815

p.238   Grant Sally Carter ltrs/admn on estate of Richard Carter decd; bond $1000 with Benjamin Roberts & Coonrod Richardson her securities.
Appt Benjn Roberts & Coonrod Richardson to lay off one years provision for support of Sally Carter relict of Richd Carter decd.
Appt Molly Adkison guardian to Lucy Adkinson minor orphan; bond $300 with Amos Bullock & William May securities.
Grant Robert McFadden ltrs/admn on estate of James McFadden decd; bond $500, Hugh F Bell & Saml Edmiston securities.
Grant Joshua Dod ltrs/admn on estate of Kinchan Dod decd; bond $500, Hugh F Bell & Saml Edmiston securities.
Grant Wm Neelly ltrs/admn on estate of Robert Neelly decd; Bond $500, Chas Robertson & Edward Swanson securities.
Grant Elizabeth Norris ltrs/admn on estate of Jas Norris decd; bond $500, Daniel White & Amos Bullock securities.

Elizabeth Lewis between age 2 & 3 years bound unto Nathan Adams until age 18 or marriage, to be taught art & mysteries of a housewife and to read & write.
William Lewis about age 14 bound unto Jason Adams until age 21 years to learn art & mystery of a cabinetmaker & to give him at expiration of time $30 worth of tools.

Order William Anthony & Oliver Williams Esqrs settle with Garner McConnico relative to his admn on estate of Richard Puckett decd.
Order Archibald Lytle oversee road from McGavocks branch; those in bounds from John Bridges to Moses Davis to John H Nichols to Widow Marshall work thereon.
p.239   Order Adam Coon oversee road to 5 mile tree on Hayes Crk as far as McConnicos Mtg house; hands...Drury Pulliams to David McEwen to Wm Marshall & hands that heretofore worked under Henry Ingram & John Wheat as overseer work thereon.

Justices returned lists of Taxables for 1815: Collin McDaniel in Capt McKeys Company; Gersham Hunt in Capt Barns; Hendley Stone in Capt Richardsons; Wm Banks in Capt C A Dabneys; Eleazer Hardeman in Capt Dilliards.

Certificates issued: John Rainey for killing an old wolf; Archibald Gray for killing an old wolf; scalps produced.
Thomas Hardeman Yancy Powers Thomas Barnet Langthurn T Walton John Thomas, apptd last Court to alter road from Franklin to Herron Settlement which passes through James Boyds land, report they marked road agreeable to order.
p.240   Settlement, Hendley Stone gdn for Green Pryor & Peter Pryor retd.
Order John Reed oversee road from Holly tree Gap lately laid out.
[Marginal note: Error. See opposite page.]

Order John Witherspoon Sion Hunt Robt McMillin on 20 April 1815 meet with Thos Garrett 640 acres granted by NC to John Pearce to examine witnesses as to beginning corner for purpose of perpetuating testimony establishing lines of sd grant.

Order John P Irion sell chattel estate of Philip J Iron decd.
Order Isaac Bissell oversee road from Andw Cowsarts to ford on Gideon Road; hands from Cowsarts to Moses Adams & John Hughstons to Bufords Ford to Pattons Road work thereon.
Court adjourns till tomorrow nine O Clock.   G Hulme HDY Stone Robert McMillin.

APRIL 1815

Tuesday 4th April 1815. Present George Hulme Hendly Stone Robert McMillin Esquires.
Deed Edward Swanson to Richd Swanson 221 acres ackd.
Deed Saml Edmiston atty/fact for Elijah Montgomery to Saml Perkins 429 acres ackd.
Deed Edward Swanson to James Swanson 236 acres ackd.
Deed Wm Banks to James Armstrong 123 acres 4 poles ackd.
p.241   Deed David Dunn to Jacob Cash 313 acres proven by Turner Saunders & Joshua Torrington.
Deed George Shannon to Stephen Johnston 100 acres ackd.
Deed George Shannon to Josiah Wood 52 acres ackd.
Deed Wm Shute to Newton Edney 99½ acres ackd.
Deed Tristram Patton to Edward Hood 61 acres ackd.
Deed William Shute to James Armstrong 128 acres ackd.
Deed John Morow to Zachary German 92 acres proven by Sion Hunt & Daniel German.
Deed Harrison Boyd to Wm McGilbry 2 Town Lots ackd.
Deed David Dunn & Turner Saunders to Jacob Cash 6 acres proven by Wm Maning & John W Manning.
Deed Wm Stephens to John Stephens 100 acres ackd.
Bond Matthias B Murfree James Mancy[?] & Isaac Hilliard to George Hulme Chairman/ County Court proven by John Watson.
Bond Matthias B Murfree James Maney & Isaac Hilliard to George Hulme Chmn/County Court proven by John Watson.
Bond James Maney Matthias B Murfree & Isaac Hilliard to George Hulme chmn/County Ct proven by John Watson.
Bond Isaac Hilliard James Mancy & Matthias B Murfree to George Hulme chmn/County Ct proven by John Watson.
Bill/sale Samuel Upry to David Cummins ackd.
Order James McLaughlin oversee road whereof Henry Slator was formerly overseer.

Order Alexander Wood oversee road from Wilsons road to Arringtons Crk leaving Wm
p.242   Denson Michael Kinnard & John Richard on south then up Hays Crk to Frederick Davis's to near Alexr Simpson to Dann Hill incl Lewis Stephens work thereon.
Order Wm Harrison oversee road from Henry Childress to near John Witherspoon; hands from Robt Grinders to Wm Whites incl Wm Childress work thereon.

Order John P Iron oversee road from Nolens shop to Davidson County including Nathan Stansell to Wm Nolens to G L Nolens mill to Wm Fielders to Archibal Cannacks work thereon.
Order Burgess T Hall oversee road from where John Andrews formerly lived to David Dickinsons to Elijah Hunters incl Willie Meatt to John Belcher to Andw Roundtree down Barr Crk incl Joshua Tarkington work thereon.
Order Stephen Pigg oversee road from where John Andrews formerly lived to James Piggs incl James Skelly to Joseph Wittinntons to Benj Mayes to John Andrews to John McCaslin to Jay Vestals work thereon.
Order Josiah Wilson oversee road; all west of Franklin road opposite head of Rutherfords Crk incl Richd Simpson Zacheus Wilson.
Order Richard Reynolds oversee road to Fishing Ford; hands from Wm Moody Spencer Reynolds Chas & Wm Legate John Tapley Thos Wilson Jr & Thos Wilson and David Riggs hands work thereon.
p.243   Inventory/estate of Henry White decd retd by Wm Neelly admr.

APRIL 1815

Acct/sales of estate of David Lewis decd returned.
Inventory/estate of James Moore decd returned.
Order Obadiah Driskill oversee road from Harpeth Lick rd to Big Harpeth James Prices ford; hands from Harrisons incl James Carothers M Greer Jno Ascue Neelly Branley widow Smithson work thereon.
Grant Wm Neelly ltrs/admn on estate of Henry White; bond $200 with Saml Edmiston & Danl Perkins securities.
Grant John P Iron ltrs/admn on estate of Sarah Iron decd; bond $2500, Josiah Knight & John Waters security.
Grant John Moore ltrs/admn on estate of John Moore decd; bond $3000, Saml Ackin & Jesse White securities.

Benjamin Lewis orphan age 12 yrs bound unto Alexr Ralston until age 21 to learn occupation & mystery of a cabinet maker, to give him 12 months schooling at one time and three month schooling at age 18 and a good freedom suit of homespun cloaths at age 21.

Licence William S Webb to keep an ordinary at his dwelling house; bond $2500 with John H Eaton security.
Licence John D Hill to keep an ordinary at his dwelling house; bond $2500, William Anthony his security.
License Francis Giddens to keep an ordinary at his dwelling house; bond $2500, Caleb Mandley his security.
Appoint Nelson Chapman constable in Capt Daltons Company; bond $1250, Wm Wilson & Thos Ridley security.
Appoint Frederick Ivy constable in Capt W O Perkins company; bond $1250, Thos Garrett & Burwell Temple security.
p.244   Appoint James J Thomas constable in Capt Edmistons company; bond $1250, Burwell Temple & Thos Garrett securities.
Appt Daniel Perkins County Trustee; bond $3000, Thos H Perkins Nichs Perkins Senr & Robert McLemore security.
Appt Wm Hulme Collector for 1815, bond $5000, Jno J Henry James Gray James & John Witherspoon securities.
Order Thos Wilson Wm Logan & Wm Nunn Esqrs settle with James Joyce relative to his admn on estate of Littleberry Epperson decd.
Archer Jordan Esqr returned a fine of 87½ imposed on Wm Hill for profane swearing.

Order John Manier Moses Ridley Mark Jackson John Webb Saml Gentry Francis Nunn James Buckley James Ridgway Chas Calhoon & John Hail any 5 alter Franklin rd near Geo Gentrys to intersect Nashville rd near Francis Nunns and to intersect Franklin rd near James Mayfields.

Andw Goff Jas McEwen David Squire John P Broadnax Martin Standley apptd to view a road report...by side of Thomas Williamsons fence, the place where Hood lives, thence to present road where it passes the 4 mile tree.

Order Joseph Crockett John Gray Senr Saml Crockett Andw Crockett James Crockett Andw Ewing Thos Walker any 5 alter road to Liberty Mtg House where it runs through land of Ephm W Beasley if they think it as good.
Deed Angus McPhail to Wm McGilvery part of Lot ackd.

APRIL 1815

Order John Nichols Joseph Braden Alexr White Jas G Jones David Squire Benjn White Jas McEwen lay off a road from bridge to intersect road from Jefferson & Murfreesborough at a branch that empties into north side of Harpeth.

p.245   Order John P Broadnax George Hulme David Squire Henry Walker let to lowest bidder the erection of a bridge across branch that empties into Harpeth.

Order Saml McCutchen Saml Edmiston Chas Brown Ephm Brown Wm Neelly Jno Motherel Joseph Motherel & Thos Berry any 5 view Natchez rd from Robt McFaddens to cross Little Harpeth at some better ford so as to intersect the road on the other side of sd river.
Order Andrew Goff John Wilson Robert Patton Jas G Jones David McEwen Thos Walker & John P Broadnax any 5 alter road from Franklin to Liberty Mtg House where it runs through land of Michael Long provided they think the alteration necessary for benefit of the public.
Order Wm Allen Clem Walls Stephen Hargrove Andw McCaskell Archibald Lytle John H Nichols & Thos Hardeman any 5 extend the road by Thomas Hardemans to Thos Herrons on Duck River ridge to County line near David Gillaspies to Warners Ferry on Duck River.
Appt George Hulme John Witherspoon & Hendley Stone Esqrs settle with Thos T Maury relative to his admn on estate of Jane Wheaton decd.
Order John Holt Spencer Hill John Hamer John Edmiston B H William Stone David Nolen & Joshua Cannon lay off a road from Turbefield Burns Shop near Liberty mtg house to County line at David Cummins.
Order Thos Cash released from appraised value of horse by him heretofore posted.
Appt Thomas Wilson Wm R Nunn & Wm Logan to settle with Diana Elam and Moses Ridley relative to their admn on estate of Stephen Elam decd.

Jurors to July Term: Wm Armstrong Joel Stephens Moses Chambers Thos B Walthal Thos Gooch Geo Stramblar Richd Reynolds Joseph Philips Demsey Nash David Cummins Daniel Hamer Thos P Keassly Geo Oliver Johnson Jordan Wm Jordan Thos Jordan Nathan Adams Wm Spencer Jordan Phipps Elijah Hamilton Henry Lyon Jonathan Currin Alexr McCown Thos McCrory Jnr Wm Moore John Carothers. Constables Nelson Chapman Fredk Ivey.

p.246   Agreement signed by Thos Jordan Stephen Johnson Patsey Johnson proven by Thomson Wood & Benj Jordan; the same article also signed by George Jordan Johnson Jordan ackd John Johnson Anne Johnson proven by Wm Wilson & John Buchanan also signed by Thos Walker & ackd.

Petition of Wm Willett for writs of certiorara & supersedias in the case of Nichs Tomlin agt him granted.

Justices made return lists of Taxable property for 1815: Archer Jordan in Capt Garretts Company; Jesse White in Capt Simpsons; Robert McMillin Capt Anglins; Wm Wilson in Capt Daltons; Saml Wells in Capt Wells; Francis Jackson in Capt Carsons; George Tilman in Capt Hookers; Thos Wilson in Capt Ridleys old company; Alexr Mebane in Capt Mebanes; Sion Hunt in Capt McRorys; Wm Anthony in Capt Johnsons; Isham R Trotter in Capt Maddins; Isham R Trotter in Capt Rees's.

Bond of Abram North & Stephen Spain for support of Elisha Hood an object of Charity

APRIL 1815

returned by I R Trotter & T Patton.
Bond of Samuel Pratt & James Boyd for support of Solomon Porch an object of Charity retd by A Mebane.
Court adjourns till tomorrow nine O Clock.   G Hulme John J Henry John Witherspoon.

Wednesday 5th April 1815. Present David R McEwen only; no other justices being present the Court adjourned till tomorrow nine OClock.

Thursday 6th April 1815. Present John Witherspoon George Hulme John J Henry Esqrs.
Deed Abram Maury to Thos Crutcher Town Lot 117 ackd.

p.247 State vs James Short. James G Jones & Hinchey Pettway bring James Short into Court; John Nichols & Joseph Braden appearance bond.
Richd Sutton vs Thomas Hiter. Debt. Geo Hulme John Witherspoon John J Henry.[blank]

Josiah Wooldridge vs Jesse Johnson. Geo Hulme Jno Witherspoon John J Henry. Dft came not; Plf recovers agt dft; damages to be ascertained at next Court.

William Hooker vs Isaiah White. Appeal. Geo Hulme Jno Witherspoon Jno Henry. Isaiah White made default. Judgt of Justice/peace affirmed agt him with interest and costs of suit.
David Craig vs Josiah Wooldridge. Debt. G Hulme J Witherspoon J J Henry. Jury Wm Shute Joseph Love Thos Old Joseph Braden Wm Hemphill Benjn White James Cavenaugh Jacob Gray John Carothers Jas Jordan Wm House John Fuzzell. Plf recovers debt, damages, & his costs.
Saml Jackson & Sarah Jackson vs Young A Gray. G Hulme J Witherspoon J J Henry. Jury
p.248   [above]. Plfs recover agt dft damages, costs afsd, and costs of suit.
Deed Samuel Winstead to Luke Pryor Jr 125 acres ackd.

Order Wm Shute oversee road from near Thos H Perkins to Franklin; those from Capt McKeys incl M Porter & Boyds, hands that live on the place that Col P Perkins died on, then to incl Thos H Perkins hands, to Parrishes mill work thereon.

Order James McEwen oversee road; hands incl Andrew Goff David McEwen & Isaac Marrs, & those south of his branch, & those between Spencers creek & Big Harpeth west of Liberty Mtg House work thereon.

Order John Marrs oversee road from 2 mile tree on Nashville rd to Holly tree Gap; hands that worked under Andw Ewen work thereon under his direction.

Order Shff summon a jury of twelve freeholders to inquire what damages Wm Hemphill has sustained by the alteration of Nashville road through his lands.

Settlement with Henry Cook gdn for Salla N Sharp retd by Wm Banks John Witherspoon & Hendley Stone.
[Same wording, Henry Cook as gdn for Searcy D Sharp, Sumner Martin Sharp, Peggy N
p.249   Sharp.]

APRIL 1815

Licence Peter Potts to keep an ordinary at his dwelling house; bond $2500, Wm Evans & John Carothers securities.
Grant Ltrs/admn to Wm Brock on estate of Barit Brock decd; bond $500, Wm Griffin security.
Inventory/estate of Lucy D Kearney decd retd by Peter R Booker exr.
Bond James Biddick & Jno R Biddick to chmn/County Court for support of Ruth Biddick an object of Charity.
Lists of Taxable property returned by John Witherspoon in Capt W O Perkins Compy, Oliver Williams in Capt Shannons company.

Pleasant Russel vs James Salisberry & Joel T Rivers. Appeal. Geo Hulme John Witherspoon John J Henry. Plf no further prosecutes. Dft recovers costs.
John Den lessee of John McSwine vs Keneth Morrison. Ejectment. [Justices above]. Death of plf John McSwine is suggested.
Henry Ingram vs James Short. A&B. [Justices above]. Plf no farther prosecutes; dft recovers of plf his costs.
State vs Henry Ingram. A&B. [Justices above]. County Solicitor enters nolle prosequi; James Short in proper person assumes all cost.
p.250   State vs John Fussel. A&B. [Justices above]. Solicitor prosecutes no farther; dft assumes costs.
State vs Saml & Polly Findley. A&B. [Justices above]. Nolle prosequi.
Caleb Manley vs Thos Cash. A&B. [Justices above]. Plf in proper person no farther prosecutes. Dft recovers costs.
Thomas Cash vs Caleb Manley. A&B. [Justices above]. Plf no further prosecutes. Dft recovers costs.
Richard Sutten vs Thos Hiter. Debt. Plf nonsuited; dft recovers costs.
Court adjourns itll tomorrow nine OClock.   G Hulme John J Henry John Witherspoon.

Friday 7th April 1815. Present George Hulme John Witherspoon Berry Nolen.
Lists of taxable property retd by John J Henry in Capt Jones Company; George Hulme in Capt Edmistons company.
p.251   John Den lessee David Mason vs George Andrews. John Witherspoon Berry Nolen Collin McDaniel. Jury Joseph Love John Nichols Wm Shute Thos Old Josiah Knight Henry Cook Henry B Jackson Saml Wood Wm Martial Jacob Halfacre James Craig John McClelland. Plf recovers damages & costs of suit & his term yet to come in the premises.
Licence Thomas L Robinson to keep an Ordinary; bond $2500 with John H Eaton & Nicholas Perkins securities.
State vs James Short. A&B. [Justices above]. Joseph Braden & John Nichols surrender James Short to sheriff.
Ltr/atty John Dabney to Charles A Dabney ackd.
State vs James Short. A&B. [Justices above]. Jury Joseph Love Jno Nichols Wm Shute Thos Old Josiah Knight Wm Martial Jacob Halfacre Jno McClelland Ewen Cameron Joseph Branden Geo Andrews Wm Sample find dft not guilty. Order James S Carrol prosecutor pay all costs.
James Allison Esqr returns fine imposed upon Wm Woodson for profane swearing on information Wm Alexander, the half fine amounting to $8.25.
State vs Thomas S West. A&B. [Justices above]. Nolle Prosequi. Dft pays costs.
p.252   Deed W B Eaton to Jno H Eaton 1421½ acres proven by A Potter & W

APRIL 1815

Smith.
Reed and Washington vs Kinchen P Bass. Debt. Geo Hulme C McDaniel James Allison. Jury Hugh Barr Saml F Glass Jonathan Currin Matthias B Murfree Robt Sawyers Andw Herrin Andw Campbell Jas Jordan Alson Edney Martin Standley Jos Braden John Nicholas. Plfs recover of dft their debt, damages, and costs of suit.

Pettway & Maury vs James G Jones. Debt. John Witherspoon Collin McDaniel J Allison. Jury Hugh Barr Saml F Glass Jno Bittick Matthias B Murfree Robt Sayers Andw Herrin Andw Campbell Jas Jordan Alson Edney Martin Standley Jos Bradon John Nichols. Plfs recover of dft their debt, damages, and costs of suit.

Albert Russel vs Henry Rutherford. Debt. [Justices above]. Jury[above]. Plfs recover residue of debt, damages, and costs of suit.

Grant James McEwen & Mary Mairs ltrs/admn on estate of Samuel Mairs decd; bond $1000, Martin Stanley & Alson Edney securities.

p.253   Order Jacob Halfacre receive ltrs/admn; bond $500, Joseph Love & Wm Marshall securities.
Licence Athelston Andrews to keep an ordinary at his dwelling; bond $2500, John J Henry & John Witherspoon his securities.

Garner McConnico admr of Richd Puckett decd vs Henry Lyon & John J Henry. Debt. John Witherspoon Collin McDaniel James Allison. Jury[above]. Plf recovers of dft his debt, damages, and costs.

Samuel Crockett vs Ewen Cameron. Debt. J Witherspoon G Hulme C McDaniel. Dft in proper person cannot deny plf debt $150. Plf agrees to stay of execution until after next Court.

John Sample surviving partner &c vs John H Eaton. Debt. Justices[above]. Jury [above]. Plf recovers of dft debt, damages, and costs of suit. Appeal granted.

Inventory/state of David Terry returned by Thos Terry admr.
p.254   Court adjourns till tomorrow nine OClock.
                                    G Hulme I R Trotter James Allison.

Saturday 8th April 1815. Present George Hulme James Allison Isham R Trotter Esqrs. Oliver Williams Esqr resignes commission as a Justice of the Peace.
Nichs Scales Esqr returns list of taxable property in Capt Fitzpatricks company.

John Sample Jnr part &c vs Jno Smith Saml McBride & Nelson Fields. Debt. Justices [above]. Plf recovers of dfts his debt, damages, & costs.
Deed Wm Hulme Sheriff to Boyles & Lytle 640 acres ackd.
Deed Joseph Ledbetter Amze Jones to Andrew Campbell 1 Lott proven by David Anderson & A Potter.
Deed Wm Hulme to John Sample & John H Eaton 1 Lot proven by A Potter & Wm Smith.
Deed Henry Cook to Thomas Reynolds 203 acres ackd.
Deed Charles Boyles to Andw Campbell 320 acres proven by Wm Hulme & David Anderson.

JULY 1815

Grant John Andrews & Samuel Andrews ltrs/admn on estate of John McSwine decd; bond $1000, Thos H Perkins & Andrew Dorton securities.
Court adjourns till Court in Course.   James Allison C McDaniel I R Trotter.

p.255   Monday 5th June 1815. a Call Court of Oyer & Terminer consisting of David Mason Sion Hunt and James Boyd Esquires Justices & Hezekiah Puryear Henry Cook Samuel Benton and James Gideon all freeholders and owners of Slaves, sworn to try a negro man slave named Sherwood the property of Oliver Williams for an assault on Joannah Thompson with attempt to commit a rape on sd Joannah; charged, pleads not guilty; upon hearing testimony as well in behalf of the prosecution as defendant, on oaths do say the deft Sherwood is not guilty, but there is probable cause that Sherwood might have committed the assault, wherewith he stands charged; adjudged sd Sherwood to receive 39 lashes on his bare back and the owner of the deft be taxes with costs, and same be immediatelay carried into execution.

Monday 3d July 1815. Williamson County. Court of Pleas and Quarter Sessions. Court House in Franklin. Present the Worshipful Geo Hulme John Witherspoon Berry Nolen. Jurors summoned Wm Armstrong Joel Stephens Moses Chambers Thos B Walthal Thos Gooch Geo Strambler Richd Reynolds Jos Philips Dempsey Nash David Cummins Danl Hamer Thos P Kersey Geo Oliver Johnston Jordan Wm Jordan Thos Jordan not found Nathan Adams Wm Spencer Jordan Phipps Elijah Hamilton Henry Lyon excused Jonathan Currin Alexander McCown Thos McCrory Wm Merritt John Carothers. Constables Nelson Chapman Fredk Ivy.
p.256   Grand Jury   Joel Stephens George Oliver David Cummins Dempsey Nash Thomas McCrory Jr Johnston Jordan William Jordan Daniel Hamer Moses Chambers William Allison Joseph Phillips George Strambler Thos P Kersey Fredk Ivy constable. Discharged 6th day, petit jury also.

Deed Samuel Shelburne to Clement Smithson 125 acres ackd.
Deed Thos G Wilkins by atty in fact O Williams to Samuel Shelburne 573 acres ackd.
Deed Wm Williams to Elijah Williams 107 acres ackd.
Deed Samuel Jackson to James Williams 49 acres proven by O Williams & Wm Williams.
Deed Samuel Rogers to Archilaus Hughes 4½ acres proven by Jno Dalton & Robt Rogers.
Deed Thomas Prowell to Sampson Prowell 100 acres ackd.
Deed Saml Jackson to Geo Woodfin 498 acres proven by O Williams & Garner McConnico.
Deed Robert Carothers Sr to Robert Carothers Jr 125 acres ackd.
Deed John Smith to Peter Smith 132 acres ackd.
Deed John Smith to Samuel Smith 130 acres ackd.
Deed Saml Rogers to Alex M Rogers 233 acres proven by Jno Dalton & Watson Gentry.
Deed Thos Shute to Thos Prowell 100 acres proven by Sampson Prowell & Jas Thompson.
Deed Geo Mansker to John Garner 52¾ acres ackd.
Deed John Johnston to Robert Johnston 69 acres 70 poles ackd.
Deed John Smith to Abraham Chrisman 102½ acres ackd.

JULY 1815

p.257 Deed Michael Kinnard to Henry Brown 240 acres ackd.
Deed Saml Jackson to Richard S Lock 40 acres proven by O Williams & R L Abernathy.
Deed Thomas Prowell to James Thompson 100 acres ackd.
Deed Samuel Shelburne to Wm Williams 103½ acres ackd.
Deed John Moody to John Johnston Senr 69 acres 70 poles proven by Enoch Heaton who saw John Johnston sign his name as witness thereto, also proven by Matthew Johnston to be the handwriting of Johnson.

Deed James G Jones and Elisa Jones his wife to Andrew Morrison 133 acres ackd by James G Jones. John Witherspoon and George Hulme took privy examn of Elisa Jones who had freely executed sd deed, after which Elisa Jones appeared in open Court and acknowledged it to be her act and deed.

Will of Littleton Brown proven by Wm Bond Senr and Morris L Bond.
Will of Absalom Taylor proven by Needham Bryan and G West; Larry Taylor one of the executors therein named qualified.
Bill/sale John Johnston Sr to Robert Johnston four negroes ackd.
Bond James Rogers to Archilaus Hughes 50 acres proven by A N Rogers & Robt Rogers.
Bill/sale John Moody to John Johnson proven by Matthew Johnson.
Grant David Edmiston ltrs/admn on estate of James E Edmiston; bond $500 with Nichs Perkins & John Walker his security.
Appt Thomas Reynolds guardian for Bythenia Reynolds; bond $1500, John Witherspoon
p.258 Caleb Mandley & David Mason security.
Peggy Carson and James Benges granted ltrs/admn on estate of William Carson decd; bond $1000, Joseph Reed & James Carson security.
Joseph Reed granted ltrs/admn on estate of Edmond Reed decd; bond $500, James Benges & James Carson security.
Malinda Parks and Jas B Thompson granted ltrs/admn on estate of Wm Parks decd; bond $1000, Henry Cook & Martin Standley security.
John Walker granted ltrs/admn on estate of Hance Walker decd; bond $500, Nichs Perkins & David Edmiston security.
Robert Rogers granted ltrs/admn on estate of James Rogers decd; bond $2000, John Dalton & Watson Gentry security.
Pryor Reynolds granted ltrs/admn on estate of George Reynolds decd; bond $600, Henry Cook & Robt Guthrie security.
Elizabeth Moreton & Barnet Donelson granted ltrs/admn on estate of Thos Morton decd; bond $1000, Saml Andrews Andw Dorton & Beckley Donelson security.

Inventory/estate of Richard Carter decd returned.
Appt Thomas Reynolds guardian for Sally Reynolds; bond $1500 with John Witherspoon Caleb Mandley & David Mason security. [Same wording, gdn for Richard Reynolds].

Inventory of chattel estate of Hance Walker decd returned.
Inventory of chattel estate of John McSwine decd returned.
Inventory of chattel estate of James Rogers decd returned.

p.259 Acct/sales estate of Richard Carter decd returned.
Inventory estate of James E Edmiston decd produced.
Acct/sales estate of James Moore decd produced.

JULY 1815

Order Thomas Wilson Esqr Jesse Bugg Ephriam Bugg lay off one years provision for support of widow & orphans of Willis Carson decd.

Order Saml Shelburne & Oliver Williams Esqrs settle with Garner McConnico relative to his admn on estate of Richard Puckett decd.

Order Wm Wilson Nichs Scales & Archer Jordan Esqrs settle with admx & admr estate of Wm Barry decd.

Order Sion Hunt John Witherspoon & Robt McMillin attend at house of Thos Garrett on 15 August next; 640 acres granted by NC to John Pierce heir of Hardy Pierce #2422 issued 21 Decr 1793, it being where sd Thomas Garrett now lives, there to examine witnesses relative to beginning corner and other specialties.

Order Basil Berry Saml Shelburne & Jacob Garrett lay off one years provisions for support of Mrs Carter widow of Richard Carter decd.

Nancy Lewis about age nine bound unto Thomas Jackson until age 18 to learn mystery and occupation of a housekeeper, to have one years schooling at one time between age 12 and 14; when she comes of age to give her a good feather bed and sufficient quantity of furniture and two nice homespun and one new calico suits of cloths with other suitable articles for each dress.

Order Oliver Crenshaw oversee road to dividing line between Crenshaw & John Carothers, hands of Henry Rutherford John Blair John Johnson Sr Thomas McCrory Sr Thos McCrory Jr James Crockett Matthew Johnson & John White work thereon.

p.260 Order Evan B Ormes oversee road from between Oliver Crenshaw & John Carothers to forks of road towards Franklin, hands of Joshua Burnham Jr Catoes & balance of hands that worked under Robert Johnson work thereon.

Johnson Jordan vs Daniel Potts. Appeal. David Mason Saml Shelburne Jacob Garrett. Deft confesses judgt for $15 & interest 36 cts. Plf recovers also his costs.

Thomas Bradley surviving partner &c vs John Neelly Jr. Debt. D Mason Geo Hulme S Shelburne. Plf no further prosecutes. Dft assumes all costs.
Court adjourns till tomorrow 9 O Clock.   G Hulme Saml Shelburne Robert McMillin.

Tuesday 4th July 1815. Present George Hulme Robert McMillin Saml Shelburne Esqrs.
Deed Chas Adams to Hartwell Hyde 55 acres proven by Christopher Williams & B Hyde.
Deed Andw Steele to Hartwell Hyde 325 acres proven by Jno Bostick & Wm Edmondson.
Deed Benjamin White to Lawrence Murphy 87 acres ackd.
Deed Thomas Alexander to Andrew Castleman 40 acres ackd.
Deed John Freeman to Saunders Freeman 100 acres ackd.
Deed John Witherspoon to Richard Hughes 21 acres ackd.
Deed Frederick Davis to Isaac Neelly 64 acres ackd.
p.261   Deed Edward Gossage to John Dunagan 50 acres proven by William Dunagan and Lott Griffin.
Deed John West to Philip Beasley 109 acres 35 poles ackd.
Deed William Black to David Houston 153 acres proven by M L Bond & H R W Hill.
Deed John Byrd to John Fitzgerald 142 acres ackd.

JULY 1815

Deed James Black to John McLellan 170 acres ackd.
Deed Edward Gossage to Wm Dunagan 50 acres proven by Jno Dunagan & Lott Griffin.
Deed James Black to Donalson Potter 100 acres ackd.
Deed Joseph Winslow to John Byrd 142 acres proven by Tristram Patton and John Fitzgerald.
Deed William Stevens to Wm Ridley 7½ acres proven by Frederick Lewis & Wm Hamilton.
Deed Gregory Wilson to Wm Ridley 38½ acres proven by Fredk Davis & Beverly Ridley.

Inventory chattel estate of William Owens decd produced.
Inventory chattel estate of William Parks decd produced.
Inventory chattel estate of John Shores decd produced.
Settlement with James Joice admr of Littleberry Epperson decd produced.
Inventory chattel estate of George Reynolds decd produced.
Account of hire of slaves of Benjamin Bugg decd produced.
Inventory of chattel estate of Joseph Hall decd produced.
p.262   Inventory of chattel estate of James McFadden decd produced.
Settlement with Moses Ridley admr/Stephen Elam decd produced.
Settlement with Garner McConnico admr/Richard Puckett decd produced.

Robert Walker Carlisle age 8 bound to Cordil Faircloth until age 21 & six months to learn mystery & occupation of house carpenter, to learn to read write and cypher to rule of three, to give him $50 at his freedom together with a good suit of clothes.

Grant Terry Bradley & Sally Carson ltrs/admn on estate of Samuel Carson decd; bond $500 with John Carothers and James Carson securities.
Grant Robert McLemore & Sion Hunt ltrs/admn on estate of Joseph Hall decd; bond $300 with Nicholas Perkins D R security.
Account of hire of slaves belonging to estate of Isaac Crow decd produced.
Grant Mordeca Kelly ltrs/admn on estate of Wm Owens decd; bond $500, Spencer Bateman and Genl Lee Nolen securities.

Order persons who failed to give in taxable property to Justices apptd to receive same, give lists to Clerk this session.
Grant Samuel Mays ltrs/admn on estate of John Shous[Shores?] decd; bond $500, Robt McMillin & Newell Gracy securities.
Court elected Philip Bryan constable in Capt Anglins company; bond $1250, Thos Alexander & James Davis securities.
Court elect Samuel Benton coroner; bond $4000, Robt McLemore & Jas McEwen sec.

p.263   Order William Allen oversee road to Warners Ferry from near Thos Mayfield lives, head of Rutherfords Crk to Allens Mill branch work thereon.
Order Wm R Nunn & Wm Logan Esqr let to lowest bidder Elizabeth Epperson an object of Charity for her support for one year.

Order Elijah Hamilton oversee road from Isaac Pattons to near Andw Cowsarts; hands from north of Thos Aydelottes with Murfrees boundary across West Harpeth incl Andw Nails old place to Davis branch to Robert Reeds to Duck River Ridge leaving out Colwell & including James Gideons work thereon.

Ephriam M Bugg released from payment of value of a mare by him posted; afterwards

JULY 1815

proven to be property of George Grissam.
James Davis released from payment of value of a mare by him posted; afterwards proven to be property of John Stephens.
Jonathan Potts released from payment of value of horse by him posted; afterwards proven to be property of Littleton Henderson.
Hadijah Collins released from payment of value of horse by him posted; afterwards proven to be property of Thomas Latta.
James Caperton released from payment of value of mare by him posted; afterwards proven to be property of William Mayberry.
James Oakley Wood released from payment/value of mare, colt & horse by him posted; afterwards proven to be property of David C Lewis & Wm Bradshaw.
James G Jones released from payment of appraised value of sow by him posted; died before expiration of twelve months.
p.264   Daniel Clifft released from value of cow by him posted; afterwards proven to be property of Wm Malugin.

Order Jesse Kennedy oversee road from Maury County line to Duck River ridge; hands on Flat Creek except David Christman work thereon.
Wm Simmons granted certificate for killing 5 wolves under 4 mos old in this county.

Order John Harden oversee road from East of Joseph Love to James Neelly.
Order Edmund Wall oversee road from John Evans to John Witherspoon; hands down West Harpeth incl John Achols & Hy Cook then with Natchez rd incl Martin Trantham Peter Holliday Bradford Ballance & Thomas Walthal work thereon.
Order Gustavus Holland oversee road from John Currys to Widow Woods; residents from plantation where John Curry lived to George Manskers to Fredk Davis to Jason Wilsons work thereon.
Order Woodson Hubbard Wm Alexander Andw Criswell Benjah Goodman Clem Hall Geo Tillman & David Chrisman any 5 alter Harpeth Lick road towards Warners Ferry on Duck river where it runs through land of Edward Ragsdale if they think condusive to public good.
Wm Neelly John Motheral Thos Berry Saml Edmiston & Ephriam Brown apptd last Court report they marked road beginning at Robert McFaddens to lane between Timothy Shaw and James J Thomas, crossing Little Harpeth with Betts fence to Natchez rd.

p.265   Order John Hall oversee road from Hightower to ridge between Little Harpeth & Hays Crk; hands from Smiths mill incl Andrew Crockett Henry Tally James Cockrel Mr Blair Hugh R Orr and his tenants Jason Wilson John Wilson and their tenants...Joseph Crockett & Ephriam Beasley work thereon.

Order Beverly Ridley oversee road to main Hays Crk at Eatons plantation; hands east of Rounsevalls incl Thos Wilson and on north of Hays Creek ridge work thereon.

Fine $1.50 imposed on Thomas Farmer by John Hill for profane swearing returned by Richard Jackson.

Report of Wm S Allen Clement Walls Stephen Hargrave Andrew McCorcle Thomas Hardeman apptd last Court to extend road to Thomas Herrons on Duck River ridge: begin near Loves plantation by Thomas Hardemans to Thomas Herrons by Thomas Wallace crossing Rutherford Crk near Hudson Dawson by David Gillaspie; order sd road be cut. John G

JULY 1815

Love prayed appeal to Circuit Court; bond $200, Eleazer Hardeman & Thos Wilson sec.

Jurors to next Circuit Court: Kemp Holland Thos H Perkins Thos Wilson John Witherspoon Wm Logan James Boyd Wm Anthony Amos Rounsevall Elisha Davis Geo Barnes John J Henry Eleazer Hardeman Geo Hulme Angus McPhail Stephen Childress Saml Shelburne Jas McEwen Wm Wilson Jesse Benton Robt McMillin James Neelly Cain Wm R Nunn Alexr Mebane Henry Cook Isham R Trotter Hezekiah Puryear. Constables Jeremiah Trantham and Andrew Carothers.

Jurors to next County Court: Elisha Williams Jr Geo Bennet Horatio Pettice Watson Gentry Nicholas Gentry Moses B Francis Henry Walker David Gillaspie Joel Dilliard James Andrews John Walker Wm Groves Joshua Farrington Josiah Knight Henry Lyon Danl German Wm Hope Adam Berry James Hardgraves Joseph Hassel Wm Jones Hadijah Collins John Thompson Thos Herron James Caperton Wm Bond on Columbia road. Constables Saml Cox Philip Bryan.

p.266 Nicholas Lanier vs John Ostin[?]. Plf in proper person no further prosecutes; Dft recovers of plf his costs.
Moses Gordon vs Thos Stephens & Thomas Neelly. Debt. Plf no further prosecutes. Dft Stephens in proper person assumes costs.
Report of Jury apptd to view Franklin rd: begin at Geo Gentry, intersect Nashville Rd at Francis Nunn, intersect Franklin Rd near James Mayfield.
Court adjourns till tomorrow 9 OClock.   G Hulme G Hunt Robert McMillin

Wednesday 5th July 1815. Present George Hulme Gersham Hunt Robert McMillin Esqrs.
David Mason, apptd deputy sheriff, qualified.
Whittson Gambill vs Jesse Wharton. G Hulme R McMillin J Witherspoon. Jury Jonathan Currin John Carothers Elijah Hamilton Thos B Walthal Harvey Puckett Henry Cook Joseph Crockett Henry Rutherford Saml Cummins Richard Hughes Isham House Abner Vaughan. Dft recovers agt plf his costs of defence.

Elijah Mayfield vs Wm Alexander. Certiorara. [Justices above]. Jury Thomas Ridley Spencer Bateman Thos Jones Abraham Walker Thos Reynolds Oliver Williams Benjn White Joel Stephens Geo Oliver Wm J Boyd Johnston Jordan Wm Jordan. Plf(sic) Wm Alexander
p.267 recovers of dft his damages.

Samuel Wilson vs Laurance Bass admr of John Patton decd. Covenant. G Hulme R McMillin Gersham Hunt. Jury Jonathan Currin Elijah Hamilton Joseph Crockett John Stacy John Creek Thos B Walthal Harvey Puckett Richd Hughs Gabriel Buford Wm Saunders John Carothers John Nichols [blank] The Court adjourns till tomorrow nine.

Grant Nancy Vinatta & George Ralston ltrs/admn on estate of Christopher Vinatta; bond $800, Thomas Wilson and George Oliver securities.
Deed Elisha Davis to William Dunagan 60 acres ackd.
Deed James Hardeman to Wright Williams 106 acres proven by Oliver Williams and Rice Williams.
Grant Wm J Boyd & Paul Dismuke ltrs/admn on estate of Armistead Boyd decd; bond $10,000, Henry Cook and John Witherspoon securities.
Inventory/chattel estate of Sarah Iron decd produced.

JULY 1815

Inventory/chattel estate of Philip Jacob Irion decd produced.
Inventory/chattel estate of Armistead Boyd decd produced.

Order writs/certiorara & supersedeas issue upon petition of Abraham Smith Alexr Smith in case of Samuel Andrews vs Alexr Smith the sd Andrews having obtained judgt agt sd Alexr Smith before Sion Hunt Esqr on 27 May 1815.

p.268   Order Isaac Ledbetter oversee road from Franklin to Murfreesborough between Arringtons Crk & Wilsons Crk; hands from Wilsons Crk to Wilsons mill rd south to Nelsons Crk work thereon.

Order William King oversee road; residents from Widow McKnight on Arringtons Crk to Benjamin Russels old place with Stewarts Crk ridge to Mill Crk incl Thomas McGaugh work thereon.
Report of jury to view a road from Turbefields Shop near Liberty Mtg house to near David Cummins. Joshua Cannon Spencer Hill John Edmiston Wm Stone John Hamer. Order David Cummins oversee sd road; residents within bounds from County line to Dr Dicksons to Richd Hubbards to David Bells to William Stones to Wm & Daniel Hamers work thereon.
Court adjourns till tomorrow nine OClock.   G Hulme   Robert McMillin   G Hunt

Thursday 6th July 1815. Present George Hulme Robert McMillin Gersham Hunt Esquires.
Samuel Wilson vs Lawrence Bass admr John Patton decd. Covenant. [Justices above]. Jury Jonathan Currin Elijah Hambleton Joseph Crockett John Stacy John Creek Gabriel Buford William Sanders John Carothers Thomas B Walthall Harvy Puckett Richard Hughs John Nichols say dft hath performed his covenant; dft recovers agt plf his costs.

p.269   Order David McEwen Alson Edney Martin Adams set apart one years provision for support of widow & children of James Mairs decd.
Order John Witherspoon Robt McLemore & Henry Cook settle with Nicholas Scales & Nicholas Perkins(D R) exrs of Peter Perkins decd.
Inventory/chattel estate of Hugh Henderson decd produced.
Deed David McEwen to Christopher E McEwen 130 acres ackd.
Deed Alexander Crafford to Andrew Roundtree 11½ acres proven by Chas Robinson & Wm Sparkman.
Grant James McEwen ltrs/admn on estate of Peter Potts decd; bond $5000, David McEwen & Wm Peebles securities.
Grant Wm Sparkman ltrs/admn on estate of Wm Withrington; bond $8000, Charles Robinson & Andw Roundtree securities.
Inventory/chattel estate of Wm Withrington decd produced.
Bill/sale Thos W Stockett to Joseph Stockett proven by John McCutchen.
License Rodin Tucker to keep an ordinary at his dwelling house; bond $2500, Nicholas Perkins and Joshua Doyel securities.
Deed Walter McConnel to James McGuire 48¾ acres proven by James Carothers and subpoena issued to Giles County for Zachariah Parker.

Edward Russell vs James Pugh. Trespass. G Hunt R McMillin Saml Shelburne. Jury Wm Peebles Christopher E McEwen Wm Goff John R Bitticks Jesse Tarkinton Elijah Hamilton John Carothers Thomas B Walthall Saml F Glass Wm Saunders Richard Hughs Thomas

119

JULY 1815

p.270   Reynolds; John R Bitticks failing to answer to return their verdict; on motion of dft, rest of Jury discharged and plf nonsuited & pay dft his costs.

Joel Parrish vs Samuel Tripp. Appeal. G Hunt R McMillin S Shelburne. Jury Wm Peebles Christopher E McEwen Wm Goff John R Bitticks Elijah Hamilton Thomas B Walthal Thos Stacy Tandy Russell John White Wm Saunders Thomas Reynolds John Carothers. Plf recovers of dft & Ebenezer Darby his security his debt, damages, & costs.

Deed Elizabeth Spencer to Lusa Black 43¾ acres was proven by Wm Jones and Marmaduke Stanfield.
Inventory/chattel estate of Thomas Morton decd produced.
Inventory/chattel estate of John Bradford decd produced.
John McSwine vs Alexander Moore. A&B. [Justices above]. Plf is dead; suit abates.
Thomas E Simmons vs Green Hill. Debt. [Justices above]. Plf no further prosecutes. Dft recovers agt plf his costs of defence.
Claiborne Pillow vs Wm Radford. Appeal. [Justices above]. Plf came not; Dft recovers of plf his costs.

p.271   State vs David Dunn. A&B. [Justices above]. Dft came not; forfeited his recognizance. Sciri facias issues agt David Dunn.
Grand Jury presented bridge below Wm McKeys mill near Wm Shutes as being out of repair. Solicitor to commence suit upon bond of undertaker of sd bridge.
Grand Jury present bridge over Big Harpeth as being out of repair. Suit commences.

Grant Samuel Shelburne ltrs/admn on estate of John Radford decd; bond $200, Wm Williams and Nicholas Perkins securities. Order Saml Shelburne sell chattel estate of sd John Radford decd.

Turner Saunders and Wilkins Harper bound for appearance of David Dunn came not nor did they bring David Dunn; forfeited recognizance; sciri facias issues.

William M Simpkins according to law the father of a bastard child begotten of Rebecca Bryant a single woman gave bond $500 with Isaac Mason and Archelus Briant securities for keeping the child from becoming chargeable upon the County. Order sd Wm M Simpkins pay sd Rebecca Briant $20 annually until child is age eleven.

State vs James Carothers. A&B. [Justices above]. Solicitor enters nolle prosequi; dft assumes all costs.

p.272   State vs Nicholas Tomlin. Assaulting officer. [Justices above]. Solicitor enters nolle prosequi; State recovers of dft costs expended.
State vs James Carrell. A&B. Samuel Shelburne J Witherspoon R McMillin. Solicitor enters nolle prosequi. Dft in proper person assumes all costs.
State vs Matthew Patton. A&B. G Hunt R McMillin S Shelburne. Dft in proper person says he is guilty; fined $12.50 and costs.

Order Edmund Lawrance Edward Elam & George Hays lay off one years provision for support of Nancy Vinnatta widow of Christopher Vinatta decd.
Ltr/atty Elizabeth Moor to Wm J Boyd ackd by sd Elizabeth Moore.
Court adjourns till tomorrow nine OClock.   G Hulme   John J Henry   Jas White

JULY 1815

Friday 7th July 1815. Present Gersham Hunt Robert McMillin George Hulme.
Charles Zachery vs Peter Potts. G Hunt R McMillin Jesse White. Dft being dead, and James McEwen having recd ltrs/admn agrees cause may come to trial.

Charles Zachery vs Peter Potts admr. Jury Josiah Knight Jonathan Currin Thos B Walthal Elijah Hamilton John Carothers Spencer Bateman Lawrence Thompson John P p.273 Broadnax John Douglass James Tomlin John K Campbell Amsey Jones. Dft's admr recovers of plf their costs of defence.

Inventory/chattel estate of Robert Neely decd returned.
Settlement with Thos T Maury admr of Jane Wheaton decd returned.
Grant John Gray ltrs/admn on estate of Alexander Gray decd; bond $500, James Smith & Nicholas Perkins securities.
Grant James Smith ltrs/admn on estate of William Smith decd; bond $400, John Gray & Nicholas Perkins securities.
James Pugh vs Hansel Ezell. Jesse White R McMillin G Hunt. Plf in proper person no further prosecutes; dft recovers of plf his costs.
Grant General Lee Nolen ltrs/admn on estate of Robert Murray; bond $400, Joseph H Scales & Nichs Perkins securities.
Order Mordica Kell sell chattel estate of Wm Owen decd.
Deed David McEwen to Stephen Childress 46½ acres ackd.
Inventory/chattel estate of Samuel Mairs decd produced.
Order admrs of Saml Mairs decd sell chattel estate of decedent.

On petition of John P Irion Geo A Iron Ann & others, order Wm Anthony Nathan Stancil Nelson Fields Thos Simmons Saml McBride divide estate of Philip Jacob Iron consisting of ten Negroes & other property among the legatees agreeably to his will.

p.274 John Den lessee of John McSwine vs Kenneth Morrison. Ejectment. G Hulme G Hunt R McMillin. Jury Joseph Crockett Thos Ridley Allen Hill Ruffin Brown Wm Peebles Chrisr E McEwen Jos H Scales John R Bitticks Henry Cook Thos Reynolds Newton Cannon John Douglass. Plf recovers agt dft his time yet to come to premises besides his damages and costs.
Inventory/chattel estate of Robert Murry decd returned. Order admr sell estate.

John Witherspoon vs Charles Gerrard. Caveat. G Hulme James Boyd G Hunt R McMillin. Jury Jonathan Currin Elijah Hamilton John Carothers Thos B Walthal Wilkins Harper Jacob Gray Archd Potter Spencer Bateman Jas Jordan Jas Short Robt Sayers & Benj Gholston. Cause adjourned till tomorrow eight oclock.

William Edmiston apptd guardian to Thomas Berry a minor orphan; bond $1000 with Jno Boyd and Robert Sayers his securities.
William Wilson apptd guardian to Robert Berry and James Berry minor orphans; bond $2000, Robert Sayers & Chapman White securities.
Grant Joseph H Scales ltrs/admn on estate of Susannah Barnes decd; bond $200, Newton Cannon & Watson Gentry securities.
James Black vs James Pugh. Si fa. G Hulme G Hunt J Boyd. Dft came not; plf recovers of dft balance of debt, damages, and costs.

p.275 Geo Hulme chairman vs George Strambler Oliver Williams Thomas McCrory &

JULY 1815

Moses Chambers. Debt. Gersham Hunt James Boyd Robt McMillin. Plf no further prosecutes. Defts assume payment of all costs.
Douglass J Puckett vs Stephen Thomason. Certiorara. G Hulme J Boyd R McMillin. Plf came not; plf may be suited, pays to dft his costs of defence.

John Taylor admr of Henry Taylor decd vs James Jackson Daniel Perkins Danl A Dunham Burwell Temple & Robert McMillin. Motion. G Hulme J Boyd G Hunt. Plf by atty suggests that James Jackson has died; plf moved to have judgt entered agt Danl Perkins Danl A Dunham Burwell Temple & Robt McMillin for $121.04 amt of judgt plf recovered agt sd Jas Jackson. Dft on 6 April 1814 was surrendered by appearance bail & ordered into custody; on 6 April 1814 gave bond with securities Danl Perkins Danl A Dunham Burwell Temple & Robt McMillin for keeping within prison bounds until discharged by course of law. Sd James went out of bounds. Plf recovers of dfts sd debt and costs. Plf releases debt except $44.09.

State vs Bernard Donelson. Solicitor enters nolle prosequi.
Court adjourns till tomorrow eight O Clock.
G Hulme John Witherspoon James Boyd Robert McMillin

p.276 Saturday 8th July 1815. Present John Witherspoon James Boyd Robt McMillin.
Henry Cook who was guardian for Sala N Sharp Searcy D Sharp Sumner M Sharp & Peggy N Sharp resigns his guardianship.
On petition of Moore Bragg, order writs issue in case of Alexander Moore agt Moore Bragg and John Davis.
On petition of Harrison Boyd, order writs issue in case of John Johnston agt Harrison Boyd.

Simeon Spruel vs George Oliver. Appeal. [Justices above]. Jury John K Campbell Terry Bradley Saml Moore David Anderson Metcaf Degraffenreid Moore Bragg Sterling Gunter Richard Hughs John Rolons Matthew Wiggs James Tomlin Morris L Bond. Plf recovers of dft his damages and costs.

John Witherspoon vs Charles Gerard. Caveat. G Hulme J Boyd R McMillin. Jury Jonathan Currin Elijah Hamilton John Carothers Thos B Walthal Wilkins Harper Jacob Gray Archibald Potter Spencer Bateman James Jordan James Short Robert Sayers Benjamin Gholson cannot agree; cause transferred to Circuit Court.

Francis May vs Henry Lyon. Debt. G Hulme R McMillin S Hunt. Jury Joel Stephens Geo Oliver Thos McCrory Johnson Jordan Wm Jordan Moses Chambers Wm Moore Joseph Philip George Strambler Thomas P Kensey Daniel Hamer David Cummins. Plf recovers his debt damages & costs.

Joseph Thompson vs Joel T Rivers. Appeal. G Hulme R McMillin Sion Hunt. Jury Joel
p.277 Stevens George Oliver Thos McCrory Johnson Jordan Wm Jordan Moses Chambers Wm Moore Jos Philips Geo Strambler Thos P Kensey Danl Hamer David Cummins find for plf. Judgt affirmed agt principal and Harrison Boyd & Peter Estes.

Lawrance & Joseph Thompson vs Joel T Rivers. Appeal. G Hulme S Hunt R McMillin. Jury Joel Stephens Wm Jordan Thos McCrory Johnston Jordan Joseph Philips Moses

JULY 1815

Chambers Wm Moore Daniel Hamer George Strambler Thos P Kensey Geo Oliver David Cummins. Judgt affirmed agt principal Harrison Boyd & Peter Estes his securitys, and plf recover of dft and securities his debt.

Inventory/chattel estate of Peter Potts decd returned; Order/sale issues.
Grant ltrs/admn to John H Eaton on estate of George Neelly Jnr decd; bond $500 with Nicholas Perkins his security.

Lawrance & Joseph Thompson vs Joel T Rivers & William Clark. Appeal. G Hulme Robert McMillin S Hunt. Jury Joel Stephens George Oliver Thomas McCrory Johnson Jordan Wm Jordan Moses Chambers William Moore Joseph Philips Geo Strambler Thos P Kensey Danl Hamer David Cummins. Judgt affirmed agt principal and Peter Estes and Harrison Boyd his securities for debt damages and costs in favour of the plf, and that he recover of dft and his securities his debt damages and costs.

Metcalf Degraffenreid vs James G Jones. Debt. J Boyd R McMillin S Hunt. Jury Joel Stevens Geo Oliver Thos McCrory Johnston Jordan Wm Jordan Moses Chambers Wm Moore Joseph Philips Geo Strambler Thos P Kensey Daniel Hamer David Cummins. Plaintiff p.278 recovers of dft his debt and damages.

Wm S Lewis vs George Gollady. Certiorara. G Hulme S Hunt R McMillin. Plf came not. Dft recovers of plf his costs.

John Johnson vs Andrew Dorton. Certiorara. G Hulme R McMillin S Hunt. Motion to quash the execution; execution quashed and set aside.

Order Benjn Evans Robt Hodge & John Mairs lay off one years provisions for support of Polly Potts and children widow of Peter Potts decd.
Ltr/atty James Henry & John Oliver to Jeremiah Dunn proven by Alfred Bridges.

George Bennett vs Lewis Stevens & Michael Kinnard admrs. S Hunt R McMillin G Hulme. Plf in proper person no further prosecutes; Dft Michael Kinnard in proper person assumes payment of all costs.
William Parham vs Spencer Bateman. Debt. G Hulme R McMillin S Hunt. Dft came not; plf recovers of dft his debt damages & costs of suit.
Oliver Crenshaw vs Joseph Crenshaw. G Hulme R McMillin S Hunt. Dft came not; Jury at next Court to determine concerning the premises.

p.279 Wm Parham vs Wm Peebles. Debt. G Hulme R McMillin S Hunt. Dft came not; plf recovers of dft his debt, damages and costs.
Thomas W Casby vs Jesse Benton. Debt. G Hulme R McMillin S Hunt. Dft made default; plf recovers agt dft his debt, damages, and costs.

Nelson Chapman constable proved his attendance for 5 days.

Report of Jury apptd to mark a road from Big Harpeth bridge to road to Jefferson & Murfreesborough: signed Benjamin White John Nichols Joseph Braden Alexander White David Squire James G Jones.

S Hunt Robert McMillin G Hunt.

OCTOBER 1815

Williamson County. Court of Pleas & Quarter Sessions, at Court House in Franklin, Monday 2d of October 1815. Present the worshipful John J Henry, Archer Jordan, Wm Anthony, Alexr Mebane.
Jurors summoned: Elisha Williams George Burnet Horatio Pettis Watson Gentry exd Moses B Francis Henry Walker David Gillaspie Joel Dilliard James Andrews John Walker Joshua Farrington Josiah Knight Henry Lyon Danl German Wm Hope Adam Berry exd James Hadgraves Joseph Hassel William Joice Hadijah Collins John Thompson Thos Herrin Jas Caperton Wm Bond. Constables Samuel Cox Philip Bryan.
p.280   Grand jurors: Joshua Farrington foreman Daniel German William Hope James Andrews John Thompson James Carpenter Joseph Hassell William Jones George Burnett Hadijah Collins Thomas Herrin John Walker Henry Lyon Saml Cox constable. Discharged 6th day, Petit Jury also.

William Stewart vs Meredith & Fielder Helms. J J Henry Alexr Mebane Archer Jordan. Jury Horatio Pettis Josiah Knight Henry Walker Daniel McMahan James Armstrong James Stanley Bernard Richardson James Craig George H Prewitt Mansfield House Alexander Smith William Legate. Plf recovers damages and costs. Plf remits damages to $95 and stays fifa 6 months.

Deed Henry Ingram to William Thomas 60 acres proven by O Williams & Michl Kinnard.
Deed James Giddins to William Kerr 48 acres proven by Andrew M Kerr & Zach Drake.
Deed James White & Polly White to John R Boyd for her interest in estate of Ralph Fleming her father proven by Stephen Wood & Josiah Flemming.
Deed John Hill to Samuel Britten 55 acres ackd.
Deed John A Lagrand to Solomon Whitman 55¼ acres ackd.
Deed Samuel Jackson to Fredk Taylor 19 acres proven by Wm Williams & Jas Williams.
Deed Thos H McGaugh to Robt Osborne 125 acres proven by Noble Osburn & John Dalton.
Deed Thomas G Watkins by his atty in fact Oliver Williams to Marmaduke Stacy 90 acres ackd.
Deed Thomas B Smith to Archibald Carmichael 54 acres proven by Stephen Loyd & James J Williams.
Deed John Crafton to Robert Sammans 124 acres proven by Joseph Cole & Andw Craig.
p.281   Deed George Mansker to William Warren 54 acres proven by Marshal Jamison John Jamison & Burwell Warren.
Deed Edmond Haggard to John Vaught 73 acres proven by Thos Simmons & Wm Anthony.
Deed Thomas McCoy to Knacy Andrews 179 acres proven by Richd Tanner & Geo Kinnard.
Deed Robert Shannon to Daniel White 181 acres ackd.
Deed Edmund Grigory to Daniel White 274 acres proven by Joshua White & Wm White Jr.
Deed David Shannon to Samuel Fitzpatrick 200 acres ackd.
Deed George Mansker to Jno Jamison 200 acres proven by Michael Jamison & Wm Warren.
Deed Green Hill to Eldridge Newsom 1000 acres proven by James C Hill & Edam Austin.

Bill/sale Bartholomew Stovall to William McCline ackd.
Inventory/William Smith decd estate produced; ordered recorded.
Inventory Charles Johnston decd estate produced by Andrew M Johnston exr.
Supplemental inventory/James E Edmiston decd produced by D Edmiston admr.
Acct/sales estate of James Norris decd retd by Elizabeth Norris Adams.
Balance/acct of sales estate of Wm C Devereux decd returned by Wm Wilson.
Acct/sales estate of Willis Carson decd returned by James(?) Burgess admr and Peggy Carson admx.

OCTOBER 1815

Acct/sales estate of Susanna Barnes decd retd by Joseph H Scales admr.
p.282   Will of Frederick Browder decd proven by Alexr Ralston & W H Downing; Archer Jordan & Saml Perkins, executors named, qualified.
Will of Thomas Cole decd proven by James Bevins Jr & Wm Philips.
Will of Charles Johnston decd proven by Wm Anthony & Bartholomew Stovall; Andrew M Johnston one of executors qualified.
Will of Benjamin Humphreys decd proven by Henry Lawrance & John P Iron.
Will of Loumi Stephens decd proven by Richard Tanner & Charles Stephens.

License William Peebles to keep an ordinary at his dwelling; bond $2500 with Harrison Boyd & Martin Adkins securities.
License Samuel Martin to keep an ordinary at his dwelling; bond $2500 with Josiah Knight security.

Grant Jonathan Stapleton & Mary Kinny ltrs/admn on estate of James Kinney decd; bond $500 with David Montgomery security.
Grant Wm Bond & Francis Coleman ltrs/admn on estate of Henry Coleman decd; Bond $200, Jno Bond and Bernard Richardson. [A second, identical item, omitted here.]
Grant Judith Southall ltrs/admn on estate of James Southall decd; bond $500 with James Southall & Bernard Richerson her securities.
Grant John McKeny ltrs/admn on estate of Ebenezer McKeny; bond $600, Moses Oldham and David Craig securities.
Grant Mary Stephens ltrs/admn on estate of Loumi Stephens decd; bond $1000, Joel
p.283   Stephens and Michael Kinnard securities.

Order Robert Rogers oversee road from James Allisons branch to Harpeth ford at Robt Rogers; hands in bounds from Chas Calhoons to Goose crk to Overalls crk to Francis Young to Kimbro Ogilvie work thereon.

Order Henry Stephens oversee part of road to Buchanans between Hayes crk & Commissioners crk; hands from Hayes crk to Harpeth incl John H Eatons plantation & Fredk Davis work thereon.

Order George Critz oversee road of which Robert H Warren was former overseer; hands from Hinchey Pettway with Natchez rd to near Alexr Lesters to north of George Hulmes & Mrs Gray to John Minters & Robt H Warren to Alexr Lester work thereon.

Grant Jobe H Thomas ltrs/admn on estate of Anthony H Thomas decd; bond $2500, Phineas Thomas David Craig John Thomas & Finch Scruggs security.

Order James Caperton oversee road from Gideons on Fountain Crk to County line; hands from old Indian boundary to settlement of Enon Spring to Amos Duncan & Widow Johnson to settlement of the Staggs & Benj Curtis work thereon.

Order Wm G Boyd & hands & Robert Sharp work on road under Thomas E Sumner.

Order Samuel Williams John Edgar & William McMullin set apart for widow and orphans
p.284   of James Kensey decd one years provisions of his stock on hand.

Order Gersham Hunt and George Barnes settle with William and Jane Stone relative to

OCTOBER 1815

their admn on estate of Wm Stone decd.

Lansford M Bramlett admitted to practice law; qualified.

Order Eleazer Hardeman and Samuel Merritt settle with James Craig & Samuel Buchanan relative to their admn on estate of David Craig Jr decd.

Jesse Blacksheres heirs vs George Strambler. Daniel McMahon one of dfts bail surrenders him; Moses Chambers and Isaac Mairs special bail.

Petition of Rebecca Berry widow of James Berry decd for her dower of 240 ac whereon decd lived conveyed by Thomas Berry & 50 acres conveyed by Wm Berry adj same, order writ issue to Sheriff to lay off according to law the one third part of sd tracts.

Permit Sarah Slater gdn of Jonathan Slater to sell interest which Jonathan Slater has in two tracts of land in Montgomery County Maryland, also his interest in lots in City of Washington which belonged to heirs of Joseph Slater decd, also one which sd Jonathan has in his own right, and that his part of the profits arising from the sales be appropriated to support sd Jonathan a minor.

Appearance bond of William H Downing, securities Saml B McKnight & Alexr Ralston, to January Court, begetting a bastard on Susanna Wade.

Petition of Wm Wilson & Wm Edmiston gdns, order James Miller surveyor & Nicholas Schales John Buchanan & John Bostick freeholders lay off 50 acres at West end of p.285 tract where William Berry lived agreeably to bond given by Wm Berry to Charles McCord and assigned to James Berry dated 7 Novr 1803.

Metcalf Degraffenreid assignee vs Samuel Jobe & William McKey. Debt. Archer Jordan Alexr Mebane John J Henry. Defts in proper person cannot deny $50 balance of debt besides $4.62 5 mills damages. Plf stays execution until 1st March next.

Metcalf Degraffenreid assignee vs Samuel Jobe & Wm McKey. Debt. [Justices above]. [Worded as above].
Metcalf Degraffenreid assee vs Saml Jobe & Wm McKey. [As above].
Metcalf Degraffenreid assee vs Henry Lester. Debt. [Justices above]. Dft in proper person cannot deny $151.33½ part of debt, also damages & costs. Plf stays execution until 1st Feby next.

p.286 Alexander Moore vs Moore Bragg & Jno Davis. Certiorara. [Justices above]. Moore Bragg in proper person; plf Alexr Moore dismisses suit; dft assumes costs.

Nicholas Lanier vs John Osling. Attachment. [Justices above]. Jesse Bugg garnishee hath $4.93¾ property of John Osling, a note on himself for £4 7s 3d Virginia money or 104½ bushels of corn, empty chest, saddle without stirrips or other fixings, one book; he knows of property in William Wilsons hands 8 1/8 bushels of corn, also a sword & cocked hat and some clothes not liable for debts.

Deed Sarah Slater to Henry Slater Charles Slater David H Slater Edward A Keeling in right of Ann his wife Lunsford M Bramlett in right of Sarah his wife and Jonathan

OCTOBER 1815

Slater for sundry lots in Washington City ackd by Sarah Slater.
Letter/attorney Charles Slater E A Keeling Lunsford M Bramlett Sarah Slater to
Henry Slater & David H Slater ackd.
Court adjourns until tomorrow 9 0 Clock.   A Jordan James Boyd Robert McMillin

Tuesday 3d October 1815. Present Archer Jordan James Boyd Robert McMillin Esquires.
Bill/sale Archer Nolins to John Johnston proven by Wm R Nunn.
Depositions of John Davis Newton Edney Burwell Temple & Robt Thompson returned by
Sion Hunt & Robt McMillin Esqrs.
Will of Ephriam Stanfield proven by Henry Tally & James Brooks.
p.287   Deed Henry Rutherford admr of John Crawford decd to Zacheus German 80
acres ackd.
Deed George Tilman to Haden Tilman 104 acres ackd.
Deed James Frasher to Jacob Garrett 555 acres proven by David McEwen & Andrew Goff.
Deed William Hemphill to Jonathan Cooper 10 acres 46 poles ackd.
Bill/sale David Stewart to Moses Steele proven by David Christman also a condition
thereof Moses Steele to David Stewart proven by David Christman.
Deed Henry Lyon to William Easton 1 Lot ackd.
Deed Robert McClelland to Isham Mathis 134 acres ackd.
Deed John C McLemore to John Bostick 14 acres proven April by Charles Goode & Octr
by Josiah Cates.
Deed Andrew Steele to William Jordan Jr 78¾ acres proven by Stephen Johnson & John
Bostick.
Deed Martin Trantham to John Gracy 50 acres ackd.
Deed George Parks to Rebecca McLin Catharine Anderson John Anderson Robert Anderson
Margaret Anderson Agness Anderson Elizabeth Anderson Mary Anderson & Thomas Anderson 200 acres proven by William B Anderson & John C Goudy.

Deed William & Mary Neely to Nicholas P Hardeman 375 acres proven by David Squire &
Thos H Perkins.
Deed Cornelius Wilson to Thomas Staggs 70 acres ackd.
Deed/mortgage William Banks to David Dickinson 425 acres proven by David Mason and
Archibald Potter.
Deed Daniel McMahan to William Hemphill 21 acres 44 poles proven by Sion Hunt & W
Stemlay[Stencilley?].
Deed Abram Maury to John Reed 230 acres ackd.
p.288   Deed Henry Inman to Andw Donley 18 acres 136 poles ackd.
Deed Henry Inman to Caty McCluken 30 acres 122 poles ackd.
Deed Martin Stanley to Daniel McMahan 21 acres 44 poles ackd.
Deed Robert Corlett to Cornelius Wilson 110 acres 111 poles ackd.
Deed John Reed to Robert Corlett 117 acres 142 poles proven by John Tassell &
Cornelius Wilson.

On motion of William Tait by atty John White a deed/sale for 2180 acres from
William McClellan of Scotland in Great Britian to sd William Tait. Subscribing
witnesses William McNeel William Walker & James Walker are in another government so
that sd Tait cannot have them before this court to make probate, but that James
Gordon who is also a subscribing witness to sd deed has made oath that he saw sd Wm
McClellan sign & acknowledge same; James Gordon further saith he saw the other

OCTOBER 1815

witnesses subscribe their names thereto; oath of James Gordon is taken agreeably to above facts; order clerk certify same to be registered.

On motion of William Tait by atty John White a deed/sale for 1000 acres from Andrew Meir Jnr of Scotland North Britian; witnesses Alexr McClellan Wm Twinance and James Walker are in another Government; James Gordon also a subscribing witness made oath he saw sd Andrew Muire Jnr sign & ackg same; oath taken; order deed be registered.

Order William Wilson Thomas Wilson & Wm R Nunn set apart one years provisions for support of widow and orphans of Abram Anderson decd.

p.289   Release Wm McEwen from payment of tax on stud horse for this year.

Jurors to next Court: Knacy Andrews Jas Ridley Nathl Smithson Arthur Fulgham John Buchanan Christopher E McEwen Elisha Williams John Waters Enoch Bateman Tapley B Andrews Wm Hope John Smith David Gillaspie Britian Adams John L Fielder Jas Terner Archd Lytle Adam Berry Zacheus German Saml F Glass Benjn White Michl Kinnard Wm McKey Wm Shute John P Broadnax Abner Vaughan. Constables Wm Williams Jas Carothers.

Order Joseph Reed oversee road from Wolf pit by Bullers Horse mill to County line; hands on south side Big Harpeth in bounds of Capt Carsons company work thereon.

Order Peter Pinkston Geo Shannon & Thos Wilson lay off one years provisions for widow & orphans of Wm Stephens decd.
Order Clerk receive list of taxable property upon oath.
Order Nichs Perkins Sr Saml Moore John Witherspoon Wm J Boyd Robt McMillin John Porter Elijah Hamilton & Joseph Philips any five lay off a road from South Harpeth ridge to Franklin.

Appoint following persons to take list of taxable property and persons for 1816. Sherwood Green Esqr in Capt S Smiths Co; Robt McMillin, Anglins Co; Wm R Nunn, Capt Biles Co; Francis Jackson, Carsons Co; Samuel Merritt in Capt Hardemans Co; George Barnes, Capt Frosts Co; David K McEwen, Capt McEwens Co; Alexr Mebane, Andrews Co; Samuel Wells, Capt Wells co; Isham R Trotter in Capt Rees Co; Tristram Patton, Maddings Co; Collin McDaniel in Thos McCrorys Co; Sion Hunt in Capt McKeys Co; William Wilson, Capt Wilsons Co; Berry Nolen, Pinkstons Co; Edward Ragsdale in Hookers Co; George Hulme, Edmistons Co; Wm Banks in Capt Duberrys Co; John Witherspoon, Perkins Co; Nicholas Scales in Fitzpatricks Co; Archer Jordan in Gaults Co; Jesse White in Simpsons Co; Hendley Stone in Capt Richardsons Co.

Allotment for support of Polly Potts & children widow of Peter Potts decd returned. Order James Pavett have certificate for killing old wolf in this County.
p.290   Appt James Wilkins Newel Gracy & Hugh Dobbins lay off one years provisions for support of Frances Coleman widow of Henry Coleman decd.
Order John Aaron Wm Anthony & Thos Simmons settle with Mordecai Kelly relative to his admn on estate of Wm Owen decd.
Order David Mason & Sion Hunt settle with David Squire relative to his admn on estate of Gurden Squire.
Order Paul Dismukes and Wm J Boyd admrs/estate of Armistead Boyd decd sell so much of estate as may be sufficient to discharge debts.

OCTOBER 1815

Division/estate of Philip Jacob Iron decd among legatees returned.
Order Chapman White Wm White Wm Ashlin John Witherspoon Nicholas Perkins Sr & Robt McLemore any three lay off for Mary Boyd & family widow of Armistead Boyd decd provisions & crop sufficient for their support for one year.

Order Peter Hardeman oversee road from five mile creek to James Boyds; hands of Thos Barnet Elias Mayfield & James Boyd work thereon.

Order Archibald Lytle oversee road from five mile creek in addition to his former part of sd road.

Order John Gray James Carothers John Carothers Wm Reed James Cockrell David Johnston & Robt Johnston any five alter road from Nichols Mill to Nashville known as Commissioners trace beginning south of Mrs Reads house to hollow tree gap by way of Robert Carothers Senr.

Order Joseph Braden Henry Walker Wm McEwen David McEwen Martin Stanley Danl McMahan & Thos Haynes any five alter road on line of Benjn White beginning near Sharps branch on McConnico Mtg House Rd so as not to interfere with plantation of Mr Donnelson.

p.291 Order Collin McDaniel & Gersham Hunt let to lowest bidder John Wilson an object/Charity for his support one year.
Order Nancy Epperson allowed $40 for support of Elizabeth Epperson object/Charity for last year.
Order David Mason & Wm Banks settle with Sherwood Green relative to his guardianship for children of Samuel Clark decd.

Appt Alexander Smith guardian to Shadaric Lavina & Robert Reed minor children of John Reed decd; heirs of sd John petition for division of land belonging to estate.

On petition of Pryor Reynolds, order Samuel Moore Wm Ashling Edward Warren Joel Hobbs Wm Bonds Sr & Richd Steele partition 108 acres beginning at Hendley Stones lane on Henly Stones line to an old corn crib to back line George Reynolds to Stones line between the brothers & sisters of George Reynolds Jnr decd.

Order Jesse Jackson oversee road from Franklin to Murfreesborough beginning at McConnicos Mtg House; hands in bounds including Wm Marshall Wm Thomas to Plummers branch at upper end of David McEwens plantation to Hays Crk to John Richards plantation incl Michael Kinnard Chas Harald & Wm Denson work thereon.

Order Henry Swisher oversee road to Henry Childress; hands that worked under Thos Patton except those on plantation of Geo Hulme work thereon.

Order David Pinkston oversee road from Hurricane crk to George Kinnards still house; hands from Knacy Andrews incl Esqr Garretts leaving out David Anderson & F Taylor incl Richard Tankersly work thereon.

Order Jason Wilson oversee road from Berrys ford on Harpeth to Russells on Nash-
p.292 ville Rd; hands on Big Harpeth & Nelsons Crk incl Wm Wilsons work thereon.

OCTOBER 1815

Order James Armstrong oversee road to James Terrells mill; hands from Cowsarts to Edward Swansons to Terrells mill to Gray to Huggins to Sweeneys work thereon.

Order James Gambill oversee road to Shelbyville; begin at Harpeth River to Moses Ridley to Saml Gentry to Francis Nunn & Jas Gambell to Willis Carson work thereon.

Order George Allen oversee road from Columbia to Warren Court house, include all Tillmans Esrad Philip James Joseph & Ephriam Mair the Stephens John Smith Jesse Kennedy & David Riggs all hands in said bounds work thereon as far as Wm Logans.

Woodson Hubbard Clem Wall Andw Creswell Wm Alexander & Benijah Goodman apptd to alter Harpeth Lick rd towards Warners ferry on Duck River where it runs through land of Edward Ragsdale report in favour of the petitioner.

Order James Marchant & Azariah Anderson have ltrs/admn on estate of Abraham Anderson; bond $200 with Wm R Nunn & Benjn Russell securities.

License Edwd Harris to keep an ordinary at his dwelling house; bond $2500 with John House & Daniel Dean security.

Appt Matthew Elam guardian to Joel Elam a minor orphan; bond $500 with Robt Elam & Jeremiah Rope security.

Appt Spencer Reynolds guardian for Millage T Durham minor orphan; bond $1000, Wm Legate & Wm Logan securities.

Grant ltrs/admn to Thos Nolin on estate of Mark Thomas decd; bond $200, Berry Nolen & Kemp Holland his security.

Grant Enoch Bateman ltrs/admn on estate of Parker Bateman; bond $800, Henry Stephens & Wm Stephens security.

p.293 Grant Allen Hill ltrs/admn on estate of Elisha M Hassell; bond $300, Thos Garrett & Thos Ridley security.

Grant Lewis Stephens & Joel Stephens ltrs/admn on estate of William Stephens decd; bond $14,000, Garner McConnico Saml Shelburne & Wm Reed security.

Appt Robert Elam guardian for Elizabeth Elam minor orphan; bond $500, Thos Wilson & Moses Ridley security.

Grant Mary Tapley ltrs/admn on estate of John Tapley decd; bond $1200, Wm Legate & Wm Logan security.

Appt James Carothers constable in Capt McCrorys company; bond $1250, Andrew Carothers & Oliver Crenshaw security.

Appt Wm Williams constable in Capt Hardemans company; bond $1250, Samuel Shelburne & Alexr Mebane security.

Appt John Stacy constable in Capt McEwens company; bond $1250, Andw Goff & Joseph Braden securities.

Appt John Blythe constable; bond $1250, Alexander Mebane and Tapley B Andrews securities.

David Lewis age six bound unto William Carson until age 21 to learn occupation of a stone & brick mason, to read & right and to know arithmetic perfect to the double rule of three, to give him a good suit of homespun clothes a horse saddle and bridle worth fifty dollars.

p.294 Allotment for support of Mary Mairs & children widow of Samuel Mairs decd one years provisions produced and ordered to be recorded.

OCTOBER 1815

Allotment for support of widow and orphans of Willis Carson decd one years provisions produced and ordered to be recorded.

Bond for support of Elizabeth Eperson object/Charity for one year produced.

Acct/sales estate of John Shores decd produced by Saml Mays admr.
Acct/sales estate of Samuel Mairs decd produced by James McEwen & Mary Mairs admx.
Inventory/estate of James Rogers decd produced by Robert Rogers admr.

John Johnston resigns commission as a Justice of the Peace.

Acct/sales estate of Peter Potts decd produced by James McEwen admr.
Acct/sales estate of Thomas Simmons decd produced by Thos Simmons admr. Order John P Iron & Gersham Hunt settle with admrs or exors of Thos Simmons decd.

Inventory/estate of Parker Bateman decd produced by Enoch Bateman admr.
Bill/sale Andrew Goff to Peter R Booker ackd.
Acct/sales estate of James Rogers decd produced.
Acct/sales estate of James Carson decd returned into Court by Terry Bradley admr.

Bond John Crawford to John Armstrong for transfer of 128 acres proven by Charles Robinson.
Acct/sales estate of William Owen decd produced by Mordecai Kelly.
Inventory/estate of John Tapley decd produced by Mary Tapley admx.
p.295   Acct/sales estate of James McFadden produced by Robt McFadden admr.
Addl inventory/estate of Robert Murray decd produced by Genl L Nolen.
Inventory/estate of Anthony H Thomas decd produced by Jobe H Thomas admr.
Acct/sales estate of George Reynolds Jr decd produced by Pryor Reynolds.
Court adjourns until tomorrow morning 9 OClock.   S Hunt   Saml Perkins   Thos Wilson

Wednesday 4th October 1815. Present Sion Hunt Samuel Perkins John Wilson Esquires. Elizabeth C Childress widow of Henry Childress decd presented two petitions praying she might have dower allotted to her in 200 acres whereon sd Henry Childress formerly lived immediately before his death. Order Sheriff summon 12 freeholders to allot to sd widow one third part of the land afsd to include the house in which sd Henry formerly lived and the outhouses thereto belonging and also lay off to sd Elizabeth one fifth of chattel estate.

Deed Samuel Benton to John Campbell 140 acres in Dixon County proven by William Smith and James McCracken being dead his handwriting was proven by Wm Hulme, and same was ordered certified to Dixon County for registration.

Deed Charles Campbell to James Campbell 500 acres in Dixon County proven by George Hulme & William Smith witnesses thereto each of them saying it was their hand writing and that they did not know of ever signing their names as witnesses without it was really so but that they did not know when this writing was executed; Court then ordered same certified to Dixon County there to be registered.

p.296   Deed Samuel Barton to Charles Campbell 500 acres in Dixon County proven by

OCTOBER 1815

Archibald Potter and William Smith and ordered to be certified to Dixon County and there to be registered.

Transfer or endorsement on Grant #1383 from North Carolina to John Setgrave made thereon John Setgrave to Samuel Barton with H Murfree witness; death of sd Murfree being known, handwriting of sd Murfree was proven by Archd Potter & Robert P Currin and ordered to be certified to Dixon County there to be registered.

Settlement with Sherwood Green guardian for heirs of Samuel Clark decd produced by David Mason & Wm Banks.
Inventory/chattel estate of Absalom Taylor decd produced by Lany Taylor extx.
Inventory/estate of Jonathan McPherson decd produced by Hannah McPherson admx.

Order Levin Cator Charles Brown & Samuel Edmiston lay off one years provision for support of Hannah McPherson widow of Jonathan McPherson decd.

Bill/sale John Buchanan Senr to John Buchanan Jr ackd.
Acct/sales estate of Thomas Morton decd produced by Elizabeth Morton & Barnard Donelson admrs.
Grant Hannah McPherson ltrs/admn on estate of Jonathan McPherson decd; bond $300, John Carothers and Sampson Gray securities.
Grant Nathan Stuart ltrs/admn on estate of Lawrence Newsom decd; bond $1500, John H Eaton & Henry Walker securities.

Deed/gift John Buchanan Senr to John Buchanan Jr 600 acres ackd.
Deed John Reed to Cornelius Wilson 104 acres ackd.
Deed Guilford Dudley Reed to John Lemmons 100 acres proven by Moses Turner at July session 1813 and by Bethell Allen at October session 1815.

Gideon Pillow vs Charles Kavenaugh. Debt. Sion Hunt Saml Shelburne Collin McDaniel. Jury Henry Walker Alexr Smith William Morris Horatio Pettice Philip Malory Lawrence p.297   Thompson Josiah Knight James Cockrill Wm Shute Geo Strambler John Winn Wm McKey. Plf recovers agt dft debt and costs.

George Strambler assee vs John Mairs. Debt. [Justices above]. Jury Henry Cook John Sample Thos Ridley Martin Stanley Joseph Braden Jas Gray Page Bond John R Betticks Francis Gunter Geo Brooks Thos West Enoch Bateman. Plf recovers of dft his debt, damages, and costs.

Francis May vs Edward Warren. Debt. [Justices above]. Jury [above]. Plf recovers of dft debt damages & costs.

Wm Banks assee vs John J Henry. Debt. [Justices above]. Jury [above]. Plf recovers of dft his debt, damages, and costs.

p.298   Metcalf Degraffenreid assee vs John J Henry. Debt. [Justices above]. Jury [above]. Plf recovers agt dft his debt, damages, & costs. Dft prayed appeal.

Henry Lyon vs John P Broadnax. Case. [Justices above]. [Same jury except Thos Bradley for Thos Ridley]. Plf recovers of dft damages and costs.

OCTOBER 1815

Commissioners of Pulasky vs Henry Rutherford admr of Jane Crawford decd. Debt. Sion Hunt Saml Shelburne Collin McDaniel. Jury Henry Cook Martin Standley Page Bond Geo Brooks John Sample Jos Braden John R Bettick Thos West Thos Ridley Jas M Gray Francis Gunter Enoch Bateman. Plfs recover of dft balance of debt, damages, costs.

p.299 Isaac Roberts & others vs David Shannon & Robert Sayers. Debt. [Justices & jury above]. Plfs recover of dfts balance of debt, damages & costs.

Isaac Roberts & others vs David Shannon & Robt Sayers. Debt. [Justices & jury above]. Plfs recover of dfts debt, damages, and costs.

William Perry vs Sarah Slater & Henry Slater. Debt. [Justices & jury above]. Plf recovers of dfts residue of their debt, damages and costs.

Harry Lyon vs Wm W Cunningham appellant Wm B Eaton Archibald Potter his securities in appeal]. Motion of plf by atty John White. Justice/Peace before whom suit was
p.300 tried had not returned the papers to the Clerk within the two first days of this Term, order Judgt rendered agt dft Wm W Cunningham and security.

William Perry vs Sarah & Henry Slater. Debt. [Justices above]. Wm Mairs special bail for deft Henry Slater surrenders him.

Stephen Smith vs Ewen Cameron. Trespass. [Justices above]. Suit referred to determination of Joshua Farrington David Mason Geo Hulme & John J Henry or any three of them, their award is to be judgment of this Court.

Bass & Bedford vs Wm Hulme Shff. Not executing a writ on James Crawford at suit of Bass & Bedford. Motion overruled; dft recovers of plf his costs of defence.
Court adjourns until tomorrow 9 O Clock.   Saml Shelburne Saml Perkins C McDaniel

Thursday 5th October 1815. Present Saml Perkins Samuel Shelburne & Collin McDaniel.
Edward Swanson and Polly his wife to Joseph Phillips ackd by sd Edward Swanson. Polly his wife privily examined; ordered certified to Davidson County where the land lies for registration.

Deed William Hulme sheriff to James Gordon Stephen Childress & Robert P Currin lot #129 in Franklin ackd by Wm Hulme as Sheriff.
Inventory/estate of William Wethering decd produced by Wm Sparkman admr.
p.301 Acct/sales estate of Wm Wethrington decd produced by Wm Sparkman admr.
Deed Thomas Crutcher to Samuel Crockett Lot 117 proven by Jno H Eaton & John White.
Deed/gift John Rogers to Patsey Hughes part of James Rogers estate proven by Robert Rodgers.
Deed Robert Rodgers & James Rogers to Martha Rogers 200 acres ackd by Robt Rogers & James Rogers being decd ordered registered.
Deed/gift Martha Rogers to Robert Rogers proven by John Dalton and A Hughes.
Deed/gift John Rogers and Robert Rogers for his legacy in estate of James Rogers decd proven by John Dalton & A Hughes.
Deed William Hulme sheriff to Charles Boyles 440 acres proven by Archd Potter & John H Eaton.

OCTOBER 1815

Deed Peter R Booker to John H Eaton Lot 45 ackd.
Deed David Huston to William P Duke 70 acres proven by John H Eaton & Charles McAlister.

Hinchey Pettway summoned to appear as witness behalf Oliver Crenshaw agt Joseph Crenshaw came not. Fined $125 unless he shew cause of his inability of attending.

Robert P Currin [worded as above]. On application of Robert P Currin & sufficient cause shewn, fine set aside; cost to be paid.

Nicholas Tomlin reputed father of a girl child begotten on Elizabeth Hobbs gave
p.302   bond $500 with John Nichols and Alexander McCown securities to keep child from being chargeable upon the County; Nicholas Tomlin to pay Elizabeth Hobbs $20 a year for five years.

Order Hendley Stone released from guardianship for heirs of John Pryor decd as one of them has become of age on his making final settlement.

Order Nicholas Perkins D R Daniel Perkins Robert McLemore Edward Warren settle with Hendley Stone guardian for heirs of John Pryor decd, and make division of the estate among them and divide the negroes between Peter Pryor and Green Pryor.

Petition of William Wilson and William Edmiston guardians for heirs of James Berry decd, order William S Webb Joseph H Scales John Buchanan James Patton and Nathan Adams lay off to each minor to whom sd Wm Wilson and Wm Edmiston is gdn for their part of personal estate and their proportion of 240 acres on which their father lived and 50 acres adjoining.

Order Randal McGavock oversee road from Franklin to McGavocks branch; hands on John Donelsons plantation Moses Moore and others on McGavocks plantation and Nicholas Perkins hands work thereon.

Harrison Boyd ads Henry Stewart. Certiorara. Saml Perkins Saml Shelburne C McDaniel. Plf no farther prosecutes and assumes payment of all costs.

Kemp Holland vs Saml Andrews. Appeal. [Justices above]. Plf in proper person no farther prosecutes; dft recovers of plf his costs.

Thomas Bradley vs George Hulme. Debt. [Justices above]. Jury Josiah Knight Horatio Pettice Henry Walker John Buchanan James McCombs James Gray John Buchanan Wm P Duke Page Bond Charles A Dabney Kemp Holland John Johnston. Plf recovers of dft his
p.202   debt, damages, and costs.

Thomas Bradley vs Daniel Perkins. [Justices above]. Plf no farther prosecutes; dft recovers of plf his costs.

Metcalf Degraffenreid vs John Witherspoon. Debt. [Justices & jury above].
Plf recovers of dft his debt, damages, and costs.

Oliver Crenshaw vs Joseph Crenshaw. Case. [Justices & jury above]. Plf recovers of

OCTOBER 1815

dft damages and costs of suit.

Thomas Bradley vs John Witherspoon. Debt. Saml Perkins Saml Shelburne Collin McDaniel. Jury Josiah Knight Horatio Petice Henry Walker John Buchanan James McCombs James M Gray John Buchanan Wm P Duke Page Bond Charles A Dabney Kemp Holland John p.204   Johnston. Plf recovers of dft his debt, damages, and costs.

State vs Elijah Mayfield. A&B. [Justices above]. Dft in proper person plead guilty to A&B on Wm Alexander; fined $1 and costs.
State vs George Glasscock. A&B. [Justices above]. Dft in proper person plead guilty to A&B on Wm Tunage; fined $20 and costs.

State vs Turner Saunders. Sci fa. [Justices above]. Dft in proper person not having shewn sufficient cause, fined $500 the amt of his recognizance; afterwards, Court remits sum, deft to pay all costs.

State vs Wilkins Harper. Sci fa. [Justices above]. Dft in proper person, not having shewn sufficient cause, fined $500 the amot of his recognizance; afterwards Court remit sum afsd, but dft pays all costs.

State vs Henry Lyon. Tresspass A&B. [Justices above]. State no farther prosecutes; dft pays all costs.

John Den lessee of James Armstrong vs Garland Cosby. Ejectment. [Justices above]. p.305   Dft in proper person; James Terrell is bound as his security.

Metcalf Degraffenreid vs James M Gray. Debt. [Justices above]. Plf no farther prosecutes; dft recovers of plf his costs.
Court adjourns until tomorrow 9 0 Clock.   G Hulme William Banks John J Henry.

Friday 6th October 1815. Present George Hulme William Banks John J Henry Esqrs. Order John Witherspoon Robert McLemore & Henry Cook settle with Nicholas Scales and Nicholas Perkins executors of will of Peter Perkins decd.

Acct/sales estate of Hance Walker decd produced by John Walker admr.
Inventory/estate of Christopher Venatta decd produced by Alexr Ralston admr & Nancy Venatta admx.
Bill/sale John Crafton to Danl Wilks proven by Andw Craig.
Deed John Crafton to Sarah B Shelburne 76 acres proven by Andw Craig & David Craig.
Settlement with David Squire admr/estate of Gurden Squire decd produced.
Deed John Crafton to Daniel Wilks 36 acres proven by David Craig & Andw Craig.
Deed John Crafton to George Dennis Richard and Daniel Crafton 200 acres proven by David Craig & Andrew Craig.
Deed David Craig to Andrew Craig 100 acres ackd.
Deed William Sloan by atty in fact David McEwen to Wm R Bell (illeg) acres ackd.
p.306   Deed Demsey Dunn to Wm Coer[Con?] 100 acres ackd.
Deed Jacob Garrett to James Allison 555 acres ackd.

On affidavit of Hinchey Pettway; order fine agt him for not appearing as witness

OCTOBER 1815

behalf Oliver Crenshaw agt Joseph Crenshaw be set aside and he pay costs.

Acct/sales estate of John Radford decd produced.
Addl inventory/estate of John Radford decd produced.

Grant ltrs/admn to Jemima Gowing on estate of William Gowing; bond $800, Andrew Johnston and Isaac Bizzel her securities.
Order Jemima Going admx of Wm Gowing decd sell chattel estate of decedent.

Bond of Wm Walker Hervey Puckett & Daniel German heirs of Richard Puckett decd to George Hulme chmn and his successors in office produced by Garner McConnico admr.

William Bright vs Daniel Crenshaw. Trespass. Wm Banks Saml Shelburne John J Henry. Jury Josiah Knight Henry Walker Horatio Pettice Thos Ridley Wm P Duke Robt P Currin Edwd Stephens Isaac Bizzell James Standley Moses Chambers John Nichols James McCombs. Plf recovers agt dft his damages and costs.

Carny Felts vs Henry Dotson & others. Debt. Geo Hulme Wm Banks Saml Shelburne. Jury Murrel Bressey Thos Hiter Dixon Vaughan Saml Winstead John Winstead Wm Bright Francis M Dean Nicholas Tomblin Lewis Stevens Harvey Puckett Joel Stevens Jarrad p.307   Puckett. Plf recovers of dft debt, damages and costs.

Carny Felts vs Henry Dobson & Ruben Huggins. [Justices & jury above]. Plf recovers of dfts his debt, damages, and costs.

John Barber vs William Hemphill. Covenant. [Justices above]. Plf damages satisfied; he no farther prosecutes; dft pays costs.

Ephraim Davidson vs Henry Rutherford. Debt. [Justices & jury above]. Plf recovers of dft his debt, damages, and costs.

Robert Sprigg for use Wm & John Montgomery vs Hugh F Bell. Debt. [Justices and jury p.308   above]. Plf recovers of dft his debt, damages, and costs.

Wilson Gray vs Stephen Thomason. Appeal. [Justices above]. Court orders appellant give good and sufficient security before next court, or appeal to be dismissed.

Metcalf Degraffenreid vs John J Henry. Debt & Judgt. [Justices above]. Dft offers James G Jones and John P Broadnax as his security; plf by atty objected to security as insufficient; overruled.

Hinchey Pettway & Co vs Robt R Richards. Deft came not. Plfs damages to be determined by jury at next Court.
Court adjourns until tomorrow 9 O Clock.   G Hulme James Allison John J Henry

Saturday 7 Oct 1815. Present George Hulme James Allison William Banks John J Henry. Deed Abel Oliver to Tracy Carter 150 acres in Lincoln County proven by Richard Hightower and John Hightower.
Deed Abel Oliver to Tracy Carter 98 acres in Lincoln County [witnesses above].

OCTOBER 1815

Deed John Blackman to James Hicks 190 acres proven by Joel Hobbs & James Southall.
p.309   Deed John J Henry and Sally his wife to Benjamin White 52 acres ackd; privy examn of Sally; She appeared in open Court and ackd her act.

Order Hendley Stone and John Witherspoon settle with James Wilkins admr of John Dowd decd.

James Bradley vs Jordan Solomon. Si fa George Hulme James Allison Wm Banks. Plf by atty John White. Dft made default. Plf granted judgt and execution agt dft Jordan Solomon for balance of his judgt and also costs of suit.

Hugh Henderson admr vs William Hemphill. Depositions behalf dft to be taken of James W Batcheler James Johnston and John Morast[Mosart?] of Halifax North Carolina; plf admitted to take depositions [illegible].

Bill/sale James Bridge to Thos L Robinson proven by Peter Estes.
Bill/sale Jacob Garrett to Thos L Robinson proven by James Gordon.

Henry Cook apptd guardian to Sala N Sharp; bond $3000, Henry Lester Daniel Perkins Henry Walker & Andrew Goff security.

Celia Cross vs James Wilson. Order dft give bond by first day of next Term.

Lazarus Parkins vs Jesse Benton. Debt. [Justices above]. Dft came not; Plf recovers of dft his debt.

p.310   Grant ltrs/admn to Robert Bates on estate of Richardson Perry decd; bond $300, Jesse White and Caleb Mandley securities.
Deed Joseph Crenshaw to Clarissa Deshawney 1 Lot proven by Saml F Glass and Henry Hill.
Appt Henry Cook guardian to Searcy D Sharp; bond $3000, Henry Lester Danl Perkins Henry Walker & Andw Goff security.
Appt Henry Cook gdn to Sumner M Sharp; bond $300 [security above].
Appt Henry Cook gdn to Peggy N Sharp; Bond $300 [security above].
Deed/release John Sample for John Sample & Co and James Hicks to Peter Edwards ackd.
Court adjourns till Court in Course.   G Hulme   William Banks   James Allison.

A   George Mansker is released from payt of double tax on 177 acres and one slave for present year.
B   Order Beverly Reece oversee road from Legate & McCrackens mill to Edward Ragsdale and hands of Jordan Reece & Elisha North work thereon.
C   Ordered John Williamson Jones Glover John Roberts Richard Tanner David Lancaster George Kinnard & Frederick Taylor any 5 lay off a road from Glovers Gap duck river ridge to intersect with Harper Lick road between James Gibsons and Hurricane Creek.

OCTOBER 1815

p.311 D   Michael Kinnard Jacob Halfacre Robert Crafton Owen T Watkins and James Price apptd last Court to lay off a road from William Marshalls fence to road from Franklin to Murfreesborough on Commissioners creek report they had done so.
E   John Dalton Robert Rogers Spencer Reynolds Watson Gentry & Joseph Davidson apptd to alter road to Fishing Ford where sd road runs through land of Richard Oglevie report having turned sd road.
F   Order James Southall oversee clearing of road from Baileys ford on West Harpeth to big bridge as laid off by last jury.
G   Order William Bond oversee road from Frankin to Naches beginning at Baileys ford on West Harpeth and ending at bridge near Saml Bentons old place; hands in bounds from Saml Bentons old place thence to Leepers thence to Jonas Meadows to Elijah Hunters to Baileys ford to Leepers Fork to South Harpeth ridge to beginning work thereon under his direction.
H   Collector for 1814 vs Thomas P Curry. William Hulme Sheriff and Collector made report to January Session 1815 that sd Thomas P Curry reputed owner of 250 acres on Mill Creek hath not paid taxes due thereon; Shff cannot find goods & chattels whereon to distrain; to recover of sd Thomas P Curry 90 cents 6 mills and costs, order of sale issues.

[The rest of this book is blank].

--, Letitia 28
--pson, William 98
AARON John 128
ABERNATHY R 114
ACHOLS John 79 117
ACKIN Samuel 108
ACKINS John 86
ACLIN Christopher 97+ 105
ACOLS John 2
ADAMS Britain/Britian 2 17 23 32 33
  128 Charles 19 115 Jacob 69+ 91
  Jason 106 John 43 Martin 62-64 80+
  87 88 92 119 Moses 106 Nathan 45 72
  89 106 109 134 William 25 31
ADAMSON Loyd 9 10
ADKINS Martin 125 Thomas 58 68 74 97
ADKINSON Lucy 106
ADKISON Molly 106
AIKINS Samuel 58
AKIN/AKINS Samuel 4 13 14 16 25 58
ALEXANDER Captain 1 80 Ebenezer 30
  Nathaniel 80 Thomas 13 47 101 105
  115 116 Alexander 16 18-20 29 31+
  48 51 82 111 117 118 130 135
ALFORD John 39 83 104 William 89
ALFRED 96
ALLEN Bethel/Bethell 9 14 15 132
  George 37 45 52 53 71+ 130 Hany 92
  Henry 103 John 20 28-30 Thomas 14
  Valentine 48 74 William 35 80 90 95
  109 116 117 branch 116
ALLFORD Bentis/Burtis 37 John 40
ALLISON James 6+ 16+ 18 24 26 28 34
  38 40 43 47+ 49 54 55 66 70 73 74
  79+ 90 111-113 125 135-137 John 66
  branch 79
ALLMAN Thomas 81
ALMON Thomas 81
ALMOND Thomas 23 73 92
AMELIA COUNTY VA 6
AMY 73
ANDERSON Abraham 130 Abram 128 Agness
  127 Azariah 130 Branch 87 Catharine
  127 David 28 30-32 43 78 112+ 122
  129 Elizabeth 127 John 30 47 70 127
  Margaret 127 Mary 127 Robt 127 Saml
  54 Thos 27 79 94 127 William 12 127
ANDREW James 6
ANDREWS Athelston 48-50 55 62 65-68
  83 112 Athelstone 75 77 Atholston
  21 32 Capt 128 E 18 Eleazer 26 89
  Ephriam 10+ 13 14 22 36 40 42 47+

55 59 62 65-68 80 87 88 94 Ethelston 10 George 14 17 23 32 34 38 39
  48 50 58 71 84 89 94 95 111+ James
  25 118 124 John 36 37 39+ 59 63 71
  79 82 84 107+ 113 Knacy 2 18 22-24
  29 32 35 37 40 47+ 61 73 89 98 124
  128 129 Mark 24 72 Samuel 1 14 25
  52 82 84 113 114 119 134 Tapley 5
  22 51 52 60 128 130 Taply 89
ANGLIN Capt 18 55 91 92 109 116 128
  James 5 26 76
ANTERBURY Archibald 20
ANTHONY William 5 10 18 26 34 35 38
  40+ 50 57 63 65 75-77 80 82 91 96
  97 106 108 109 118 121 124+ 125 128
ARCHER B 28
ARMSTRONG James 39 107+ 124 130 135
  John 30 32 36 41 49 61 131 William
  88 109 113
ARRINGTONS CREEK 2 4 12 19 29 36 40
  46+ 47 56 57 69 75 81+ 107 119
ASCUE John 108
ASHLEY James 102
ASHLIN William 40 71 77 129
ASHLING William 129
ASHMAN -- 21
ASKEE Aaron 46
ASKEW Aaron 88
ASLIN William 40
ASTAN William 37
ATKINS Thomas 71 77 89
ATKINSON John 33+ 39 57 58 67 69 89
  91 blacksmith shop 37 45
AUSTIN Edam 124
AYDELOTTE Thomas 74 116
AYRES Polly 91
BADLEY Terry 90
BAILEY Henry 14 34 John 14 ford 81
  138+ pond 76
BAIRFIELD Stephen 57
BALANCE Bradford 45 79 Henry 29
BALCH Alfred 6
BALDRIDGE John 23
BALEY Henry 79 ford 78
BALLANCE Abram 79 Bradford 117 Henry
  30 65 Richard 52
BALLOW Ann 38 Thomas 38 39 50 Wm 72
BANKS William 18-21 23 28 33 41 45 53
  60 63+ 66+ 69 72+ 74-77 82-87 91 97
  98 100-102+ 105-107 110 127-129
  132+ 135-137
BARBER John 136

BAREFIELD Stephen 100
BARFIELD Stephen 1 17 86 91 92 94 102
BARHAM Ivy 5 Joshua 5
BARKLEY John 18
BARNES Capt 47 55 70 91 George 18 45
   72 91 118 125 128 Henry 1 Nathaniel
   25 91 Susanna/h 121 125   -- 80 89
BARNET James 52 Thomas 77 106 129
BARNETT George 14 Solomon 17
BARNS Captain 106 shop 91
BARR Hugh 58 112 creek 107
BARRINGTON James 55
BARROW Charity 70 Henry 70 Matthew
   70+ Milly 70 Rebecca 70 Susan 70
   William 70
BARRY William 115
BARTON Gabriel 31 Nathaniel 47 Samuel
   92 131 132
BASS Benjn 70 80 87 92-94 Kinchen 18-
   20 83 84 87+ 112 Laurance 118 Law-
   rence 63 73 119 Uriah 64 -- 133
BATCHELER James 137
BATE David 58+
BATEMAN Beniah 76 Bimah 76 Enoch 3 57
   58 91 128 130-133 Henry 32 Isaac 3
   26 91 Jonathan 76+ Parker 130 131
   Simon 65 76 Spencer 116 118 121-123
   William 1 7 8 10 11 29 50 76
BATES Robert 63 137 mill 88
BAYNEY John 2
BEARFIELD -- 92
BEASLEY Ann 68 Archer 30 33 E 57
   Ephraim 68 102 108 117 John 68
   Philip 99 100 115 Phillip 68
   Robert 68
BEDDIX Ruth 98
BEDFORD Benjamin 65 -- 133
BEDFORD COUNTY 12
BELCHER John 63 107
BELDEN John 63
BELL Carey 32 David 119 Hue 80 81+
   Hugh 71 76 101 105 106+ 136
   Joseph 56-58 71 Samuel 75 105
   Thomas 11 17 26 67 69 103 W 7 81
BELLOW William 3
BELLS ROAD 81
BENGES James 114+
BENNET George 118
BENNETT Alexr 61 Drury 26 George 27
   54+ 55+ 92 123 Jno 36 58 66 69 81
   89 Solomon 65 Thos 98 Walter 58 66
BENSON John 88+ 97 Labon 88

BENTEN John 28
BENTON Jesse 12 60 61 64 92 101 105
   118 123 137 Nathaniel 55+ 59-63 67
   95 97 103 Samuel 26 45 46 55 78 101
   113 116 131 138 Thomas 10 12 18 55
BERK Joseph 66
BERKLEY John 8 13 19 20 31 41 42 59
   77 86 103 -- 76 77 85
BERRY Adam 118 124 128 Basil 98 99
   115 Bazil 88 James 14 36 42 88+ 98
   99+ 105 121 126+ 134 Poley 100 Re-
   becca 88+ 98 99+ 126 Robert 121
   Thomas 29 32 39 40 47 70 71 81 85
   88 92 93 98 100-102+ 109 117 121
   126 Wm 98 100 105 126+ ford 81 129
BERRYMAN Anderson 35 76+ 87 Andw 14
BESHAN Benjamin 91
BETTICK/BETTICKS John 132 133
BETTS William 51 75 Zachariah 8
   -- 117 mill 56 88
BEVELL/BEVILL Edward 16 35
BEVINS James 125
BEZZEL David 28 Isaac 58
BIBB Cary 4 12 14 Carey 61 75
BIDDICK James 111 John 111 Ruth 111
BIDDIX John 97
BIDGES John 88
BIG CARTER 4 46 98
BIGER/BIGGER Robert 14+ 105
BILE Captain 128
BILES Stephen 43
BILLINGSLEY James 46 70
BISSELL Isaac 106
BITTICKS John 119-121
BIZZEL/BIZZELL Isaac 6 68 136
BIZZLE Isaac 69
BLACK David 27 33 34 James 5 8 18 26
   27 38 39 45 51 55 64+ 70 83 88 90
   93 95 98 116+ 121 Lusa 120 Mark 7
   Thomas 80 87 William 4 44 115
BLACKBURN Gideon 27 36 Samuel 16 29
BLACKMAN John 16 17 24 71 77 81 137
BLACKSHARE Jacob 103
BLACKSHERE Elijah 90 Jesse 126
BLACKSHIRE David 95 Elijah 95 Ezekiel
   94 95 Jacob 95 Jesse 95 Luke 95
BLAGRAN Harrison 102
BLAIR Harpeth 95 John 115 Mr 117
   Samuel 79 Thomas 24 74 80 95
BLOUNT Isaac 89 Jackey 100
   John 33 61 104
BLYTHE John 130 Samuel 40

BOB 73 82
BOILS Charles 44 61
BOIND William 14
BOLAND James 83 93
BOLIN William 88
BOMAR William 39
BOND Frances 98 104+ Harrison 54 J
  68 John 8 17 19 21 23 26 37 45 57
  78 125 Joseph 80 M 115 Maurice 82
  Morris 114 122 Morrison 83 Page 59
  75 132-135 W 48 William 5+ 6+ 14 16
  24 26 27 29 33 38 44+ 48 55 67 70+
  71 73 75-78 82-84 90 91 101+ 104+
  114 118 124 125 138
BONDS William 62 64 129
BOOKER Peter 30 31 100 102 111 131
  134
BOREN/BORIN/BORING William 14 29 98
BORRIS William 14
BOSTICK Absalom 73+ 81 Don 34 John 4
  19 27 35 70 75 79+ 88 89 94 100+
  101+ 115 126 127+
BOYD Armistead 97 118 119 128 129
  Armstead 65 Burnet 52 Harrison 8 12
  60 67+ 76+ 77 85 107 122+ 123+ 125
  134 James 11 12+ 24 25 28 30-32 34
  42-44 47 55 60 62 67-69 72 77 97-99
  101 106 110 113 118 121-123 127 129
  John 4 19 121 124 Mary 129 Rebecca
  97 William 1 8 12 55 62 65-68 78 88
  91-93 95+ 97 98 100 118+ 120 125
  128+ -- 110
BOYLES C 7 Charles 7 11 12 15 32 42
  54+ 55 60-64 78 85 112 133
  -- 13 112
BRADEN Joseph 7 8 37 45+ 53 59 60 61
  82 91 97 105 109-112 123 129 130
  132 133
BRADFORD John 120 Samuel 76+
BRADLEY James 45 53 137 Robert 99
  Terry 16 90 101 116 122 131 Thomas
  20 42 51 54 57 59 67 90 101+ 115
  132 134+ 135 -- 76 77 85 96+ 103
BRADLEYS MILL 51
BRADLY Thomas 105
BRADSHAW Saml 47 Wm 8 75 89+ 100 117
BRADY Murrell 64
BRAGG Moore 24 74 105 122+ 126
BRAK Mark 80
BRAMLETT Lansford/Lunsford 126 127
  Sarah 126
BRANCH John 59 84 Nicholas 45 47 53
  67+ 80 99
BRAND Joseph 90
BRANDEN Joseph 111
BRANDON Thomas 67
BRANLEY -- 108
BRANTLEY Abraham 5 34 Abram 34
  John 63
BRECK Walter 81
BREES Henry 80
BRENTHALL Edward 103
BRESERE Murrell 64
BRESS Henry 90
BRESSEY Murrel 136
BRIANT Archelus 120 Rebecca 120
BRIDGE James 137
BRIDGERS Joseph 29
BRIDGES Alfred 123 John 8 9+ 21 26
  30+ 88+ 106
BRIGGS David 17
BRIGHT Jane 99 Wm 60 83+ 103 136+
BRISBEY James 16 Rosey 16
BRITTEN Samuel 124
BROADNAX Jane 67 92 93 John 60 67 80
  87 92 93 98 101 103 105 108 109+
  121 128 132 136
BROCK Barit 111 William 111
BROOKS George 6 55 62 65-68 132 133
  James 23 127 Thos 11 21 William 57
BROWDER Frederick 81 92 125
BROWN Anna 81 Archibald 63 Benjamin
  45 53 68 69 95 100 Charles 8 23 71
  77 82 83 88+ 91 97 109 132 Daniel
  2+ 15+ Ephriam 9 17 23 24 34 55 62
  65-68 78 81 82 95 102+ 109 117
  Fredk 73 George 102 Henry 100 114
  Joseph 11+ 81 90 Littleton 114
  Moses 92 Nathaniel 82 88 Richard
  14+ Robert 32 Ruffin 22 29 31 48
  65+ 69 82 121 Samuel 5 16 20 35 45
  53 71 77 86 Sterling 65 Thomas 102
  William 34 43 91
BRUFF James 104
BRYAN Needham 114 Philip 116 118 124
BRYANT David 65 Rebecca 120
BRYTSAS John 17
BUCHANAN John 2 17 18 23 25 26 28-33
  35 40 46 109 126 128 132+ 134+ 135
  Samuel 17 126
BUCHANNON -- 88
BUCK Mark 90
BUCKLEY James 79 108
BUFORD Chas 3 Edwd 25 33 36 42 48+ 50

52 55 56 60 71 80 87 89+ 92-95
  Gabriel 10 72 90 118 119 James 89
  Spencer 25 44 64 72 91 97
BUFORDS FORD 24 68 72 106
BUGG Benjamin 2 11 22 24 34 43+ 63 88
  116 Ephriam 24 43+ 88 115 116 Jesse
  14 24 28 29 115 126 Lucy 43 Nancy
  24 43+ 88 Patsey 43 Polly 43 Sally
  43 -- 98
BUKLEY John 13 20 41
BULLERS HORSE MILL 128
BULLOCK Amos 15 54 97 106+ James 29
  Lewis 77 Nathan 15 29 54
BURGER James 101
BURGESS Abraham 28 James 105+ 124
BURNES George 37 42
BURNET George 124
BURNETT Drury 66 George 14 15+ 92-95+
  124 John 47 51 68 69 Walter 14
BURNHAM James 70 Joshua 70 115
BURNS Chitwood 37 George 105 Horatio
  100 Turbefield 109
BURROWS Francis 39 45 65 70 87
BUTLER John 28 Samuel 63 72 81
BUTT Archer 70
BYER Robert 105
BYRNS John 40 41
CAHOON Charles 49 79 88 George 54 55
  66 John 66 Wilson 61
CAIN James 118
CALDWELL David 8 14 25 Thomas 74 95
CALENDER Thomas 28
CALHOON Charles 14 29 98 108 125
CALHOUN Charles 79 George 3 63
CAMBELL John 100
CAMERON Dancan 101 Ewen 1 4+ 5 13 32
  36 45 58 68 69 76 83-85 95 101 111
  112 133 Frankey 36
CAMP John 9
CAMPBELL Alexander 51 Andrew 41+ 47+
  112+ Catlet 101 Charles 131 David
  26 Edward 46 Hugh 13 James 2 54 131
  John 27 35 39 45 48 51 55 62 76 92-
  95 121 122 131 Patrick 56 William
  39 47 75 -- 11+ 13 32 41+ 42
CANADAY Jesse 71 80
CANNACK Archibal 107
CANNON Clement 17+ Joshua 80 109 119
  Minos 24 69 72 80 Newton 2 11 13 27
  32 33 38 40 48+ 50 51 72 89 105
  121+ mill 17 24
CANSBY Jalund 61

CANTRELL Stephen 41
CAPERTON James 80 117 118 124 125
CAREY Thomas 105
CARLILE Betsey 3 Robert 3
CARLISLE Robert 116
CARMICHAEL Archibald 124
CAROTHERS Andrew 90 91 97 118 130
  James 59 61 73 108 119 120 128-130
  John 36+ 42 48 55 62+ 90+ 101 109-
  111 115+ 116 118-122 129 132
  Robert 90 100 101 113 129
CARPENTER James 124
CARR Joseph 55 mill 44 73
CARRELL James 120
CARROL/CARROLL James 50+ 111
CARRUTHERS John 62
CARSON Capt 72 81 109 128 James 17+
  28 38 46 49 62 79 90 114+ 116 131
  John 44 Joseph 19 22 39 44 Peggy
  114 124 Sally 116 Samuel 66 79 116
  Thomas 46 62 William 114 130 Willis
  90 115 124 130 131 -- 8
CARTER Benjamin 10 Daniel 11 20-22 25
  51 58 59 75 Francis 77 87 John 11
  21 Margaret 51 Mrs 115 Richard 106+
  114+ 115 Robert 23 100 103 Sally
  106+ Sarah 51 Tracy 136+
CARTTON Benagy 65
CARTWRIGHT Vincent 2
CARUTHERS James 32
CASH Dr 45 Jacob 107+ Thomas 6 14 36
  42 71 77 85 94 109 111+
CASBY Thomas 123
CASTLEMAN Abraham 5+ 16 Andrew 115
CASWELL -- 80
CATES Isaiah 50 Josiah 127
CATHEN Joshua 53
CATHEY Alexander 15 22 Andrew 3
CATOE -- 115
CATOR Levin 132
CAUSBY Jalund 61
CAVENAUGH James 110
CAVENDER/CAVINDER James 4 29-31 65 70
CERBY Thomas 91
CHAFFIN Nathan 23
CHAMBERS Moses 1 6 13 14+ 21+ 25 28
  29 31 38 48 50+ 51 71 77 83 85 109
  113 122+ 123 126 136 Samuel 12
  ferry 4 22 46 56 98 shop 65 69
CHAPMAN Nelson 6 36 67 108 109 123
  Samuel 91
CHEATHAM William 52

CHESTERFIELD COUNTY VA 6
CHILDRESS Edmund 94 Edwin 70+ Eliza 72 Elizabeth 76 131 Henry 38 46 66+ 68 72 76 83 86 94 107 129 131 John 66 68 Reps 19 Sally 94 Stephen 6 20 31 57 80 101 118 121 133 Thomas 94 William 107
CHITWOOD Edmond 23 Edward 63
CHRISMAN/CHRISTMAN Aaron 5 15 20 Abraham 113 David 5 15 35 36 117 127 William 63
CHRISTMAS William 14
CLAIBORNE William 32 61
CLARK A 83 Alexander 40 56 68 69 76 John 72+ 78 80 Samuel 44 49 92 93 129 132 William 60 61 123
CLAY Mary 59
CLEM/CLEMM James 1 5 12 42 55 62+ 83 90 91 97 101
CLEMON James 36
CLICK John 24 72
CLIFFT/CLIFT Daniel 27 117
COCHAN John 80
COCKREL/COCKRELL/COCKRILL James 57-60 117 129 132 John 13 21
CODDINGTON Benjamin 40 57 Jacob 57 John 57 Joseph 99
COER William 135
COFEE/COFFEE/COFFEY John 23 27 73 100 Reuben 35
COLE Abimelich 104 Andrew 16 Isham 22 29 30 58 Joseph 124 Sarah 16 Thomas 125
COLEMAN Ebenezer 33 41 Frances 128 Francis 125 Henry 86 125 128 Joshua 37 45 53
COLES Isham 68
COLESO[illegible] James 28
COLLENTON Benjamin 50
COLLINS Erastus 84 Hadijah 17 117 118 124
COLWELL -- 116
COMPTON John 60 Richard 29
CON William 135
COOK Edward 65 73 George 65 73 Henry 5 7 11-13 20+ 22 23 32 33 41+ 45+ 47+ 57 60 65 71 73+ 79 87-89 91-93+ 95+ 101-103 110-114+ 118+ 119 121 122 132 133 135 137+ Hy 117 John 65 73 89
COON Adam 106
COONROD David 4+

COOPER Jonathan 85 127
CORDELL Elizabeth 89
CORLETT Robert 127+
COSBY Garland 135
COTES Isaiah 50 51
COTTON Allen 4
COUNCIL Jesse 25
COVEY Thomas 105
COWAN Joseph 3 22 24 56
COWDEN Thomas 32
COWSAR/COWSART Andrew 15 37 48 54+ 55 68 74 104 106 116 130
COWSER -- 83
COX James 25 95 John 28-31 35 36 38-41 48 50+ 60 67 84 95 Samuel 1 10 11 17 26+ 27 31 74 77 100 101 118 124 Thomas 69 74 104
CRADOCK John 79
CRAFFORD Alexander 119
CRAFTON Daniel 15 30 135 Dennis 15 30 135 George 15 30 135 James 9 15+ 16 30 35 John 9 15+ 47 64 124 135+ Richard 15 30 135 Robert 15 19 40 64 86+ 138 Sarah 16 -- 2
CRAIG Andrew 14 17-20 23 32 64 67 85 86 124 135+ Archd 32 61 104 Aveline 86 Colonel 2 David 2 14 15 17 27 39 51 70 75 86 110 125+ 126 135+ James 17-19 23 46 70 124 126
CRANE Widow 64
CRAWFORD Elizabeth 39 45 Henry 24 98 James 24 111 133 Jane 133 John 18 21 24 25 27 34 39+ 45 74 82 127 131 Patrick 88 Washington 24 98 William 102 -- 93
CRAWLEY Benjamin 6
CREEK John 118 119
CRENSHAW Daniel 136 Henry 22 James 46 65 John 24 69 Joseph 10 24 65+ 69 95 123 134+ 136 137 Oliver 24 69 73 115+ 123 130 134+ 136
CRESWELL Andrew 130
CRISMAN Abram 37
CRISWELL Andrew 117
CRITCHLOW Henry 16
CRITZ George 125 Jacob 91+
CROCKETT Andrew 108 117 Captain 17 55 David 63 James 108 115 John 46 68 69 Joseph 18 32 36 108 117-119 121 Samuel 35 57 80 82 90 108 112 133
CROSS Celia 137
CROUCH John 73+ 79 88 90 96 103+

Solomon 73 Susannah 73 88 90 96 103
CROW Bryant 90 Isaac 9+ 10 16+ 22 30+
   31+ 40 48 53 57-59 65+ 82 90 92 116
   Polly 90 Thomas 90
CRUMP Fendall 34
CRUNK John 19 69 72 91 97 William 2
CRUTCHER Thomas 18 110 133
CRYTZ Jacob 104
CUCHEN Joshua 2
CUFF Andrew 21
CUMMINS David 1 37 45 80 89 91+ 100
   107 109+ 119 122 123 Samuel 28 47+
   55 69 76 100 101 105 118
CUNNINGHAM John 58 59 William 21 44
   45 59 74 75 133
CURRIER Jonathan 50 80 R 47
CURRIN Jonathan 83 109 112 118 119
   121 122 R 76 Robert 2-5 8+ 10 13
   17 18 23 26 27+ 31 35 36+ 40 41 45
   65+ 72 75 83 85+ 100 103 132-134
   136 -- 19 75
CURRY Bennett 104 John 5 39 44 78
   117 Thomas 138
CURTIS Ben 59 Benjamin 125
CUTCHEN/CUTCHIN Joshua 48 49+ 79 81
   100
CUTCHER Joshua 45
DABNEY Capt 76 91 106 Charles 45 53
   60 61 65 91+ 96 97 102 111 134 135
   John 71 81 84 111
DACON William 98
DALTON Captain 28 73 108 109 John 18
   36 48 55 56 62 71 74 113+ 114 124
   133+ 138
DAMIND John 63
DARBEY/DARBY Ebenezer 27 73 120
DARNAY William 90
DAVIDSON Charles 95 Ephraim 136
   Joseph 138
DAVIDSON COUNTY 9 83 133
DAVIES David 63
DAVIS Capt 5 David 63 Elisha 79 80
   118+ Frederick 36 39 44 46 48 63
   69 78 88 107 115-117 125 James 18+
   23+ 25+ 28 29+ 34 37 38 42 69 99
   100+ 116 117 John 23 32 89 100 104
   122 126 127 Jonathan 32 61 Moses
   8 88 106 Robert 16 25 30 86 99
   Sterling 8 10 -- branch 116
DAWSON Hudson 117
DEACON William 63 99
DEADRICK -- 19 75

DEAKINS William 25+
DEAN Daniel 130 Demsay 6 Francis 8-10
   13 67 103 104 Joseph 2
DEASON William 36
DEFRIES John 25
DEGRAFFENREID A 46 Abram 38 Allen 11
   Christopher 11 M 102 Metcaf 122
   Metcalf 7 16 20 58 76 77 83 85 87
   123 126+ 132 134-136
DEMOSS William 2 47
DEN John 40 42+ 60 68 75 85 93 96 97
   111+ 121 135
DENIKIN Amos 59
DENS -- 47
DENSON William 4 8-10 17+ 23 25+ 32
   33 50 57+ 67 69 71 77 98 107 129
DENTON Joseph 17
DEPRIEST Jno 1+ 11 89 91 100 Sarah 97
DERRIKIN Amos 59
DESHAWNEY Clarissa 137
DEVEREAUX/DEVEREUX/DEVEROUX/DEVEROX
   William 31 90 99+ 124
DEVERS BRANCH 37 74
DEVLIN Patrick 70 87
DIAL Joshua 105 Kinchin 105
DICKINSON David 1 5 8 21 24 28 40 43
   45+ 54-56 63 71 85 86+ 88 93 101
   107 127 Fanny 28
DICKSON Dr 119 Francis 72
DICKSON [DIXON] COUNTY 131+ 132+
DIERS -- 47
DILLEN John 92
DILLIARD Capt 18 26 56 91 106 Joel
   27 58-60 71 74 77 82 83 86 118 124
   Nicholas 32 56 58-61 84 95
DILLINDER Joseph 56 71 91
DINWIDDIE COUNTY VA 5 41
DISMUKE/DISMUKES Paul 118 128
DIXON Tillman 19 William 7
DOBBINS Capt 91 David 36 37 79
   Hugh 24 27 55 58 62 76 101 105 128
DOBSON Henry 25 58 93 102 136
   -- 15 54
DOBTSON Samuel 89
DOD Joshua 106 Kinchan 106
DODSON Elisha 54 83 Hightower 37
   Joseph 57 Lazarus 40 Paisley 74
   Reuben 83 Samuel 6 William 98
DOE John 31 39 83
DOHERTY Mrs 44
DOLOLDSON Barnet 79
DOLTON Capt 55

DONALDSON Berry 51
DONALSON/DONELSON Barnard 132 Barnet/Barnett 6 13 14 82 114 Beckley 114 Bernard 122 John 30 82 83 134 Rpbert 45 53 creek 24 78
DONLEY Andrew 127
DONNELSON Mr 129
DOOLEY William 74 78
DORCAS 82
DORTON Andrew 14 18 19 22 29+ 38 60 68 94 113 114 123
DOTSON Henry 136 Lazarus 97
DOUGLASS John 1 49 89 121 Jonathan 43
DOWD John 137
DOWDY William 5+ 6 14 16+ 18-20+ 76
DOWNING W 125 Wm 27 80 87 100 126
DOYEL Joshua 119
DRAKE Zachariah 67 96 124
DREW Newit 7 Nuvit 7
DRISKILL Obadiah 108
DUBERRY Capt 55 128 Charles 4 21 John 4 William 4
DUDLEY Francis 76 G 52 Guilford 9 17 23 56 71 84 Theoderick 15
DUFFILL John 37
DUKE William 134+ 135 136
DUMES David 63
DUNAGAN John 115 116 Wm 115 116 118
DUNAGEN -- 46
DUNCAN Amos 125 Matthew 92
DUNERGUT Leonard 34
DUNESS Thomas 54
DUNHAM Danl 93 122 Jno 103 105 Wm 105
DUNN Capt 28 David 6 15 18 20-24 28+ 29+ 32 33 39 44 45 51-53 55 65 66 72-74+ 86 99 100 102 107+ 120+ Demsey 135 Francis 12 Jeremiah 123
DUNNRIGHT William 34+
DURHAM Millage 130
DURNINS John 63
DUTY Thomas 15 54
DYER Joel 63 John 57 Steven 82 -- 81
DYSART/DYSERT Robert 15 54
EACHOLS John 45
EAKIN Samuel 64
EASON Joseph 104
EASTON William 127
EATON John 19 26 30 34 36 37 40 42 45-47 63 64 66 88 99 100 102-104+ 108 111+ 112+ 123 125 132-134+ Myra 104 W 111 William 102 104 133 -- 2 117

ECHOLS John 25
EDGAR jOHN 1 125
EDMINTSTON John 45
EDMISTON Capt 70 108 111 128 D 124 David 7 16 46 47 70 71 77 80 114+ James 114+ 124 John 1 80 89 91 109 119 Moses 70 Samuel 4 23 69 71-73+ 75 81 83 95 106-109 117 132 Wm 44 55 74 89 121 126 134 -- 40 89
EDMONDSON Captain 91 David 1 John 23 37 William 37 100 101 115
EDMONDSTON Captain 55 Thomas 49 Samuel 68 William 62 65-68
EDNEY Alson 5 36 42 43 70 71 77 103 112+ 119 Newton 107 127
EDWARDS Adonijah 68 75 Peter 36 90 137
ELAM Diana/Dianna 24 47 109 Edward 1 7-11 13+ 73 91 97 120 Elizabeth 130 Joel 130 Matthew 130 Robert 91 130+ Stephen 24 47 109 116
ELLISTON Joseph 15+ 16
ENGLEMAN Joseph 55
ENON SPRING 59
EPERSON/EPPERSON Anderson 80 90+ Betsey 80 Elizabeth 116 129 131 Littleberry 2+ 16 27 44 56 72 108 116 Nancy 129
EPPS John 9 30
ERVIN William 97 -- 90 105
ERWIN Christopher 79
ESTES Peter 30 122 123+ 137 Robert 12 Samuel 10 11 81
EVANS Benjamin 48 123 Isam 90 Jesse 104 John 45 48 51 67 79 81 100 117 William 111
EVENS David 66 John 73 Martha 66
EVERETT John 79
EWEN Andrew 110
EWIN -- 105
EWING Andrew 92 104 108 -- 101
EZELL Baalam 15 54 Hansel 121
EZZEL Mr 104
FAIRCLOTH Cordil 116
FARMER Richard 37 Thomas 117
FARMINGTON Joshua 91
FARRAR Clement 97 Joseph 34 98
FARRIER Joseph 63
FARRINGTON Joshua 71 91 118 124 133
FELLMAN George 3
FELTS Carny 136+
FEN Richard 42

FERGUSON Isaac 27 34
FIELDER Elizabeth 97 Jane 1 John 1
  23 28 37 45 48+ 72 80 89 91+ 95 128
  Nimrod 25+ 37 45 89 William 107
FIELDS N 65 Nelson 5 17 25 79+ 112
  121
FILLIS 51
FINDLEY Polly 111 Samuel 111
FINLEY -- 98
FIPPS/FIPS Jordan 80 82 83 85 101
FITZ John 97
FITZGERALD John 3 97 115 116
FITZPATRICK Captain 69 91 100 112 128
  Samuel 124
FIVES William 71
FLEMING Ralph 124
FLEMINGS Mrs 73
FLEMMING Josiah 124
FLETCHER Thomas 48
FLOURNOY Francis 14
FLOYD William 2 59
FLY Elisha 25 80 91 Jeremiah 102
  John 102 Lawrence 63 William 102
FOREHAND Thomas 35
FORGERSON Isaac 3
FOSTER Anthony 48 86 Ephriam 99
FOWLER Richard 69 105
FOX Hugh 77
FRANCIS Moses 28 69 99 118 124
FRASHER James 127
FRAZIER James 16
FREEMAN Jeremiah 90 John 57 115
  Saunders 57 115
FRIERSON David 93 Moses 36 Wm 11+
FROST Captain 128
FULGHAM Arthur 14 29+ 82 128
FULLERTON Thomas 84
FUSSEL/FUZZELL John 110 111
FWER William 71
GAINES Anthony 28
GALLOWAY Enoch 3 4 44 45 82
GAMBELL James 130
GAMBILL James 130 Milton 94
  Whittson 118
GAMBLE Milton 67
GANTTS James 18
GAREY John 1
GARNER John 113 Roberta 82 William 99
GARRETT Abel 73 89+ Able 24 Capt 5 18
  55 109 Esquire 129 Jacob 5 8-10 25
  26 28-30 34 40 44 47-49+ 51 52 56
  57 59 64 67 72 73 102 115+ 127 135

  137 James 68 Lerois 34 Squire 37
  Thomas 18 30 45 50 53 55 65 70 74
  77+ 106 108+ 115 130 -- 56
GARY John 8 69
GATLIN William 40 41
GAULT Captain 63 70 91 128
  James 18 27 42 96
GEE David 36 91 96 102 James 8-10 24
  74 102 John 8-11 13 18-20
  Neavel/Nevil 34+
GENTRY George 46 79 95 97+ 108 118
  James 40 76 79 83 89 93 94 Nicholas
  46 62 71 79 97+ 118 Saml 7 17 46 90
  97+ 108 130 W 88 Warren 71 Watson
  56 88 89 113 114 118 121 124 138
GERARD Charles 122
GERMAN Daniel 3 45 53 63 70+ 71 91 97
  107 118 124 136 Elizabeth 71 Joseph
  21 100 Matilda 71 Michael 71
  Zachary 107 Zacheus 17 23 32 34 35
  39 55 71 127 128
GERRARD Charles 121
GHOLSON Benjamin 6 14 36 48 50 51 54
  76-78 83 90 101 122 John 16 22
GHOLSTON Benjn 42 50 52 55 62+ 83 121
GIBSON James 26 37 99 137 John 16 37
  63 90 Patrick 70 90
GIDDEN Captain 5 70 James 68 -- 67
GIDDENS Francis 64 70 72 108 James 18
  26 27 33 38 45 56+ 62 64+ 66-68 71
  74 89+ road 24
GIDDINS James 83 124
GIDENS Francis 59
GIDEON Captain 55 James 55 62 113 116
  road 106
GILBERT 82
GILBERT William 38
GILES COUNTY 104 119
GILLASPIE David 5 6 16 20 36 71 78 84
  89 94 109 117 118 124 128 George
  53 67 Isaac 6 20 John 6 15 32 61
  94 Thomas 20 27 -- 15 54 72 84
GILLIAM Anthony 13 James 89
GLASCOCK George 100
GLASS Samuel 6 14 18-21+ 45 53 59-61
  74 85 91 94 103 112 119 128 137
GLASSCOCK George 68 86 94 101 135
GLIMP George 105
GLOVER James 45 Jones 26 37+ 57 90
  137 Lancaster 7 10 14 16 21 22 25
  36 95 Wm 6 9 10 15+ 25 33 40+ 41+
  42 57 78   gap 26 37+ 45 57 90 137

GOCEY, James 16
GOFF Andrew 14+ 15 17 21 25 54 57 67+
  74 80 82 98 108-110 127 130 131
  137+ John 15 53 Thomas 43 52
  William 48 82 100 119 120 -- 15
GOFORTH George 64 117
GOING Jemima 136
GOLLADY/GOLLIDAY George 61 123
GOOCH Thomas 4 15 17 109 113
GOODE Charles 127 Squire 76
GOODMAN Benijah/Benjah 117 130
GOODWIN Samuel 101
GORDON James 3 10 15 16 21-23+ 27 43
  49 64 72 76+ 77 85+ 127 128+ 133
  137 John 58 Moses 97 118
GORE Edward 97
GOSSAGE Edward 14 17 21+ 26 29 33 35
  39-41+ 50+ 51 69 100 115 116
  John 48
GOUDY John 127
GOWING Jemima 136 William 136+
GRACY Newel/Newell 74 116 128
GRAHAM Edward 4 Ezekiel 22 John 89+
  Richard 24 29 94 101 Robert 89+
  Samuel 87 Thomas 4
GRAY Alexander 121 Archibald 106
  Deliverance 5 16 Jacob 3 6 31 51
  54 64 73-75 80 87 88 90 91 97 101
  110 121 122 James 1 31 36 39 86 89
  102 105 108 132-135+ John 15 23 24
  29 53 57+ 68 108 121+ 129 Mrs 125
  Robert 22 31 40 58 94+ Sally 30 31+
  39 40 51 Sampson 132 William 102
  Wilson 136 Young 27 30-32 36 40 51
  59 66+ 86 90 101 110 -- 83 130
GREEN Esqr 76 James 39 82 87 S 65 66
  Shearwood 57 79 92 Sherrod 44 Sher-
  wood 6 45 48 49 55 63 65 67 73-75
  92 96 101 105 128 129 132 Vincent 5
GREER M 108 Vincent 9 45
GRESLEY Benjamin 17
GRIFFIN Lott 115 116 William 111
GRIFFITH John 35
GRIGORY Edmund 124
GRIMES William 67
GRINDER Robert 107
GRISSAM George 117
GROVES William 118
GUCH Thomas 91
GULLETT James 15+ 22+
GULLEY Jesse 88
GUMAN Daniel 3

GUNTER Charles 101 Francis 22 48 53
  78+ 82 85 92 132 133 Michael 24
  Sterling 101 122
GURLEY Benjamin 26 James 76
  Jeremiah 30 31 William 30
GUTHRIE Robert 14 24 58 71 74 77 79
  86 96 101 114 Sam 94 !
HADGRAVES James 124
HADLEY Ambros/Ambrose 54 80 87 88 94
HAGGARD Edmond 124 Samuel 5 23
HAIL Stephen 29 John 64 72 80 108
HAILE Stephen 14 88 William 14+
HAILEY John 36 42 William 53
HAINES Thomas 60
HALBERT William 99
HALE E 87 Elihu 19 44+ 54+ Moses 43
  Stephen 14 98
HALEY John 3 Richard 94 William 45
  creek 88
HALFACRE Jacob 17 29 30 35 64 80 87
  111 112 138
HALIFAX COUNTY NC 74 89 137
HALL Burgess 107 Clem 117 Clement 28
  Elihu 94 100 John 100+ 117 Joseph
  116+ Stephen 105
HALS H 100
HALSEY Charles 33
HAMBLETON Elijah 119
HAMER Andrew 34 Daniel 25 29 89 102
  109 119 122 123 Harris 25 John 25
  37 45 89 93 109 119 Susannah 93
  102 William 25 89 119
HAMILTON Elijah 55 62 67+ 98 109 116
  118-122 128 Wm 63 94 116 -- 38
HAMMOND John 28 -- creek 37
HANES George 81
HANKS George 102
HARALD Charles 129
HARDEE James 52 59
HARDEMAN Bailey 15 Captain 128 130
  Constant 100 Eleazer 6 46 63 69 91
  101 106 118+ 126 James 118 John 2
  3 6 12 22 25 27 35 42 47 49 51 60
  102 N 34 82 83+ Nicholas 2 22 32
  36+ 38 42 56 60 65 95 99+ 127
  Peter 55 62 64-68 77 92-95 129
  Thomas 15 98 100 106 109 117
HARDEN Jacob 40 James 30 Jeremiah
  31 Jesse 29 John 31 32 60 61 67
  97 117 Mark 67 Thomas 97
HARDER Jacob 7+ 8 11 13 41 65
HARDGRAVE/HARDGRAVES James 5 10 118

HARDGROVE James 10
HARDIN Jeremiah 25   John 29 33 47 58
  Presley 27   Thomas 80
HARDING John 88   Thomas 3
HARDRICK Thomas 24
HARGRAVE Stephen 117
HARGROVE John 28   Stephen 109
HARLEY John 90
HAROLD Captain 91
HARPER Wilkins 100 120-122 135
HARPERS LICK 137
HARRALD Charles 17
HARRELL Abraham 35   Charles 35 36 64
  69   Mary 35
HARRIS Andrew 15   Charles 55   Ede 15
  Edith 27 43   Edward 130   George 81
  Josephine 27   Josephus 35   Patsey 43
  Samuel 55   -- 66
HARRISON Allen 64   Ann 3 4 15 64
  Nathaniel 4   Widow 37   William 4 30
  42 64-66 73 76 78 94 107   -- 108
HARRISS Andrew 14 27   Eli 92
HART Joseph 51   William 104
HARWELL Bucknell 39   Buckner 43
HASSEL/HASSELL Elisha 24 130   Joseph
  5 7 8 71 76+ 77 86 118 124+
  Zebulon 104
HAWES FORD 90
HAY Baalam 33 69   John 15 54
  Richard 37 45 57 63 72 78 90
HAYES John 18 104   Wm 32   -- 7 creek
  2 4 17 30 57 69 71 88 98 106 125
HAYNES George 73   John 38   Thomas 18-
  20 25 29 42 51 85 86 129
HAYS George 120   O 64   John 7 12
  creek 36 46 57 107 117+ 129
HAYWOOD John 48
HEATON Enoch 114
HELM/HELMS Fielder 60 74 77 93 94 101
  124   Meredith 13 22 45 101 124
HELVE Thomas 90
HEMPHILL William 28 29 31 110+ 127+
  136 137
HEMPHREYS Solomon 25
HENDRICKS Thomas 64
HENLEY John 59
HENDERSON Ann 102   Archibald 28   Benjamin 70   Hugh 102 119 137   James 100
  Littleton 117   Samuel 89   Wm 70
HENDRIX Thomas 63 68 69 72+
HENRY Isaac 17 18 23   James 123   John
  7-14 16 17-22 31-33 37 45 48 49 55

58 63-67 76 80+ 88 91-93+ 95 98-
100+ 103-105 108 110-112+ 118 120
124 132+ 133 135-137   Lavenia 93
Mary 93   Sally 11 92 93 137   Sarah
67   Thomas 63
HERBERT John 31 39 89   Nathaniel 4 91
  Richard 4 31 39 58 75 89
HERNDON James 9
HEROLD Charles 98
HERON SETTLEMENT 98
HERRALD Charles 57
HERRIN Andrew 33 57 58+ 69 91 97 112
  James 24   Thomas 124
HERRON Andrew 68 97   James 97
  Thomas 57 75 97 101 109 117 118
  settlement 106
HEWS Richard 58
HEWSTON John 68   Lidia/Lydia 62 63 67
  Samuel 62 63 64
HICKMAN Captain 30 55   Wm 18 47 93 95
HICKS James 4 11 34 36 47 68 71 77 81
  96 102+ 137+   William 67
HIDE Richard 80
HIGGINS Albert 78   John 78   Philemon 78
HIGHTOWER John 136   Richard 6 14 24
  45 50 52 80 101 136   -- 117
HILBOURN Ambros 77
HILL Abraham 61   Abram 7   Allen 45 53
  56 61 66 71 84 99 121 130   Capt 49+
  55   Daniel 68   Dann 69+ 76 81 107
  Denne 36   Green 22 120 124   H 115
  Henry 34 82 137   James 3 6 27 34
  65+ 67 78 124   Jimmey 6   John 11 19
  24 27-29 35 37 38 41 44-46 49+ 51
  53 55 56 59 64+ 65+ 70 73+ 78+ 79+
  80+ 84 87 108 117 124   Joe 6+   Jorden 22   Joseph 3   Moses 6+   Rebecca
  76   Robert 35 41 45 50+ 79   Sally 3
  6   Sarah 6   Spencer 91 109 119   Thomas
  57   Walter 16 17 26 31 38   Will 3 6+
  William 8-10 17 20 26 31 34 38 62
  73 105 108
HILLIARD Isaac 28 102 107+   John 87
  Micajah 84
HINDS Polly 37
HINE William 34
HINSON Thomas 95
HITE Thomas 91
HITER Thomas 72 74 84 94 97 101 104
  110 111 136
HOBBS Elizabeth 134   James 36   Joel
  14 22 24 34 36 52 55 73 76 81+ 82

83 94 102 129 137 Jno 36 Solomon 36
HOBS Joel 64
HODGE Francis 64 John 64+ 72 Robert
 123 William 64
HOGAN David 60 74 77
HOGES -- 78
HOGG John 101 Robert 54 Thomas 3
HOGIN Isaiah 26
HOGUE -- 24
HOHN John 85
HOLLADAY Peter 9
HOLLAND Gustavus 117 James 38 Kemp
 8 57 73 76 77 83 118 130 134+ 135
HOLLANSWORTH Joseph 97
HOLLIDAY David 70 92 Mary 92 Peter
 45 53+ 79 117
HOLLOWAY John 13
HOLLINSWORTH Joseph 105
HOLLTIME Kemp 5
HOLM Meredith 6
HOLMAN Daniel 86
HOLMES Isaac 61 Moses 15
HOLSTEAD Elizabeth 86
HOLT Harden 64 John 50 109
HOOD Edward 72 91 97 107 Elisha 63
 66 99+ 109 -- 108
HOOKER Captain 17 49 55 56 70 91 109
 128 William 6 18 26 39 94 110
HOOKS Curtis 22 102
HOPE Eli 38 46 98+ James 104
 William 1 13 60 62 63+ 71 80 81 92
 93 97 101 105 118 124 128
HOPKINS James 54 99 Jason 16 21 23+
 31 36 40 41 45 45 53 76 77+ 90 94
 95 100-105 John 2 17 26 33 62
 Widow 56 88
HORBERT Richard 14
HOUSE Green 32 35 Isham 26 118 James
 10 12 15+ 16 20 32 54 72 84 John
 43 78 82 84 85 91 130 Mansfield 124
 Nicholas 84 William 17 26 32 110
HOUSTON David 18-21 26 27 67 88 89
 115 Samuel 67 William 5 8
HOWDESHALL Jacob 16
HOWELL Buckner 75 Joseph 37 mill 65
HOWELS MILL 69
HUBBARD Richard 119
 Woodson 14 117 130
HUGGINS Reuben/Ruben 65 136
 -- 83 130
HUGHES A 133+ Archilaus 113 114
 Elizabeth 22 James 47 73 76 81

Owen 22 Patsey 133 Richard 1 13
 24+ 58 74 100 105 115 118 119
 -- 81
HUGHS Owen 22 Richard 101 122
HUGHSTON John 106
HULME George 1-7 12 14 16 18-23 25
 27+ 29-36 38 41-45 49-51 55 56 58
 60-63+ 65-69+ 75-78 81-89 91-95 97
 98 100-107+ 109-115 118-123 125 128
 129 131 133-137 John 78 Margaret
 87 Mrs 74 Peggy 67 68 102 103
 Robert 1 47 Thomas 2 16 21 27 75
 William 4 12 21 23 27+ 32 33 47 48
 54 64 68 72 73 78 88 91 93-95 99
 100 104 105 108 112+ 131 133+ 138
HUMPHREYS Benjamin 25 125
HUNT Elisha 64 G 7 53 89 Gersham 7
 10+ 17 20 25 31 34 37 45 50 55 63
 70 89 98 106 118-123 125 128 131
 Sion 1 3 7 8 16 17 25 27 32 42-45
 55 61 62 64+ 68 70 73+ 74 80 87-89
 92-95 98+ 106 107 109 113 115 116
 119 122 123 127+ 128+ 131-133
HUNTER Abraham 39 Andrew 81 97
 Elijah 23 39 58 63 78 82 107 138
 Henry 26 35 58 59 70 76 83 105
 John 4 26 William 21 trace 36
HURRON James 72
HURST William 104
HURT Bird 64 Elisha 64 Henry 64 Is 64
 James 64 Jo 64 John 64 Milly 64
 Moses 64 Sally 64 William 64
HUSS Bryant 89
HUSTON David 134 John 2 William 38
HUTCHINSON William 70
HYDE B 115 Hartwell 46+ 73 93 115
 Richard 2 18 23+ 27 37 44+ 46 73+
 87 100+ 101 105
INDIAN BOUNDARY LINE 44 59 125
INGRAM Henry 30 71 75 93 106 111+ 124
INMAN Henry 2 33 35 38-41+ 127+
INOIS John 58
IRION Ann 121 John 5 76 79+ 106 121
 Philip 119 Sarah 79
IRON George 121 John 107 108 125 131
 Philip 106 121 129 Sarah 108 118
ISSELS Frederick 83
IVEY/IVY Frederick 35 108 109
JACKSON Francis 64+ 65 79 90 91 109
 128 Henry 97 103+ 111 James 35 74
 85 93 96 122 Jesse 35 129 John 44
 103 Mark 108 Richard 64 117 Samuel

29 33+ 40 61 110 113+ 114 124
  Sarah 110 Thomas 115 William 14
  105+ Zachariah 44 53 80 88 92
JACOBY Jacob 33 86
JAMES George 22 51 58 60 61 86 101+
  105 Moses 71 Mr 49 Philip 80
  -- 75 96+
JAMISON John 124+ Marshal 124
  Michael 124
JARMAIN Joseph 64
JARMAN Zacheus 34
JEFFERSON COUNTY, VIRGINIA 102
JENNY 82
JERMAN Daniel 64
JINKINS Dempsey 28
JOB Aron 99
JOBE Samuel 126+
JOHNSON A 47 Alexander 29 69 99 Anne
  109 Andrew 1 8+ 13 25 27 Benjamin
  28 Capt 91 109 Charles 17 18 26 73
  Jesse 110 John 10 23 36 90 109 114
  115 123 Matthew 29 114 115 Patsey
  109 Polly 23 Robert 15 115 Stephen
  109 127 Swanson 14 36 94 Widow 125
  -- 114
JOHNSTON Alexander 2 67 69 88 105+
  Andrew 5 26 32 47+ 59 80 87 88 124
  125 136 Capt 55 Charles 17 47 124
  125 David 38 51 69+ 129 James 137
  Joel 47 John 8 9 11 14 18 19 25+ 26
  28 31 36 38 40+ 41 49+ 55 58 62 76
  80 113 114+ 122 127 131 134 135
  Matthew 25 114 Robert 15 53 69+ 71
  113 114 129 Stephen 107 Swanson 58
  Widow 59 -- 46
JOICE James 7 116 William 124
JONES Abigail 66 Amsey 66 121 Amze
  112 Arnsey 66 Capt 76 91 111 David
  2 5 Elisa 114 Eliza 75 Elizabeth 2
  66 67 83 George 99 Isaac 35 Jackey
  66 James 50 52 53 67 76 83 84 90-93
  97 105 109+ 110 112 114 117 123+
  136 Jesse 98 Joel 35 John 11 21
  23+ 35 Julia 86 Thomas 23+ 33 43
  48 55 61 62 65-68 118 William 13 23
  25 36 42 118 120 124
JORDAN Andrew 40 Archer 31 40 63 69
  70 73-75 91 105 108 109 115 124-128
  Archie 55 Benjamin 109 Benton 23
  Berton 27 31 Burton 18 19 23 George
  109 Hezekiah 4 James 110 112 121
  122 John 35 36+ Johnson 109 115 122

123 Johnston 118 122 123 Nancy 36
  Stephan 105 Stephen 47 73+ 79+ 81
  92 Susannah 36 Thomas 2 19 73+ 81
  92 105 109+ William 46+ 73+ 109
  118 122 123 127 Wiltshire 46
JOYCE James 17 26 27 44 56 72 108
JUVIS John 58
KAIGLAR David 15
KANADA Jesse 49
KATES Isaiah 91
KAVENAUGH Charles 8 9 20 29 132
  Ezekiel 55 Hezekiah 92+ James 92
KAYLAN Andrew 89
KEARNEY Henry 14 17 21 25 26 28 31 32
  Lucy 21 31 102 111
KEASSLY Thomas 109
KEELING A 89 Ann 126 E 127 Edward 126
KELLY Mordeca 116 Mordecai 128 131
  Mordica 121
KENNADY Jesse 38
KENNEDY Abraham 14 Jesse 28 49 117
  130 Miriam 97
KENSEY James 125 Thomas 122 123
KENTUCKY 14 61 62 94
KERBY Malachi 1
KERR Andrew 124 William 124
KERSHAW DISTRICT SC 10
KEY Nancy 104
KEYSTAR John 33
KID Benjamin 100 William 91
KIDD Benjn 5 65+ 76 Wm 25 43 65+
KILE Rebekah 47
KIMBROUGH James 15
KINDRICK William 59
KING William 13 47 52 119 -- 8
KINNARD George 1 7 11-13 17 25 26 29
  37+ 39 45 47 57 64+ 67 72 78 92 101
  105 124 129 137 James 35 Michael
  4 16 17 20 25+ 29 34-37 45+ 53-55
  57 58 64+ 65 69+ 73 74 82 91 97 98
  100+ 102 103 107 114 123-125 128
  129 138 Walter 68 -- 29 88 98
KINNEY/KINNY James 125 Mary 125
KIRBY Malakiah 47
KIRK Parham 29
KIRTCHER John 65
KNIGHT Josiah 5 60 84 95 108 111 118
  121 124 125 132 134 135 136
KRYTSAI John 17
KUTES Isaiah 87
LADD Jehosophat 102
LAGRAND John 124

LAMB David 63 72 78 Joseph 63 72 79
LAMBERT Abner 34
LANCASTER David 26 37+ 72 78 137
LANDRUM Merryman 78+
LANIER Nicholas 105+ 118 126
LAPP Andrew 87
LARD James 35
LATTA Thomas 117
LAURANCE Edward 81
LAW Dolly 10
LAWRANCE Edmund 120 Edward 80 Henry 125 James 19
LAWRENCE Edward 73 91 97
LAYPOOR John 39
LAYS Isaac 85
LAYTON Michael 13 20 102
LEADBETTER Joseph 85
LEDBETTER Isaac 94 101 119 Joseph 66 74 85 112
LEE Ambrose 61 62 J 79 Matthew 45
LEEPER -- 138 creek/fork 4 26+ 46 52+ 55 56 64 76 78 93 98 101 138 lease 24 74
LEGATE Charles 1 81 107 William 4 71 81 107 124 130+ -- 137
LEIGH Benjamin 59
LEMMONS John 56 71+ 86 132 Joseph 77 Samuel 56 71
LESTER Alexander 21 81 125 Henry 39 43 101 137+
LEWIS Benjamin 108 David 8 56 72 79 90 108 117 130 Elizabeth 106 Frederick 116 Joel 9 95 M 33 Nancy 115 William 7 52 106 123
LIBERTY MTG HOUSE 5 15+ 25 37 45 57 80+ 83 91 92+ 105 108 109+ 110 119
LINCOLN COUNTY 136+
LINCOLN COUNTY, KENTUCKY 61 62
LINDSEY John 11+
LINSTER John 35 Thomas 59
LITTLE Abraham 25
LITTLETON John 66
LOAL Joseph 104 Thomas 104
LOCK Richard 114
LOGAN William 6 7 18 26 44 48 49 55 56+ 66 67 72+ 80+ 90 101 108 109 116 118 130+
LOGAN COUNTY, KENTUCKY 94
LONG Michael 17 109 Samuel 75
LORD James 35
LOUISIANA 76 95
LOVATT Lancaster 34

LOVE Hugh 54 J 105 James 89 John 12 56 118 Joseph 12 15 20 31 33 52 55 62 67 77 98 101 105 110-112 117 Josh 89 William 12 20 33 -- 117
LOVETT John 105
LOWRY David 91 Sarah 91
LOYD Lewis 43 Stephen 124
LUNN David 91
LYON Harry 133 Henry/Harvy/Hany 19+ 22 30 32 33 40 66 74-77 91 105 109 112 118 122 124 127 132 135
LYSARD Henry 43
LYTLE Archibald 1 13 18-20 22 25 27 31 35 39 58 60 67 71 73 82-84 102 106 109 128 129 William 47 48 -- 17 26 32 112 knob 24 78 rd 77
MABEN Alexander 98
MACKEY Captain 55
MADDEN Elisha 54
MADDIN Captain 109
MADDING Captain 128
MADIARIS John 28
MADISON COUNTY, MISSISSIPPI 38
MAILEY Benjamin 28
MAIR Ephriam 130 Esrad 130 James 130 Joseph 130 Philip 130
MAIRS Ephriam 80 Isaac 54 95 126 James 119 John 35 54+ 55 75 80 87 89 91-95 123 132 Joseph 7 25 80 Mary 112 130 131 Samuel 68 112 121+ 130 131 William 133
MALLORY John 30 66 83 84+
MALLOY Thomas 35
MALORY Philip 132
MALUGIN William 117
MANCY James 107+
MANDLEY Caleb 108 114+ 137
MANEY James 28 107+ Sally 28
MANIER/MANIERS J 46 John 7 16 27 46 56 108 Philip 66 71
MANING William 107
MANLEY Caleb 1 5 6+ 9 13 14 20 25 68 69 82 84 90 111+
MANNING Capt 91 John 107 William 76 83 86 91-93 97 100 102 103 105
MANSCAR George 78
MANSCOE George 100
MANSES Philip 26
MANSKER Gasper 19 George 3 39 44 96+ 113 117 124+ 137 Lewis 4 William 20 29 31+
MARCHANT John 27 33 James 130

MARIAH 73
MARR William 96+
MARRS Isaac 110 John 94 110
MARSHAL/MARSHALL James 2 43 Widow 88
    106 William 2 17+ 23 30 32 36 37 42
    45 57 64 71 98 106 112 129 138
MARTIAL William 111
MARTIN Alexander 81 Ann 16 George 60
    James 28 79 Jonathan 17 Lewis 16
    Samuel 125 Thomas 86 95 96 Tignal
    17 80 90 William 6 25
MARYLAND 126
MASINE John 34
MASON Abraham 37 76 Abram 68 69
    Charles 34 82 D 49 David 12 51 53
    58+ 64 77 82 83 85 111 113-115 118
    127-129 132 133 Hak 37 Hale 37
    Isaac 37 63 120 John 34 Joseph 37
    63 Martha 88 Rebecca 63 -- 19 75
MASONIC LODGE 38
MASTERSON Thomas 16 18 49 51 83 94 95
    -- 85
MATHEWS John 43
MATHIS Isham 127 John 81
MATTHEWS Cornelius 1 Isham 57 John
    43 47 57
MAUREY Philip 56
MAURY Abraham 21 28+ 31+ 60 61
    Abram 4 8 27 35 36 43 67 77 82 83+
    85 98 101 102+ 110 127 John 23
    Philip 3 5 7 25 36 102 Thomas 18-
    22 75 78 100 109 121 -- 8 112
MAURY COUNTY 72 74 84 93 102
MAXWELL William 44
MAY Benjamin 6 13 38 80 87 88 94
    Francis 122 132 Wm 21 106 -- 30
MAYBERRY Job 79 William 117
MAYES Benjamin 107
MAYFIELD Elias 77 79 129 Elijah 43
    118 135 George 8 92 Israel 14 James
    79 97 108 118 John 4 8 48 49 Thomas
    37 45 57+ 82 116 Samuel 116 131
McALISTER Charles 3 7+ 8 11-13 18 23
    25+ 29-33 35 43-45 48-50 52 62-64
    82 93 134 Elizabeth 93 Joseph 52
    84 98 102 Thomas 52
McBANE -- 24
McBRIDE Saml 31 37 47+ 81 100 112 121
McCALISTER C 92 Charles 3
McCALL John 92 gap 17 35
McCALLISTER Charles 41
McCALPAN John 70 William 8 70

McCALPIN John 92+
McCAMNEY William 94
McCANDLASS/McCANDLESS William 35 38-
    41 50 95 -- 87
McCANS Jane 43
McCARRELL Israel 37 James 79
McCARRILL James 16
McCARTY Abhm 44
McCASKELL Andrew 109
McCASLIN John 94 96 107
McCAUL Jane 43
McCLAIN Docr 46
McCLARAN Alexander 3 27 69 80 89 Docr
    73 Franklin 69 Widow 76
McCLEARY Samuel 4
McCLELLAN Alexander 128 John 12 89
    William 127
McCLELLAND John 111 Robert 40 127
McCLEM Susanna 99
McCLINE William 124
McCLORE Mary 23
McCLUKEN Caty 127
McCOLISTER Joseph 60
McCOLLISTER Joseph 46 94
McCOLPIN William 60
McCOMB/McCOMBS James 45 53 59-61 74
    95 102 134-136
McCONNELL Walter 59 119
McCONNICO Garner 11 23 28 33 37+ 45
    50 57+ 66 69 70 73 86 99 101 106
    112 113 115 116 130 136 -- 90 101
McCONNICOS MEETING HOUSE 15 17 30 53
    57 71 98 105 106 129+
McCORCLE Andrew 117
McCORD Charles 105 126 David 3
    John 105
McCORLIN John 81
McCOWAN Alexander 54
McCOWN Alexander 21 54 55 68 69 76
    109 134
McCOY Thomas 124
McCRACKEN James 25 60 67 131 -- 137
McCRACKIN John 39 67
McCRADY Andrew 78 98
McCRORY Capt 55 67 73 130 Thomas 5+
    10+ 18 19+ 25 36 54 65 71 81 95 109
    115 121-123 128 creek 6
McCUISTON Benjamin 33 61
McCUTCHAN/McCUTCHEN David 84 Hannah
    2 27 96 James 6 7 27 31 34 66 John
    21 71 119 Patrick 2 4 11 32 35 40
    43 Samuel 2 33 34 43 70 71 81 101

105 109   creek 24 78
McDANIEL Collin 2 14 16 20-23 25 29+
   30 36 37 39+ 45 51 56 58 59 67 73+
   80 87 89 91 94 95 98 105 106 111-
   113 128 129 132-135 Francis 24+ 74
   81 105   John 24 27 35 63 74 William
   24 74   -- 39   ford 24 73
McDONNELL Collin 38
McDOWELL Joseph 75 94 105
McELWEE David 17 30 43 71   Jane 94
   Thomas 27+ 42
McEWEN Captain 128 130 Christopher 48
   80 87 88 119-121 128   David 4 17 25
   51 54+ 57 67 74 76 80 92 98 106 109
   110+ 119+ 121 127-129+ 135   James 17
   80 98 101 105 108-110 112 116 118
   119 121 131+   William 17 128 129
McFADDEN James 106 116 131
   Robert 106 109 117 131
McFAIL Angus 103
McFASHION Nathan 39
McGAN Eli 86 94
McGAUGH Matthew 63 72+ 78-80 87
   Theron 34   Thomas 34 57 119 124
   William 8 88   -- 75
McGAVOCK David 9 13 32 70   James 8-11
   50 70 80 85   Randal 134   -- 17 21
   30 105   branch 26 88 106
McGEE William 14 89
McGHEE Thomas 96
McGILBRY William 107
McGILVERY William 74 108
McGUIRE James 119
McKAY Captain 32
McKENY Ebenezer 125   John 125
McKENZIE William 7 8 32
McKEY Captain 18 73 91 106 128
   Wm 19 20 36 39 53+ 120 126+ 128 132
McKINNEY John 8-10 15 21 54 75 78 86
McKINNY John 85
McKNIGHT James 12   Samuel 8 78 126
   Widow 56 119
McKORKLE Andrew 32
McLAIN George 61
McLAMORE Burrell 4
McLARIN Alexander 87
McLAUGHLIN James 107
McLEAN Ephriam 102   George 33
McLELLAN John 116
McLEMON Bethenia 20   Robert 20
McLEMORE Bethenia 20   Burrill/Bur-
   rell/Burwell 6 9 12 14 15 21+ 22

35 40 41+ 54 55 58 67 75 85 97 John
   127   Robert 7 16 20+ 21 24 32 36 45
   55 62 64 66+ 70 71 97 108 116+ 119
   129 134 135
McLIN Rebecca 127
McMAHAN/McMAHON Daniel 10 18 19 21 92
   98 124 126 127+ 129
McMEANS John 11 21
McMILLAN Robert 5
McMEIN Joseph 51
McMILLIN Robert 5 7-13 16+ 18+ 25 26
   38-40 55 58 60 61 73 74 76 78 80
   82-86 91 93 94 96 98 100-103 106+
   107 109 115+ 116 118-123 127+ 128+
   William 58
McMINS Joseph 58
McMULLIN Robert 39 William 29-31 125
McMUN Joseph 51
McNEAL Edward 85   John 82
McNEALY Isaac 86
McNEEL William 127
McNEELY Isaac 85
McNUTT Thomas 105
McPHAIL Angus 27 48 50+ 53 60 63+ 64
   67 80 87 93 103 108 118   Anne 67
   Nancy 63+ 92 93
McPHERSON Hannah 132+   Jonathan 132+
McRORY Captain 109   -- 49
McSWINE John 29 30 48 50 52+ 54 58 60
   67 82 83 85 91 94 95 111 113 114
   120 121
MEADOWS Jonas 78 138   Joseph 60 86
MEATT Willie 107
MEBANE A 110   Alexander 5 6 24 34 55
   59 64 70 89+ 91 109 118 124 126 128
   130+   Capt 55 70 91 109   George 5
   18+ 22 24 36 42   -- 72
MEIR Andrew 128
MENTOR John 104
MEREDITH Jane 89   Thomas 89
MERRITT Benjamin 54 55 97 100 102
   James 3 27   Samuel 14 27 63 96 126
   128   Shemi 35   Shiner 10   Thomas 14
   27 33 68-70 76 80 87 88 98
METCALF Ilai/Jlai 12 14
METHODIST MTG HOUSE 35 45 79
MIAMI COUNTY, OHIO 95+
MILES Hartwell 19 23 78
MILLER Adam 63   Alexander 51   James
   59 126   John 59 68 69 73 75 76 90
MILLS Sherwood 95 97
MINOR John 54

MINOR Lanselot 54
MINTER John 81 86 125
MISSISSIPPI TERRITORY 38
MITCHELL Benjamin 68 69 John 74 102
  Joseph 28 William 21
MONTGOMERY David 125 Elijah 95 107
  John 136 L 32 Lemuel 29 William
  136 -- 15 53
MONTGOMERY COUNTY, MARYLAND 126
MOODY John 63 65 78 114+
  William 81 92 107
MOOR Amos 49 Elizabeth 120 John 46
  Polly 61 62 Robt 49 Saml 43 61 62
MOORE Alexr 68 120 122 126 Amos 48
  Elizabeth 120 Easther 49 Esther 48
  James 11 108 114 John 4 84 98 108
  Joseph 71 Moses 30 48 49 134 Robert
  75 77 Samuel 14 16 58 91 97 98 122
  128 129 William 109 122 123
MORAST John 137
MORETON Elizabeth 114
MORGAN Matthew 81
MOROW John 107
MORRIS William 132
MORRISON Andrew 114 Keneth/Kenneth 50
  51 67 85 91 111 121
MORRISS Allen 9
MORROW John 34 36 42
MORSE John 17
MORTON Elizabeth 132 John 35 Samuel
  76 Thomas 37 51 55 79 114 120 132
MOSART John 137
MOSELY William 6
MOTHERAL/MOTHERALL John 117 -- 81
MOTHEREL John 109 Joseph 109
MOTHERELL John 61 Joseph 61
MOTON Samuel 80 86 87 Thomas 80 87 88
MOVELIER John 103
MUIRE Andrew 128
MULLIN Joseph 15 William 15
MURFREE C 34 H 132 Hardy 28 66+ 86
  93 Levina 28 M 102 Martha 28 85
  99 Matthias 28 45 50 83 85 91 95
  99 102 107+ 112 William 28 -- 74
  116 fork 22 26 34 46 56 83 98
MURFREESBOROUGH 123 129 138
MURPHY Lawrence 115
MURRAY/MURRY Robert 121+ 131
MYATT Wiley 63 -- 46
MYERS Jacob 14
NAIL Andrew 116 Julian 1 29 61
NALE John 100 William 49

NALL William 6 14 49 61 86 87
NALLY George 64
NASH Isaac 47 Reuben 1+ 31 51
  Dempsey 80 81 Demsey 2 14 89 109
NATCHEZ ROAD 34-38 45 46+
NAWL Martin 35 William 10
NEAL Alexander 15 Julian 1 12 15
NEEL/NEELL James 91 William 86
NEELLY George 15 18 19 21+ 22 54 55
  71 84 104+ 123 Isaac 4 115 James
  10 12 15 17 25 28-35 42 60 67 71 72
  76 77+ 82 84 86 117 John 3+ 6 14
  115 Mary 83 Robert 10 54 106 Thomas
  97 118 William 10 55 71 81 83 87
  94 95 101 106 107 109 117 -- 108
  creek 35 67
NEELY James 17 23 36 Mary 127
  Robert 121 William 80 108 127
NEILSON Charles 11 22 23 32+ 33 38
NELSON Charles 38 Prudence 48
  Robert 75 William 90 creek 4+ 15
  19 24 36+ 46+ 72 73+ 81+ 119 129
NEW ORLEANS, LA 95
NEWMAN John 41
NEWSOM Eldridge 124 Lawrence 132
  mill 24 78
NICHOLAS John 112 mill 17
NICHOLS John 10-12 18-20 22 27-29+ 35
  38 39 61 88 101 105 106 109-112 118
  119 123 134 136 mill 26 129
NOBLES Drury 14 21+
NOLEN Anslem 23 37 B 66 67 Berry 14
  23 32 33 53-55 58 60 61 63-69 75-78
  82-87 92 96 98 101 103-105 111 113
  128 130 David 5 23 33 68 69 80 99
  105 109 G 107 General 23 44+ 65
  67+ 68 91 Joseph 105 L 14 131
  Lee 14 16 90 116 121 Stephen 63 65
  89 100 Thomas 37 W 63 William 5+
  14 63 67 68 89 91 107 shop 83 107
NOLIN Berry 17 45 David 17 Thomas 130
NOLINS Archer 127
NOLL Andrew 74
NORMAN Betsey 102
NORRIS Elizabeth 105 106 124
  James 105 106 124
NORTH Abraham 34 36 42 43 48 50 52
  100 103+ 109 Elisha 3 5+ 45 59 90
  137
NORTH CAROLINA 74 89 104 106 132 137
NORTON Eliza 54 84 85 88 William 54
  63 84 -- 15 53

NORWOOD William 104
NUNN Francis 79 90 108 118 130 John
    6 62 79 William 2+ 18 24 25 39 40
    44+ 56 66 70 72 80 84 108 109 116
    118 127 128+ 130
OGILVIE Capt 49 Harris 25 John 26 27
    34 37 46 55 56 66 Kimbro 55 79 125
    Mrs 49 Richard 24 25+ 34 46 47 56
    57 70+ 71 William 34+ 47
OGLEVIE Richard 138
OHIO 95+
OLD Betsey 5 83+ 95 Elizabeth 93
    Thomas 5 6 28 31 34 36+ 42 62 71 83
    84 95 96 101 105 110 111
OLDHAM Conaway/Conway 4 100 Elisha 4
    Moses 4+ 68 75 125
OLIVER Abel 136+ George 36 42 48 50-
    52 55 58 68 69+ 76 105+ 109 118+
    122+ 123 John 123 Levy 85
ORANGE COUNTY, NC 104
ORECH Walter 81
ORMES Evan 92 115 Ewen 70
ORR Hugh 58 59 117
ORTON Richard 11+ 17 24 25 31 69 75
    85 100
OSBORNE Noble 124 Robert 124
OSLING John 126
OSTIN John 118
OSTON Richard 57 103
OVERALL CREEK 49 79 125
OVERTON Samuel 91
OWEN Glen 14 15 56 71 84 James 41 72
    89 Walter 49 William 79 121 128 131
OWENS Clement 72 William 116+
PAGE David 35 Frederick 35 Harvey 35
    Jacob 35 John 25 35+ Lovey 77
    Patsey 35 Stokely 35 -- 2
PARHAM George 2 16 45 Sally 86 Sarah
    74 89 William 34 40 43 45+ 54-56
    62 66 71 74 80 84-89 92-95 123+
PARK John 94 Moses 94
PARKER George 29 38 46 62 Jeremiah 59
    William 8 Zachariah 59 119
PARKINS Lazarus 137
PARKS Benjamin 15 George 127 John 6
    14 17 27 36 50 73 83 Malinda 114
    Moses 36 Reuben 17 59 99 William
    8 9 10 29 114 116
PARRISH Fountain 97 103 Joel 4 8 83
    85 120 branch 87 mill 5 110
PATE Hardy/Hardey 7 36 Jesse 105+
    Nancy 7 Pason 36 Person 36

PATES Hardy 25
PATMORE Daniel 72
PATTEN Archibald 9
PATTERSON Luke 4
PATTON Andrew 102 Archibald 49 Capt
    26 55 74 Isaac 18 69 71 74 77 86
    116 Jacob 69 James 27 38 50 98 134
    Jason 46 John 63 73 118 119 Mat-
    thew 91 120 Robert 49 T 110 Thos
    46 86 129 Tristram 1 5 18 26 31 45
    55 61 74 91 93 95 97 99 107 116 128
    William 58 59 road 68 106
PAVETT James 128
PEARCE John 106
PEEBLES William 7 8 14 18-21+ 23 27
    35 40 41 50+ 87 91 102 119-121 123
    125
PENDER William 28
PEPPER Samuel 31
PENSPAR Ezekiel 64
PERKINS Capt 55 70 91 128 Charles 45
    48 53 59-61 Daniel 7 10+ 13 19 21
    24 25 36+ 42 45 62 64 67 70+ 71 80
    87 93 96+ 97 101 108+ 122 134 137+
    Elisha 74 Harden 91 96+ 97 N 7 21
    66 Nicholas 1 2 4 6-8 10 12 13+ 16
    24 29-31+ 35 36 43 45+ 53 55 60 62
    64+ 65 67+ 70 73 74 79 90 91 95+ 97
    98 101 108 111 114+ 116 119-121+
    123 128 129 134+ 135 P 110 Peter
    35 40 66 74 119 135 Samuel 6 18 34
    37 44 55 67 69 85+ 92 93 101 107
    125 131 133-135 Thomas 2 9 10+ 12
    13 21 24 36 52 78 85 108 110 113
    118 127 W 108 111 William 20 55
    62 70 75
PERRY Richardson 137 Simpson 59
    William 25 59 70 133+
PERRYMAN Jos 89
PETICE/PETTICE Horatio 118 132 134
    135 136
PETTIS/PETTUS Horatio 6 90 99+ 124
PETTWAY Hinchey 3+ 6 8+ 10-13 18-22+
    24 25 35 39-41+ 43-45 47-49+ 52 53
    62 64 66+ 80 81 83 103 110 125 134-
    136 William 57 -- 8 112
PETWAY Hinchey 18 63 103
PEWIT/PEWITT James 26 33 47 -- 46
PHENIX Henry 82
PHILIP Joseph 101 122
PHILIPS Joseph 2 45 80 87 109 122 123
    128 William 80 81 125

PHILLIPS Jasper 88   Joseph 98 133
   William 70 72
PHIPPS Jordan 5 83 84 105 109
PICKARD John 35
PICKENS John 13 19
PICKINGS John 8
PIERCE Hardy 115   John 28 115
PIG/PIGG James 107   Stephen 100 107
PILLOW Claiborne 86+ 120   Gideon 132
   John 48   Mordecai 42 64 88
PINDER John 64
PINKERTON David 45 James 13 22 39
PINKSTON Daniel 92   David 2 24 35 43
   73 88 89 129 Hugh 2 29-31 38 39+ 48
   James 49   Peter 6 56 90 128   Tenner
   38 Turner 47 65 company 128
PITTMAN Daniel 80
PLUMMERS BRANCH 129
POE Rodian 8   Rouelham 43
POGUE William 38 39
POINDEXTER George 11
POLK Richard 68 69 76 Thomas 16 Wm 12
POLLARD Joseph 33 38-41+ 83
PONDER William 28
POPE Jeremiah 130   John 34 82 100
   Lemuel 100   Thomas 80 87 88   gap 34
PORCH Solomon 98 110
PORTER A 1+   Alexander 1+   Dudley 11
   44 59   John 24 34 48 49 70 80 87-89
   97 98 128   Joseph 23   M 110   Major
   15 54 104 Reese 23   Sarah 11 44
   William 103
POTTER A 48 111 112+ Archibald 16 85
   121 122 127 132+ 133+ Donalson 116
POTTS Daniel 115   Jonathan 117 Joseph
   76+ 82   Peter 35 91+ 111 119 121+
   123+ 128 131   Polly 123 128
POWEL/POWELL Thomas 28 Edmond 9
POWERS Robert 38 40 Yancey 69
   Yancy 97 98 106
PRATT Samuel 110
PREWITT George 124   John 79   Wm 79+
PRICE Hannah 43   James 43 64 101 105
   108 138   John 17   Robert 14+ 91 105
   William 63 105
PRIESTLY James 29
PRIMM Green 89   Jeremiah 23+ 89
   John 23+ 37 45 89
PRINCE EDWARD COUNTY, VA 86
PRITCHETT Benjamin 35   James 77
PROUTHAM Martin 45
PROWELL Sampson 2 17 29 51 52+ 54+

   113+   Sarah 29   Thomas 54+ 113+ 114
PRYOR Green 24 34 97 106 134   John 24
   34 62 71 97 134+   Luke 5 15 17 23
   25 71 77 83 86 110   Peter 24 34 97
   106 134
PUCKETT Douglass 94 122   Elizabeth 70
   Harvey/Harvy/Hervey 70 71 118 119
   136+   Jarrad 136   Richard 6 9 12-15
   18 20 25+ 29-32 34 35 38 40-42 50+
   53 57 58 64+ 70+ 93 106 112 115 116
   136 Sally 70
PUGH James 26 38 80 82 85 89 119 121+
PULASKI [PULASKY] 133
PULLIAM Drury 4 6 13 14 30 33 58 64
   67 71 91 97 106   branch 17 57 98
PURYEAR Ezekiel 62   Hezekiah 83+ 93
   95 101 113 118   Matilda 83+ 95
QUILING William 2
RACORD John 36
RADFORD John 120 136+   William 42 120
RAGSDALE E 52 53   Edward 5 14 18 24+
   33+ 35 38 39 44 45 48+ 53 55 56 59
   60 62 63+ 66-68 71 72 74 75 84 92
   117 128 130 137   Thos 1+ 9   Robt 51
RAINEY John 106
RALSTON Alexander 1 36 72+ 108 125
   126 135   George 118
RAMSEY Frasis 33   Francis 61
RAP Daniel 34
RAY James 79   John 77   Nathaniel 47
READ Joseph 38   Mrs 129   Robert 37
   Widow 51   William 71
READER Jacob 61
READING Maxamilian 89
REECE Beverly 64 137   Jordan 34 137
   Patrick 34
REED Edmond 114   G 14   Guilford 132
   James 27 43 46 66 104   John 6 18
   22+ 28 53+ 106 127+ 129 132   Joseph
   114+ 128   Lavina 129   Robert 74 116
   129   Shadaric 129   Thomas 87
   William 77 129 130   -- 112
REES Beverly 62 65-67 72 Capt 109 128
   Jordan 56 83   Sally 62
REESE Beverly 18-20 35+ 36 41 54 55
   62 68 83 95 101   James 46   Jordan 8
   34 40+ 43 77   Malinda 36 Matilda 83
   Sally 36 Susannah 35 36 41   Thos 87
REEVE/REEVES Peter 40   Sarah 89
REID Andrew 15   John 30 103   M 102
   Thomas 87
REYNOLDS Bythenia 114   George 58 63

114 116 129 131 Pryor 2 58 114 129
131 Richard 1 16 28 38 80+ 92 107
109 114 Sally 114 Spencer 56 71
74+ 81 107 130 138 Susannah 58
Thomas 58 103 112 114+ 118-121
RICARD John 38 107
RICHARDS Ambrose 2 John 57 98 129
Robert 136
RICHARDSON Benard/Barnard/Bernard 27
35 36 42 47 71 76 77 101 105 124
125 Capt 44 47 55 70 73 91 106 128
Coonrod/Coorod 24 36 106+ -- 32
RICHERSON Bernard 125
RICKARDS John 17
RIDGEWAY/RIDGWAY James 79 108 Mr 49
RIDLEY Beverly 50 99 116 117 Captain
27 49 55 70+ 91 109 James 18 24 27
33 46+ 56 62 72 128 Moses 7 24 27
46 47 49 56 72 80+ 90 108 109 116
130+ Thomas 6 13 14 19 29 31 33 38
39 45 47 48 52 59 60 65 100 108 118
121 130 132 133 136 Walter 38
William 116+ -- 56
RIGGS David 15 17 55 71 80 92 97+ 107
130 Joel 6 14 16 23+ 25 33 47 80
87 Wright 15 16
RIGS Wright 55
RIVERS Jacob 65 Joel 8 14 18 21 24+
27 37 65 111 122+ 123
ROACH Simon 24 37
ROADS Elisha 2
ROBBINS William 39+
ROBERSON Benjamin 46
ROBERTS Benjamin 3 6 14 35 39 40 43
81 106+ Elijah 99 Isaac 11+ 133+
Ja 90 Jesse 89 John 26 137
Joseph 34 43 93 102 Lewis 89
ROBERTSON Charles 55 106 Christopher
43 David 83+ Henry 25 James 9 10
16 23 89 John 80 Joseph 18 23 32
52 Michael 7 8 Patsey 86 Thomas
42 86 -- 28
ROBINSON Charles 6 13 14 27 76 119+
131 David 6 13 27 36 84 John 27
43 51 87 88 92 94 95 98 Joseph 26
27 32 37 46 51 56+ 71 Michael 27
Thomas 76 111 137+
ROGERS A 114 Alex 113 James 114+
131+ 133+ John 133+ Martha 133+
Robert 24 36 39 42+ 56 68 69 71 79
113 114+ 125+ 131 133+ 138
Samuel 113+ -- 81

ROLAND/ROLLAND Jacob 22 29 James 40
Mary 22
ROLONS John 122
ROPER John 91+ Sarah 91+ -- 46
ROSENBURN Matthias 97
ROSS Daniel 34
ROUNDSEVALL Amos 63 65
ROUNDTREE Andw 54 55 63 101 107 119+
ROUNSEVALL Amos 37 45 65 69 118
-- 117
RUSSEL Albert 112 Benjamin 57 119 130
Col 44 Pleasant 111
RUSSELL Benjamin 42 81 Edward 119
Pleasant 1 5+ 13 26 33 67 79 86 101
Sander 85 Tandy 120 Wm 75 -- 129
RUTHERFORD Griffith 7 Henry 4 6 17
24+ 25 39-41 85+ 98 112 115 118 127
133 136   creek 35 78 107 116 117
RUTLEDGE William 41
RYBURNE William 92
RYNER -- 5 16
SAINT FRANCISVILLE, LA 76
SALISBERRY James 111
SALMON Edward 73 Robert 50+
SAMMANS Robert 124
SAMMON/SAMMONS John 19 Nancy 89
Newell 81 Newett 92 Robt 50 -- 90
SAMPLE James 35 John 3 4 11 12 16
18-20 23 37+ 31 33 35 36 39-43 51
53 61 62 64 66 75+ 83+ 86+ 87 94
95+ 112+ 132 133 137 Robert 36+
42 55 62 78 William 35 111
SAMPSON Ephriam 15+ 16 20 54 101
Richard 20 48 50 78 William 101
SAMSON Richard 51
SANDERS James 7 William 119
SANDRIDGE Austin 35
SANFORD James 43 90 Robert 43
SAPPINGTON John 2+ 21 36 57 59
Roger 2 64 Thomas 2 13 17 21 26
SARGANT/SARGENT William 37 104
SAUNDERS Terner 28 Turner 22+ 24 34
39 51 57 58 67 70 72 74+ 82-84 90
101+ 107+ 120 135 Wm 73 118-120
SAWYER -- 37
SAWYERS Robert 112 Sampson 1 11 29
33 44+ 47 61 81 87+
SAYERS Robert 18 19 40 74 112 121+
122 133+
SCALES J 46 Joseph 12 37 44 45 73
79+ 121+ 125 134 N 90 Nicholas 3
4 6 11 12 18 19 27+ 29 30 35-37 40

45 61 63+ 69 74 75 78 79 87 88+ 90
91 94 99 100-102 112 115 119 128
135 Robert 1 9 89 94 Thomas 35
SCHALES Nicholas 126
SCONCE Robert 104
SCOTLAND 127 128
SCOTT/SCOT Elias 48 Green 25 45 88
  James 6 John 56 71 Thomas 25 29 60
SCRUGGS Drury 14 Finch 17 34+ 51 58
  59+ 60+ 72 84 125 Nathan 30 91+ 96+
SCUGGS Finch 80
SEATON George 25 60
SEAY John 4
SECREST Abraham 31 38 49 Henry 58
SEERS Samuel 4
SENT Green 45 47
SENTER George 67
SETGRAVE John 132
SHAFFER Anne 43
SHANNON Capt 55 56 66 91 111 Charles
  102 David 1+ 23 38 44 54 55 93-96
  124 133+ George 54 56 58 69 78 80
  85 101 105 107+ 128 James 4 18 22
  24 R 15 Robert 124 Thomas 13
  -- 5+ 16 76
SHARP Anthony 11-13 15 20 29 31 38
  66-68 70 73 74 87 88 102 Grove/
  Groves 22 29 30 50 51 65 Janie 20
  John 88 Margaret 87 Nancy 20 Peggy
  11 13 20 67 88 102 110 122 137 Robt
  12 78+ 91-93 97 125 Sala/Salla 67
  102 110 122 137 Salie 20 Searcy 20
  67 88 102 110 122 137 Sumner 20 67
  88 102 110 122 137 Widow 67 92 William 37 branch 129   -- 90 101
SHARPE Sally 11
SHAW Alexander 89 Timothy 45 53 56
  89 117 William 76
SHELBOURNE Elizabeth 54 James 54 Mary
  54 Samuel 15 55
SHELBURNE James 47+ 52 54 59 John 34
  Josephine 54 Samuel 6+ 12-14 18-20
  22 26 32 34 44 45+ 47+ 52-54 59+ 72
  78 89 90 92+ 102 113-115 118-120
  130+ 132-136 Sarah 47 52 135
SHELBY David 75 road 81
SHELBYVILLE 46 56 62 79 90 99 130
SHELTON Bennett 41+ 45 George 73
SHEPHERD John 6
SHEPPERD Nancy 28
SHERALD Ambrose 2
SHERON John 59+

SHERWOOD 113
SHOEMATE James 57
SHORES John 116+ 131
SHORT James 110 111+ 121 122
SHOUP Widow 92
SHOUS John 116
SHUMATE James 16 57 58 63 Thos 57
SHUTE Asa 54 65 John 83 Thos 54+ 113
  William 1 10 11 13+ 18 19 33 41+ 43
  58 61 62 66 68 71 77 82 94 95 101
  103 105 107+ 110 111 120 128 132
SIMMONS John 84 Nancy 7 Nathaniel 8
  Thomas 5 11 17 19 45 51 76 82 100
  120 121 124 128 131   Wm 72 99 117
SIMMS James 6 18
SIMPKINS John 37 William 37 120
SIMPSON Alexr 36 61 69 70 107 Capt 55
  70 91 109 128 Charles 12 Ephriam 14
  John 32 Richard 67 107 William 4
  6 22 26 46 55 56 62 101
SITTER -- 19
SKELLY James 12 100 101 105 107
SKIRLOCK James 83
SLADE William 28
SLAKER George 41
SLATER Charles 87 126 127 David 126
  127 Henry 70 72 89 126 127 133+
  Jonathan 126 127 Joseph 126 Sarah
  70 126+ 127+ 133+
SLATOR Henry 107
SLEDGE H 90 Hany 89 Harry 89 John 90
SLESKER George 15
SLOAN William 54+ 76 135
SLOCUM Riley 105
SLUKER George 41 54 93
SMITH Abraham 119 Alexr 14 16 21 22
  36 38 39 42+ 51 55 57 62 63 100 101
  119 124 129 132 Benjamin 7 28 38 49
  Bryant 28 James 24 78 101 121+ John
  42 44 68 71 80 87 100 112 113+ 128
  130 Millington 43 Morgan 88 O 28
  Owen 86 Peter 113 Peyton 97 Richard
  65 66 74 Robert 33 42 61 83 S 128
  Samuel 113 Stephen 8+ 11 14 31 52
  54 73 76 78 87 133 Thomas 30 97 124
  W 112 Washington 55 William 16 19
  29 55 64 66 68 74 75 79 93 103+ 112
  121 124 131+ 132   mill 71 117
SMITHSON Clement 90+ 92 99+ 113 Nancy
  90+ 92 99+ Nathaniel 10 72 73 78 90
  128 Widow 108
SNEED James 6 14 33 55 92

SOLOMON Jordan 75 137
SOMERVILLE -- 75
SOUTH CAROLINA 10
SOUTHALL James 78 94 125 137 138
  Judith 125
SPAIN David 26 37 52 65 66 79 90
  Stephen 95 103 109
SPAN William 105
SPARKMAN Jesse 3 6 13 14 36 William
  6 13 14 50 51+ 55 62 119+ 133+
SPENCER Elijah 35 Elizabeth 23 35 66
  120 Stephen 100 William 22 23 35
  36 66 91 95+ 102 109   creek 15 53
  54 87 110
SPRATT Andrew 2 32
  Sam 2 Thomas 2
SPRIGG Robert 136
SPRUEL Simeon 122
SQUIER/SQUIRE David 4+ 15 17 26 36 54
  72 74 84 91 98 101 105 108 109+ 123
  127 128 135 Gurden/Gurdon 17 26+ 43
  54 65 128 135 Sarah 74
STACY Eli 12 John 118 119 130 Marma-
  duke 124 Mrs 105 Thomas 120
STAGGS Felix 19 31 38 71 77 83-85+ 95
  Thomas 127   -- 59 125
STALER Charles 87+
STALY John 91
STANCIL/STANCILL Nathan 34 121
  Nathaniel 67
STANDFIELD Ephriam 10 George 10
  Shackspier/Shack Speer 10 23
STANDLEY James 87 136 Martin 55 62
  85 92 103 108 112 114 133
STANFIELD Ephriam 127 Marmaduke 120
STANLEY James 100 124 Martin 1 10 12
  21 62 65-68 80 84 85 98 100 112 127
  129 132 Right 100
STANSELL/STANSILL Nathan 101 107
STAPLETON Jonathan 125
STATER Henry 94
STAVELL Nathan 100
STEALY John 41 42
STEEL Alexander 104 Andrew 100
STEELE Andrew 115 127 Moses 5 20 127
  Richard 4 24 25 50 61 62 65 105 129
STEELY John 105
STEMLAY W 127
STENCILLEY W 127
STEPHENS Charles 37 45 48 125 Edward
  69 136 George 74 91 Henry 74 125
  130 James 71 Joel 6 12 15 29 33 53
  65 68 69+ 82 109 113 118 122 123
  125 130 John 79 81 107 117 Lewis 6
  34 37 45 55 69 71 74 77 82 86 101
  105 107 130 Loammi 25 29 Loumi 125+
  Mary 125 Thomas 97 118 William 37
  45 77 86 107 128 130+   -- 130
STEPHENSON George 100   -- 80
STEPLETON Jonathan 1
STEVENS Charles 38 Joel 122 123 136
  Lewis 20 53 123 136 William 116
STEWARD James 84
STEWART Arthur 19 57 David 127 Henry
  134 James 5 41+ 47 69 John 89
  Thomas 89 William 124   -- 11+ 32
  41+ 42 creek 57 119
STINE William 34
STOCKETT Joseph 9 10 73 119 Stephen 9
  T 11 20 Thomas 8 11+ 18 28 48 55 67
  70-73 95 119
STONE H 67 Hendley/Henley/Henly 2 7+
  13 24+ 25 30 34 51 55 58 59 62+ 65
  67 68 70 71 73 74 76 87+ 88 91 94-
  99 101 102+ 106+ 107 109 110 128
  129 134+ 137 Jane 125 William 80
  89 109 119 125 126 creek 28
STOVALL Bartholomew 37 63+ 67 94 124
  125 Nathan 100
STRAMBLAR George 93 109
STRAMBLER George 1+ 9 10 14+ 16 18+
  21+ 38-40 68 69 76 78 86+ 95+ 102+
  103 113 121-123 126 132+
STRAMLER George 101
STRATAR George 94
STREET John 4 25
STRICKLIN Joseph 84
STRINGER Joseph 82
STUART Nathan 132 Thomas 102 Wm 69
STURDEVANT Silvanus/Sylvanus 18 19 20
SUGGS Acquilla 49 Noah 49
SUIT Green 47
SULLARDS James 15
SUMMERS Joseph 43
SUMNER Jethro 75 Joseph 56 Thomas 2
  29 31 100 125
SUTTEN/SUTTON Richard 110 111
SWAIN Samuel 102
SWANCEY John 34
SWANSON Edward 40 43 56 71 83+ 84
  101+ 106 107+ 130 133 James 54 55
  65 83 107 Mary 101 Polly 133
  Richard 15 30 54 107
SWEENEY John 59 78   -- 130

SWEENY John 79+ 101 102 104 105
SWENSON Richard 37
SWIN George 104
SWINCY 83
SWINEY/SWINNEY/SWINNY John 6 14 16 21
    71+ 77 82 84+ 85 86   -- 83
SWISHER Henry 129
TAIT William 127 128
TALLY Henry 117 127
TANKERLY Rowland 51
TANKERSLEY John 89 Richard 37 57 89
    Rowland 51
TANKERSLY John 1 15 22 47 Richard 129
TANNER D 90 Joseph 90
    Richard 26 124 125 137
TAPLEY John 71 81 107 130 131
    Mary 130 131
TARKINGTON/TARKINTON Jesse 6 7 11 14
    15 34 38 54 61+ 103 119 John 15 54
    61 Joshua 75 77 83-86 107
TASSELL John 127
TATOM/TATUM Absalom 33 61
TAYLOR Absalom 65 114 132 Billington
    36 42 Bird 3 4 44 F 37 129 Fred 90
    Frederick 26 37+ 124 137 George 23
    H 93 Henry 74 96 122 James 29 37
    John 74 93 96 122 Lany 132 Larry
    114 Thomas 25 William 23   -- 73
TEMPLE Burwell 6 29 35 68+ 69 74 91
    93 97 108+ 122 127 Captain 5
TERNER James 128
TERRELL James 48 54 71 83 130 135
TERRILL James 15 34 38 84 92 Jones 51
TERRY David 11 39 112 Jeremiah 11 21
    Thomas 3 71 77 82-85 87 101+ 112
THOMAS Anthony 125 131 James 5 108
    117 Jesse 34 59+ Jobe 125 131 John
    29 34 59 60 98 106 125 Mark 37 130
    Mary 34 60 75 Nathaniel 59 Phineas
    34 60 125 William 17 36 42 57 64
    98 124 129
THOMASON Stephen 122 136
THOMPSON J 91 James 2 7 33 38-41+ 47
    50 51 94 113 114+ Joannah 113 John
    66 104 118 124 Joseph 74 122+ 123
    L 91 Lawrance 122 123 Lawrence 74
    121 132 Moses 70 Robert 127 Stephen
    94 William 91 94
THOMSON Graves 11
THROWER Sarah 89
THURMAN Graves 21
TIGNER James 22

TIGNOR Edward 11 21 Isaac 8 Jones 11
TILLMAN Francis 28 38 71 George 15-
    17 28 35 38-41 49 54 55+ 57 69 70
    80 91 117 Haden 6 20 56 71 Harden
    80 Jacob 2 67 102 103 John 25 28
    31+ 38 49 71   -- 80 130
TILMAN George 109 127 Haden 127
    Jacob 101 103+
TOMBLIN Nicholas 135
TOMLIN James 103 121 122 Jones 103
    Nicholas 11 21+ 109 120 134
TOMPKINS Silas 8
TORRINGTON Joshua 107
TRADEWELL Daniel 48+
TRANTHAM Jeremiah 90 118 Martin 2 79
    117 127
TREMBLE James 54
TRIMBLE David 32
TRIPP Samuel 120
TROTTER Benjamin 103 Isham 25 26 33
    44 55+ 70 71 83 84 86 91 92 99+ 101
    102 109+ 110 112 113 118 128
TROWER Sarah 74
TRUETT Abraham 7
TUCKER John 60 Rodin 119 William 5 82
TUNAGE William 135
TURBEFIELD -- 119
TURNBULL -- 5 16 76
TURNER James 6 68 69 79 81 105 Moses
    3 36 42 56 84 132 Richard 34
TWINANCE William 128
UNDERHILL Daniel 5 16
UNDERWOOD P 81 Perry 47
UPRY Samuel 107
VANATTA/VANATTO Christopher 2 73
VAUGHAN/VAUGHN Abner 118 128 Dickson
    103 Dixon 7 8 10 58 105 136 Jas 14
VAUGHT John 124
VAULTS John 5
VENATTA/VENATTE Christopher 44 135
    Nancy 135
VESTAL Jay 107
VINATH C 46
VINATTA/VINNATTA Christopher 118 120
    Nancy 118 120
VIRGINIA [State] 5 6 41 86 102 126
WADE Obadiah 72 78 81 Susanna 126
WAGGONER John 58
WAIT/WAITE Robert 10 16 Wm 91
WALDRUFF James 91
WALKER Abraham 5 16+ 27+ 78 103 118
    Abram 6 Anthony 6 Freeman 4 30 52

59 101 105 H 68 Hamilton 49 Hance
114+ 135 Henry 6 12 14 37 43 45 54
55 57 59 62 65-68 79 80 84 91 92 97
109 118 124 129 132+ 134-137+ James
43 70 127 128 John 6 7 16+ 20 27
36 37 46+ 50 52 56 71 79 81 114+
118 124 135 Lucy 104 Thomas 4 6 14+
17-21+ 53+ 80 92 103 108 109+ Wm
70+ 71 74 103 127 136 -- 38 56
branch 4 22 46 56 98
WALKUP Nancy 79 Samuel 79
WALL Clem/Clement 16 130 Edmund 117
WALLACE Thomas 51 90 117
WALLS Clem/Clement 109 117
WALTHAL Thomas 17 23 36 42 48 50 51+
55 62+ 79 92 99 109 113 117-122
WALTON Jesse 34 Josiah 97 Langhorn
94 98 Langthurn 106 Thomas 45
WARNER Nathaniel 47
WARNERS FERRY 109 116 117 130
WARREN Burwell 124 Drury 2+ Edward
1 22 24 31 45 51 53-55 58 60-62 73
80 83 87 88 97 101 105 129 132 134
Nathl 47 Robt 81 83 86 125 Wm 124+
WART Robert 91 William 91
WASHINGTON Gilbert 11 47 87+ 100
Thomas 18 49 99 -- 112
WASHINGTON D.C. 126 127
WATERS John 47 108 128
WATKINS Joseph 33 61 Owen 25 35 37
38 40 65 69 96 138 Thomas 64+ 69
124 William 64
WATSON Jane 83+ 93 95 John 28 34+
36 37 42 54 67 71 82-84 86 95 101
107+ Langhorn 34 Owen 45 Thomas
15 54 William 37 91+
WATTS Benjamin 79
WEATHERS Edmund 72
WEBB James 104 John 70 108 W 35
William 89 90 108 134
WELCH Benjamin 72 95
WELLS Aaron 86 100 Capt 27 55 91 109
128 John 35 64 Samuel 25 35 45 55
64 89 90 91 98 109 128 Thomas 27
53 68 80 William 27 35 43 64 68 69
WEST G 114 John 22 35+ 57 104 115
Thos 13 35 36 53 57 97 111 132 133
WESTMORELAND Jesse 43 Thomas 43
WETHERING William 133
WETHRINGTON William 133
WHARTON Jesse 94 118 William 18 19 22
WHEALEY John 59

WHEAT John 71 106
WHEATON Jane 4 22 78 109 121
WHINTON William 18
WHITE Alexander 58 101 102 109 123
Benjamin 14 17-20 26 30 39 56 60
67-69 76 86 90 100 103 109 110 115
118 123 128 129 137 C 18 Chapman
1 7-11 13+ 15 19 25 33 49 85 92 121
129 Cornelius 91 Daniel 106 124+
E 12 Ezekiel 28 George 63 Henry
107 108 Isaiah 110 James 55 120
124 Jesse 4 18 26 38 39 51 55+ 59-
62 65 70 85-87 91+ 98 100 101 108
109 121 128 137 John 9 11+ 21 29
30+ 34 70 71 74 90 91 100 101 115
120 127 128 133+ 137 Joshua 32 124
Lemuel 31 Polly 124 Robert 63
Thomas 79 William 2 39 45 53 60 61
92 94 107 124 129
WHITEHEAD Jacob 13
WHITMAN Solomon 124
WIER, James 31
WIGGS Matthew 122
WILBOURN/WILBURN Nicholas 10 12
WILKES Daniel 9 15 17
WILKINS James 15+ 16 23 54 55 59 74
85 86 88 89 101 105+ 128 137 John
22+ 23 39 59 100 Martha 74 86 89
Thomas 113 William 16
WILKINSON James 45
WILKS Daniel 135+
WILLETT Absalom 31 Charlotte 26
Hamiah 31 Hannah 31 James 31 Joseph
31 Lewis 31 Mary 48 Richard 26
27 36 71 Sally 31 William 7 8 25
31 38 40 41 48 90 95 109 mill 35
WILLIAMS Capt 55 69 Christopher 115
Claiborne 38 Daniel 38 40 41 Elijah 89-91 97 101 113 Elisha 3 9 30
39 40 118 124 128 Isaac 62 94 James
15 17 25 32 35 54 89 92 113 124+
John 68 100 Mosson 28 Nicholas 60
O 49 52 88 89 100 113+ 114 124
Oliver 9 12 19-21 25 28 29 31 36 38
41 45 50-55+ 57-59+ 64-66+ 69 74+
75+ 90-96 98 99 102+ 105 106 111-
113 115 118+ 121 124 Rice 118 Samuel 2 9 24 25 27 38 62 75 88 102
125 Sampson 91 Tanner 57 William
24 33 35 37-41+ 45+ 47+ 53 54 57 72
78 90 92 97 113+ 114 120 124 128
130 Willis 79 Wright 35 118 -- 47

WILLIAMSON Ann 89 97 Benjamin 53 57
  John 1 16 17 26 37+ 45 57 75 86 89
  90 104 137 Thomas 37 53+ 108 William 53   mill 36
WILLIS Caleb 5 79   -- 83
WILLS John 28
WILLSON William 100
WILSON Anita 66 Archibald 3 Arissa 66
  Betsey 66 Capt 25 128 Cornelius 24
  72 90+ 127+ 132 Daniel 81 Gregory
  18 19 39 60 116 Greory 81 James 11
  16 24 32 45 50+ 53 57 59 99 100 137
  Jason 39 44 78 117+ 129 Jesse 52 54
  73 John 28 38 44 80 88 92 109 117
  129 Jonah 37 Jos 33 Josiah 16 37
  52 66 78 107 Margaret 66 Mark 70
  Martha 7 Moses 7 Peter 96 103 Robert 3 7 46+ 47 62 79 Samuel 2 7 9
  19 22 24 35 Polly 66 Sally 66 Samuel 66 79 82 118 119 Thomas 6 7+
  16+ 25-27 36+ 37 40 42 44 46-48 50-
  52+ 55+ 56 65+ 66+ 69-72 79-81 90
  91 101 107-109+ 115 117 118+ 128+
  130 131 W 100 William 1+ 11 12 21
  25 35 38 43 44+ 47-49 54 59 72 79
  80+ 81 88 90 91+ 97 99 105 108 109+
  115 118 121 124 126+ 128+ 129 134
  Zacheus 6 7 20 79 90 107   -- 49
  creek 4 12 19 29 36 46+ 56 73 119
  mill 46 72 73   road 36 69 107
WINBERNE Henry 28
WINDROW John 56 72 81
WINN John 132
WINNY 51
WINROE John 56
WINSET/WINSETT Amos 2+ 15 Jason 14
  Milly 14 15 Robert 2+ 14 15 24
  Silas 2+ 15+ 57 William 2+ 15
WINSLOW Joseph 97 116
WINSTEAD John 17 23 32 91 136 Samuel
  12 15 63+ 64 72 79 84 85 95 110 136
WITHERSPOON J 90 James 108 John 3 6-
  8 16 18-20 24+ 25 28 32 33 44 45+
  48+ 49 52 55 58+ 62 63 65+ 67-70
  73+ 75-77+ 79 80 82 87-89+ 91-95 97
  98 101-104 106-115+ 117-122+ 128+
  129 134 135+ 137
WITHRINGTON William 119+
WITTINNTON Joseph 107
WOLF William 19
WOOD Alexander 65 69 76 107 Jackson
  44 James 78 117 John 69 Johnson
19
  45 46 53 73+ 79 Jonathan 36 69
  Josiah 107 Leonard 100 Samuel 111
  Stephen 79 124 Thompson 46 Thomson 109
WOODFIN George 113
WOODS Johnston 81 93 Oliver 35 Samuel 35 Widow 39 44 78 117 gap 6 20
  28 38 horse mill 93
WOODSON William 111
WOOLDRIDGE Betsey 27 Elizabeth 22
  John 22 27 Josiah 11 14 61 75 91+
  95 110+ Keziah 61 Lovell 27 Loving 22 Mary 22 Nancy 8 Rolly 27
  Thomas 22 Tom 27
WOOTEN/WOOTON James 16+ John 40
  Moses 58 92 William 60
WORD Johnson 37 Samuel 100
WORLEY/WORLLEY Devinney 2 Francis 27
WRIGHT Elizabeth 11 Isaac 9 10 12
  John 7 12
YARBOROUGH David 98 104+ Helen 98 104
YOUNG Elizabeth 47 Ephriam 47 Francis 47 125 Howard 47 James 68 John
  17 95 Joseph 43 Michael 47 Nancy
  47 Patsey 47 Robert 43 Thomas 47
  William 1 43 47   -- 75
YOUNGER Francis 79 Samuel 25
  Thomas 10 49 60 61 86 87
ZACHERY Charles 121

Other Heritage Books by Carol Wells:

Abstracts of Giles County, Tennessee: County Court Minutes, 1813-1816 and Circuit Court Minutes, 1810-1816

CD: Tennessee, Volume 1

Davidson County, Tennessee County Court Minutes, Volume 1, 1783-1792

Davidson County, Tennessee County Court Minutes, Volume 2, 1792-1799

Davidson County, Tennessee County Court Minutes, Volume 3, 1799-1803

Dickson County, Tennessee County and Circuit Court Minutes, 1816-1828 and Witness Docket

Edgefield County, South Carolina Probate Records, Boxes One through Three Packages 1-106

Edgefield County, South Carolina Probate Records, Boxes Four through Six Packages 107-218

Edgefield County, South Carolina: Deed Books 13, 14 and 15

Edgefield County, South Carolina: Deed Books 16, 17 and 18

Edgefield County, South Carolina: Deed Books 19, 20, 21 and 22

Edgefield County, South Carolina: Deed Books 23, 24, 25 and 26

Edgefield County, South Carolina: Deed Books 27, 28 and 29

Edgefield County, South Carolina: Deed Books 30 and 31

Edgefield County, South Carolina: Deed Books 32 and 33

Edgefield County, South Carolina: Deed Books 34 and 35

Edgefield County, South Carolina: Deed Books 36, 37 and 38

Edgefield County, South Carolina: Deed Books 39 and 40

Edgefield County, South Carolina: Deed Book 41

Edgefield County, South Carolina: Deed Books 42 and 43, 1826-1829

Genealogical Abstracts of Edgefield, South Carolina Equity Court Records

Natchez Postscripts, 1781-1798

Rhea County, Tennessee Tax Lists, 1832-1834, and County Court Minutes Volume D: 1829-1834

Robertson County, Tennessee Court Minutes, 1796-1807

Sumner County, Tennessee Court Minutes, 1787-1805 and 1808-1810

Williamson County, Tennessee County Court Minutes, July 1812-October 1815

Williamson County, Tennessee County Court Minutes, May 1806-April 1812

www.ingramcontent.com/pod-product-compliance
Lightning Source LLC
Chambersburg PA
CBHW050820160426
43192CB00010B/1836